THE NAVARRE BIBLE

The Epistle to the Hebrews

THE NAVARRE BIBLE
The Epistle to the Hebrews

in the Revised Standard Version and New Vulgate
with a commentary by members of the
Faculty of Theology of the University of Navarre

FOUR COURTS PRESS

Original title: *Sagrada Biblia: X. Epístolas
a los Hebrews*. Quotations from Vatican II documents
are based on the translation in *Vatican Council II:
The Conciliar and Post Conciliar Documents*,
ed. A. Flannery, OP (Dublin 1981).

Nihil obstat: Stephen J. Greene, *censor deputatus.*
Imprimi potest: Desmond, Archbishop of Dublin, 2 October 1990.

Typeset by Gilbert Gough Typesetting, Dublin
and designed by Jarlath Hayes,
this book is published by Four Courts Press,
Kill Lane, Blackrock, Co. Dublin, Ireland.

First edition 1991
Reprinted 1993

A catalogue record for this book
is available from the British Library.

ISBN 1-85182-069-8

Printed in Ireland by
Colour Books Ltd, Dublin

Contents

Preface

In providing both undergraduate and postgraduate education, and in the research it carries out, a university is ultimately an institution at the service of society. It was with this service in mind that the theology faculty of the University of Navarre embarked on the project of preparing a translation and commentary of the Bible accessible to a wide readership—a project entrusted to it by the apostolic zeal of the University's founder and first chancellor, Blessed Josemaría Escrivá de Balaguer.

Blessed Escrivá did not live to see the publication of the first volume, the Gospel according to St Matthew; but he must, from heaven, continue to bless and promote our work, for the volumes, the first of which appeared in 1976, have been well received and widely read.

This edition of the Bible avoids many scholarly questions, discussion of which would over-extend the text and would be of no assistance to the immense majority of readers; these questions are avoided, but they have been taken into account.

The Spanish edition contains a new Spanish translation made from the original texts, always taking note of the Church's official Latin text, which is now that of the New Vulgate, a revision of the venerable Latin Vulgate of St Jerome: on 25 April 1979 Pope John Paul II, by the Apostolic Constitution *Scripturarum thesaurus*, promulgated the *editio typica prior* of the New Vulgate as the new official text; the *editio typica altera*, issued in 1986, is the Latin version used in this edition. For the English edition of this book we consider ourselves fortunate in having the Revised Standard Version as the translation of Scripture and wish to record our appreciation for permission to use that text, an integral part of which are the RSV notes, which are indicated by superior letters.

The introductions and notes have been prepared on the basis of the same criteria. In the notes (which are the most characteristic feature of this Bible, at least in its English version), along with scriptural and ascetical explanations we have sought to offer a general exposition of Christian doctrine—not of course a systematic exposition, for we follow the thread of the scriptural text. We have also tried to explain and connect certain biblical passages by reference to others, conscious that Sacred Scripture is ultimately one single entity; but, to avoid tiring the reader, most of the cross-references are given in the form of marginal notes (the marginal notes in this edition are, then, those of the Navarre Bible, not the RSV). The commentaries contained in the notes are the result of looking up thousands of sources (sometimes reflected in explicit references given in our text)—documents of the Magisterium, exegesis by Fathers and Doctors of the Church, works by important spiritual writers (usually saints, of every period) and writings of the founder of our University. It would have been impertinent of us to comment on the Holy Bible using our own expertise alone. Besides, a basic principle of exegesis is that Scripture should be interpreted in the context of Sacred Tradition and under the guidance of the Magisterium.

From the very beginning of our work our system has been to entrust each volume to a committee which then works as a team. However, the general editor of this edition takes ultimate responsibility for what it contains.

It is our pleasant duty to express our gratitude to the present chancellor of the University of Navarre, Bishop Alvaro del Portillo y Diez de Sollano, for his continued support and encouragement, and for reminding us of the good our work can do for the Church and for souls.

"Since Sacred Scripture must be read and interpreted with its divine authorship in mind,"[1] we pray to the Holy Spirit to help us in our work and to help our readers derive spiritual benefit from it. We also pray Mary, our Mother, Seat of Wisdom, and St Joseph, our Father and Lord, to intercede that this sowing of the Word of God may produce holiness of life in the souls of many Christians.

1   Vatican Council II, Dogm. Const. *Dei Verbum*, 12.

Abstracts and Sources

1. BOOKS OF SACRED SCRIPTURE

Acts	Acts of the Apostles	2 Kings	2 Kings
Amos	Amos	Lam	Lamentations
Bar	Baruch	Lev	Leviticus
1 Chron	1 Chronicles	Lk	Luke
2 Chron	2 Chronicles	1 Mac	1 Maccabees
Col	Colossians	2 Mac	2 Maccabees
1 Cor	1 Corinthians	Mal	Malachi
2 Cor	2 Corinthians	Mic	Micah
Dan	Daniel	Mk	Mark
Deut	Deuteronomy	Mt	Matthew
Eccles	Ecclesiastes (Qohelet)	Nah	Nahum
Esther	Esther	Neh	Nehemiah
Eph	Ephesians	Num	Numbers
Ex	Exodus	Obad	Obadiah
Ezek	Ezekiel	1 Pet	1 Peter
Ezra	Ezra	2 Pet	2 Peter
Gal	Galatians	Phil	Philippians
Gen	Genesis	Philem	Philemon
Hab	Habakkuk	Ps	Psalms
Hag	Haggai	Prov	Proverbs
Heb	Hebrews	Rev	Revelation (Apocalypse)
Hos	Hosea	Rom	Romans
Is	Isaiah	Ruth	Ruth
Jas	James	1 Sam	1 Samuel
Jer	Jeremiah	2 Sam	2 Samuel
Jn	John	Sir	Sirach (Ecclesiasticus)
1 Jn	1 John	Song	Song of Solomon
2 Jn	2 John	1 Thess	1 Thessalonians
3 Jn	3 John	2 Thess	2 Thessalonians
Job	Job	1 Tim	1 Timothy
Joel	Joel	2 Tim	2 Timothy
Jon	Jonah	Tit	Titus
Josh	Joshua	Tob	Tobit
Jud	Judith	Wis	Wisdom
Jude	Jude	Zech	Zechariah
Judg	Judges	Zeph	Zephaniah
1 Kings	1 Kings		

Alphonsus Mary Liguori, St
  Advent Meditations
  Christmas Novena
  The Love of Jesus Christ reduced to practice
  Reflections on the Passion
  Shorter Sermons
Athanasius, St
  De Incarnatione contra arianos
  Oratio contra gentes
Augustine, St
  The City of God
  De catechizandis rudibus
Cyril of Alexandria, St
  Explanation of the Epistle to the Hebrews
Diadochus of Photike
  Chapters on Spiritual Perfection
Diognetus, Letter to (2nd century)
del Portillo, Alvaro
  On Priesthood
Ephraem, St
  Commentarium in Epistulam ad Haebreos
Escrivá de Balaguer, J.
  Christ is passing by (followed by section no.)
  Friends of God (do.)
  In Love with the Christ (do.)
  Holy Rosary
  The Way
  The Way of the Cross
Francis de Sales, St
  Treatise on the Love of God
Fulgentius of Ruspe, St
  De fide ad Petrum
Gelasius I, Pope St
  Ne forte
Gregory Nazianzen, St
  Oratio catechetica magna
  Orationes theologicae
Ignatius of Antioch, St
  Letter to Polycarp
Irenaeus, St
  Against Heresies
John of Avila, St
  Audi, filia
  Sermons
John of the Cross, St
  Ascent of Mount Carmel
John Cassian
  Collationes
John Chrysostom, St
  Baptismal catechesis
  De sacerdotio
  Homilies on the Epistle to the Hebrews

John Paul II
  Address to young people, 3 November 1982
  Apos. Exhort. *Catechesi tradendae*,
    16 October 1979)
  Apos. Exhort. *Familiaris consortio*,
    22 November 1981
  Apost. Exhort. *Reconciliatio et paenitentia*,
    2 December 1984
  Apost. Letter *Salvifici doloris*
    11 February 1984
  Enc. *Dominum et Vivificantem*, 30 May 1986
  Homily (on date given)
  Enc. *Laborem exercens*, 14 September 1981
Justin, St
  Dialogue with Trypho
  First Apology
à Kempis
  The Imitation of Christ
Lateran, Fourth Council of the
  De fide catholica
Origen
  Against Celsus
  Homilies on Genesis
Paul VI
  *Creed of the People of God: Solemn
  Profession of Faith*, 30 June 1968
  Apos. Exhort. *Gaudete in Domino*,
    9 May December 1975
Philo of Alexandria
  De sacrificio Abel
Pius V, St
  Catechism of the Council of Trent
Pius IX
  Syllabus of Errors
Pius X, St
  Apos. Const. *Haerent animo*, 4 August 1908
Pius XI
  Enc. *Ad catholici sacerdotii*, 20 December
    1955
  Enc. *Mediator Dei*, 20 November 1947
  Apost. Const. *Menti nostrae*, 23 September
    1950
  Enc. *Mystici corporis*, 29 June 1943
Roman Missal of St Pius V
*Missale Romanum ex decreto sacrosancti
oecumenici concilii Vaticani II instauratum
auctoritate Pauli PP. VI promulgatum, editio
tipica altera* (Vatican City, 1975)
Sacred Congregation for the Doctrine of the Faith
  *Letter on Certain Questions
    concerning Eschatology*, 17 May 1979
Teaching of the Twelve Apostles, The

Teresa of Avila, St
  Life
Tertullian
  Against Marcion
  Apologeticum
Theodoret of Cyrus
  Interpretatio Epistulae ad Haebreos
Thomas Aquinas, St
  Commentary on Hebrews
  On the two commandments
  Summa contra gentiles
  Summa theologiae

Trent, Council of
  Decree *De iustificatione*
    De peccato originali
    De Sacram. ordinis
    De SS. Missae sacrificio
Vatican I
  Dogm. Const. *Dei Filius*
Vatican II
  Const. *Sacrosanctum concilium*
  Decree *Ad gentes*
  Decree *Apostolicam actuositatem*
  Decree *Nostra aetate*
  Decree *Presbyterorum ordinis*
  Dogm. Const. *Dei Verbum*
  Dogm. Const. *Lumen gentium*
  Past. Const. *Gaudium et spes*

3. OTHER ABBREVIATIONS

ad loc.	*ad locum*, commentary on this passage	f	and following (*pl.* ff)
Exhort.	Exhortation	*ibid.*	*ibidem*, in the same place
Apost.	apostolic	*in loc.*	*in locum*, commentary on this passage
can.	canon	*loc.*	*locum*, place or passage
chap.	chapter	n.	number (*pl.* nn.)
cf.	*confer*, compare	p.	page (*pl.* pp.)
Const.	Constitution	*pl.*	plural
Decl.	Declaration	par.	and parallel passages
Dz-Sch	Denzinger-Schönmetzer, *Enchiridion Symbolorum*	Past.	Pastoral
		SCDF	Sacred Congregation for the Doctrine of the Faith
Dogm.	Dogmatic		
EB	*Enchiridion Biblicum* (4th edition, Naples-Rome, 1961)	sess.	session
		v.	verse (*pl.* vv.)
Enc.	Encyclical		

11

The Navarre Bible (New Testament)

St Matthew's Gospel
St Mark's Gospel
St Luke's Gospel
St John's Gospel
Acts of the Apostles
Romans and Galatians
Corinthians
Captivity Epistles
Thessalonians and Pastoral Epistles
Hebrews
Catholic Epistles
Revelation

ESSAYS ON BIBLICAL SUBJECTS

In addition to special introduction(s) in each volume, the following essays etc. are published in the series:

St Mark	General Introduction to the Bible; Introduction to the Books of the New Testament; Introduction to the Holy Gospels; and The Dates in the Life of our Lord Jesus Christ
St Luke	Index to the Four Gospels
Acts	The History of the New Testament Text
Romans & Galatians	Introduction to the Epistles of St Paul
Corinthians	Divine Inspiration of the Bible
Captivity Epistles	The Canon of the Bible
Thessalonians	The Truth of Sacred Scripture
Hebrews	Interpretation of Sacred Scripture and the Senses of the Bible; Divine Worship in the Old Testament
Catholic Epistles	Rules for Biblical Interpretation
Revelation	Index to the New Testament

Interpretation of Sacred Scripture and its Various Kinds of Meaning

Sacred Scripture is the Word of God addressed to us in written form, and like every document it is open to different interpretations. However, some interpretations of the Bible—whose text is particularly rich—go deeper than others, and not all the interpretations are equally valid. To interpret any written text properly one has to bear in mind a whole series of factors such as the nature of the document; the kind of person the author is and the ways in which he expresses himself; the context in which he is writing; and the setting in which the text is going to be read; etc.

In the case of the Bible, we are obviously dealing with religious writing whose ultimate author, as Jews (in respect of the Old Testament) and Christians believe, is God himself: God it was who inspired the writers of the various books. Therefore, correct interpretation of Sacred Scripture must necessarily be guided by the fact that one is dealing with texts inspired by God, texts in which God is using human language to address man.

This fact, the divine inspiration of Scripture, has decisive importance when it comes to interpreting the text. Firstly, being the Word of God, Scripture contains a richness of meaning which the human reader can never totally plumb. It can be said therefore to have a number of meanings or senses: as the rabbis of our Lord's time used say, it has seventy faces. Secondly, one must start off from the fact that since God, in Sacred Scripture, is speaking through men   the hagiographers or sacred writers who wrote the text—the first thing to look for is what the writer intended to convey by the words he set down. This meaning is what is known as the "literal" or historic sense; and it is this sense that we shall examine first.

THE LITERAL SENSE

Let us take a particular passage—for example, the one that deals with the Israelites crossing the Red Sea (cf. Ex 14:15f). What is the literal sense of this text? The Israelites, in their flight from the Egyptians, find their way blocked by the sea; then God works the great miracle of making a path of dry ground through the sea, and once they have crossed the waters return to normal, thereby preventing the Egyptians from continuing their pursuit, with the result that the Israelites are now safe. The literal sense of the passage is the facts as described by the words of the text.

This sense is divided into the "literal sense proper" and "literal sense improper", a distinction which applies to all types of literature. The literal sense proper obtains when the words are being used in their proper or precise meaning; the literal sense improper, when some sort of literary device is being used: when we say, for example, "the skies wept", we are not using the words in a strictly literal way; we are speaking metaphorically. Or, for example, when we speak of "drinking the cup", we are using the word for the container to mean in fact its contents. Figures of speech of this type are to be found in every language and they pose no problem of interpretation.

One has to bear in mind, also, that Sacred Scripture, like every literary work, is subject to the literary styles in vogue at the time of writing. For example, orientals are very fond of hyperbole, and therefore, when St John says that if everything Jesus did were to be written down, he doubts if the whole world would be big enough to hold the books that would have to be written (cf. Jn 21:25), he is using hyperbole: he is exaggerating; he does not mean to, and should not, be taken literally.

So, we find in Sacred Scripture the whole range of styles and devices to be found in Hebrew and Greek literature—literary narrative, poetry, parable, hyperbole etc.

BEYOND THE LITERAL SENSE

In addition to knowing what the human authors intended to convey, one must also, in the case of the Bible, look for *the* meaning—what God intended the text to mean. To discover this meaning one needs to keep very much in mind "the content and unity of the whole of Scripture, the living Tradition of the entire Church and the analogy of faith".[1]

Because Sacred Scripture has dual authorship—a divine author and a human author—it has features not to be found in other books: we need to be aware of the possibility that even though a human author is guided by God, he may not be conscious of certain things which become much clearer years later, after other events of Revelation have taken place.

For the most part the authors of the Old Testament had an incomplete view of Revelation; in this sense they were different from New Testament authors. For example, the notion of the Messiah held by the Israelites of the sixth century B.C. was very primitive compared with that of the Evangelists. Yet when the Old Testament sacred writer speaks of the Messiah, saying things which he himself does not perfectly understand, God is using him to convey ideas which we—now that the salvific events have taken place—do see.

This is why the Church interprets certain passages of the Old Testament in a messianic sense; whereas it is very unlikely that the sacred writer himself realized the full import of what he was writing. So, when we come to the text, we may be inclined to ask: How is it possible to read more into the text than was put there by the human author of the book? The answer is that the words

1. Vatican II, *Dei Verbum*, 12.

written by the hagiographer were open to taking on—later—a more profound meaning, yet one which was in some way already latent in them. This meaning is discovered in the light of the content of the whole of Sacred Scripture, just as the full meaning of something said in the first act of a play comes out only at the dénouement. Some scholars call this meaning the "plenary sense".

THE PLENARY SENSE

According to the interpretation given by the Church to certain passages of the Old Testament, the existence of this plenary sense seems to be a teaching grounded in Sacred Scripture itself and one consistent with Catholic doctrine. Since God is the principal author of Sacred Scripture he can hint at a truth at a particular point in Revelation and later reveal it more fully, thereby lighting up the meaning of the earlier revelation. However, this meaning cannot be just something which an ingenious scholar turns up: it has to be something which Revelation itself (at a later stage) makes evident.

For example: in the Genesis 3 account of the first sin, God says to the serpent, "I will put enmity between you and the woman, and between your seed and her seed; he [the descendant of the woman] shall bruise your head [a mortal wound], and you shall bruise his heel [a slight wound]." The sacred author could not have understood the full meaning of these mysterious words; God was referring, when he inspired the sacred writer, to a much later stage of salvation history. The interpretation of these words, which is given by the Church, sees them as containing the Messianic Prophecy; this descendant of the woman is pre-eminently Christ and secondarily the Virgin Mary. There was no need for the sacred writer to understand the full import of these words which he wrote under divine inspiration.

How does the Church arrive at the interpretation of a messianic passage? When the text was originally written, only God could know this dimension of the passage; the Church discovers the plenary sense of Scripture in the light of the subsequent events of Revelation, and with the help of things found in other passages of the Bible or in Sacred Tradition.

This occurs in the case of very many messianic prophecies; and therefore it is very likely that the prophets themselves did not see all the implications of what they were saying; we, however, can see them quite clearly because we have the benefit of the later Revelation, the benefit of hindsight; the authors of the New Testament, who had the charism of inspiration, have interpreted the Old Testament texts and thereby helped us to understand them.

THE TYPOLOGICAL SENSE: BIBLICAL "TYPES"

Another sense which lies behind the literal sense is the typological sense: things described in the text (and people and events reported) stand for other things—while at the same time having their own proper meaning. The word "type" means an image or figure or symbol which stands for something else. Thus the passover lamb of the Old Testament is the "type" or prefiguration of something which will later come to be: the lamb is the "type" of Christ, and Christ is the "antitype" of the lamb.

It is not for us to decide that something is the "type" of something else: this is something which is itself a matter of Revelation. In the particular case referred to, John the Baptist, as a prophet speaking under divine inspiration, states that the real Lamb of God was not the one sacrificed in the Old Testament; it is Christ.

Resort to the "typological" sense provides an explanation of a number of prophecies dealing with the suffering of the Servant of Yahweh; some of those, for example, speak of him as going like a lamb to the slaughter (cf. Is 53:7), etc. Christ accepts this as a description of himself, which shows that he is the Saviour who gives his life as a victim to atone for the sins of men and thereby bring them salvation.

The passage through the Red Sea is, in its typological sense, an especially clear assertion of God's desire for man's salvation. Thanks to this amazing event the people of Israel gained their freedom; in a similar way a person is saved by passing through the waters of Baptism. Thus, the waters of the Red Sea came to be seen as the "type" of the waters of Baptism that bring salvation.

Another outstanding Old Testament type is the ritual of the *passover lamb* (cf. Ex 12:1-28; Deut 16:1-8). Before the Israelites leave Egypt God commands all the Hebrew families to sacrifice a lamb, which they are to eat in a particular way and whose blood they are to smear on the door jambs and lintels of their houses. The effect of this is that when the exterminating angel comes to punish the people of Egypt and sees the blood of the lamb on the doors of the Israelites' houses, he will pass by, pass over, and leave them untouched. Now, if we go to the beginning of St John's Gospel, we will find John the Baptist, when he sees Jesus approaching, saying, "Behold the Lamb of God, who takes away the sins of the world!" (Jn 1:29). Just as the passover lamb was sacrificed to save the Israelites, so Jesus will die to save the whole people (cf. Is 53:7): a typological or "typical" sense has been added to the literal sense of "passover lamb".

To sum up, the typical sense has to do with the way certain Old Testament events, people or things prefigure those of the New Testament. The waters of the Red Sea are a "type" of the waters of Christian Baptism; the passover lamb of the Old Testament is the "type" of Christ, who brings true Salvation and is the true Paschal Lamb (cf. 1 Cor 5:7).

THE HOLY SPIRIT AND READING THE BIBLE

The three senses mentioned above—literal, plenary and typological—are to be found in Sacred Scripture itself and provide us with the framework for interpreting it. The Second Vatican Council reminds us that "Sacred Scripture must be read and interpreted in the same Spirit by which it was written."[2] This

2. *Dei Verbum*, 12.

ultimately means the Holy Spirit, for it was he who inspired the Old and New Testaments, who led the Apostles to understand the truth about Christ, and who moves and guides the Church to practise and to pass on this truth.

Christ and the Apostles, particularly in connexion with interpretation of the Old Testament, teach us how to appreciate the profound meaning of the Bible. There is an episode in the life of Jesus, reported in St Luke's Gospel, which shows how Jesus interpreted the Old Testament; this passage establishes the basis of Christian teaching on the subject of interpretation. It reads: "And he came to Nazareth . . . and went to the synagogue, as his custom was, on the sabbath day . . . and there was given to him the book of the prophet Isaiah . . . (and he) found the place where it is written, 'The Spirit of the Lord is upon me, because he has anointed me to preach good news to the poor. . . .' And he closed the book . . . (and) he began to say to them, 'Today this Scripture has been fulfilled in your hearing'" (Lk 4:16-21).

The basic idea is that the Old Testament finds its fulfilment in Jesus. The fulness of time has come (cf. Jn 19:30). The prophecies and figures of the Old Testament are now seen to make sense (cf. Mt 1:22; 2:15; 4:14; etc.). So, the depth of meaning contained not only in the messianic prophecies but in the Law and in sacred history, cannot be grasped without Jesus Christ.

St Paul distinguishes between the letter and the spirit of Scripture (cf. 2 Cor 3:6; Rom 2:29). By the "letter" he meant the Old Testament as understood by the Jews prior to the fulness of Revelation in Jesus Christ, whereas the "spirit" meant Scripture as understood in the light of faith in Jesus Christ. The spirit, therefore, can only be perceived within the context of Christian faith. There, the Scriptures are once more "fulfilled" as the Holy Spirit opens the minds of the Apostles so that they can "understand the Scriptures".

Thus, Jesus and his Apostles gives us the permanent, fundamental principles of Christian exegesis: Christ is the key to Scripture; he provides the explanation both of the Old Testament, which announces the future Messiah, and of the New, which reveals him in the flesh. This principle applies prior to any attempt to analyse the text: it must guide any such analysis, test whether a particular analysis is appropriate or not, and free the reader of the Bible from the exegetical short-sightedness to which sheer literalism leads. For interpretation of the Bible to be truly Christian, human reason and its tools (philosophy, history, philology etc.) must be imbued with and utilized by the Spirit, that is, by Christian faith.

TRADITION, THE MAGISTERIUM AND INTERPRETATION OF THE BIBLE

The Christian faith is grounded on apostolic Tradition, which includes the Apostles' preaching, the institutions which they gave to the Church, and the writings which they themselves, or contemporaries of theirs, were inspired by the Holy Spirit to write—the New Testament. This apostolic tradition "makes progression in the Church with the help of the Holy Spirit. There is a growth in insight into the words and institutions which are being handed on. This comes about through the contemplation and study of believers who ponder these things in their hearts (cf. Lk 2:19, 51), through the intimate sense of spiritual realities which they experience, and through the preaching of those who have received, along with the right of succession in the episcopate, the sure charism of truth."[3]

Thus it is that "Sacred Tradition and Sacred Scripture are bound closely together and communicate one with the other, flowing out of the same divine well-spring, forming one stream and moving towards the same goal."[4]

This is why the contemplation of Sacred Scripture is something which must always be done within the context of the Church's Tradition.

When a Christian is reading the Bible with a view to applying it to his own life, he needs to remember that "in the sacred books the Father who is in heaven comes lovingly to meet his children and talks to them";[5] but for any interpretation of Scripture to be correct it needs to be compatible with what is termed the "authentic" interpretation; it is for the Church, and the Church only, to provide this interpretation. The process, therefore, is as follows: the Church received the books of the Old Testament through our Lord Jesus Christ and his Apostles, and with the books their true meaning; within the bosom of the Church, God inspired further books, the New Testament; and, with the help of the Holy Spirit, the Church was able to establish which books were inspired and therefore fitted within the canon of Scripture. The Bible has been entrusted to the Church, for it to conserve, meditate upon and provide as spiritual nourishment to the faithful.

Because it is the Word of God, the treasures contained in the Bible are inexhaustible. To pass on and expound the faith, Christ endowed his Church with a special ministry, its teaching authority or Magisterium: "And his [Christ's] gifts were that some should be apostles, some prophets, some evangelists, some pastors and teachers" (Eph 4:11). What this means is that only the Magisterium—assisted by the Holy Spirit—has the role of authentically interpreting the Word of God. By divine command it "listens to this [the Word] devotedly, guards it with dedication, and expounds it faithfully."[6]

The Magisterium's interpretation of Sacred Scripture takes different forms. The most important of these is when it uses its full, Christ-given authority to propose truths of faith, to be held by all—as in the Creed, which is a kind of summary of Sacred Scripture and the key to its correct interpretation. Any interpretation, therefore, which conflicts with the content of the Creed must be seen as faulty.

The second kind of interpretation occurs when the Magisterium in its ordinary, universal teaching uses the Bible to show that what it is saying is in line with the Word of God. This is its most common use of Scripture, as can

3. *Dei Verbum*, 8.
4. *Dei Verbum*, 9.
5. *Dei Verbum*, 21.
6. *Dei Verbum*, 10.

be seen from the vast majority of the documents the Magisterium issues.

Finally, it uses Scripture when it goes out of its way to take issue with faulty interpretations of specific scriptural texts, particularly those which say that Jesus or the Apostles are referring to specific sacraments. When this does happen, it is incorrect to say that the Magisterium is curtailing individual freedom to interpret the Bible; all that it is doing is pointing out that the interpretation is in conflict with the true meaning of the text.

The Magisterium, moreover, particularly in recent centuries, has fostered and encouraged biblical studies, while providing guidelines for those working in that field.

Divine Worship in the Old Testament

The life of the people of Israel was intimately bound up with religion, and particularly with divine worship. They were a race "chosen by God"; to him they owed their very existence as a people. Divine worship, public religious ritual, has always been the external expression of man's reverence and respect for and submission to God, his Creator and absolute Lord; in Israel religious rites were also an expression of faithfulness to God who had called the chosen people into being, freed them from slavery, led them into the Promised Land and protected them by special providence from the nations round about; he had given them a Law and a kingdom and, despite their infidelity, he had brought them home from their exile in Babylon.

PLACES OF WORSHIP

In the period of the patriarchs, that is, between eighteenth and fifteenth centuries B.C., the forebears of the people of Israel fixed certain places of worship, usually because they had been the scene of theophanies, that is, special events of divine revelation. Such was the origin of cultic centres like Sheckem (cf. Gen 12:6-7) and Bethel (cf. Gen 28:10-22), both located in the mountains of Samaria, Mamre (cf. Gen 13:18), close to Hebron in the mountains of Judea to the south of Jerusalem, and Beersheba (cf. Gen 26:23-25', near the southern extremity of Palestine.

However, once the Hebrew people had been set free from the slavery of Egypt (13th-11th century) and became formally established as the people of God, that is, once the Almighty had sealed the Covenant of Sinai with Moses (cf. Ex 19-24), public worship was reserved to one specific place, the location of the tent of meeting, or the tabernacle (cf. Lev 17): this was a special tent set up in the Israelite camp during the period when they were making their way through the wilderness. Later, in their first centuries in the promised land it became a more or less fixed tent. In the reign of King David this tabernacle was moved to Jerusalem (the Jebusite city of Mount Sion which he chose as his capital) and set up there permanently (cf. 2 Sam 6), but it was still only in the form of a tent. From then on it became the place for the national liturgy promoted by the king. David's son and successor, Solomon, brought to fulfilment his father's desire by building a splendid temple to take the place of the earlier tent; this first temple of Jerusalem was a magnificent building made of the choicest materials, as specified by God himself—cedarwood, gold, silver etc.

From this point onwards divine worship at the earlier shrines went into decline; this was true both of the shrines associated with the Patriarchs and those that had been set up by various Israelite tribes in the time of the Judges. The first to disappear were those located in Judea; historical circumstances, such as the invasion and destruction of the Northern Kingdom by the Assyrians, were later responsible for the disappearance of the rest. After the return from Babylon, it was established that the temple of Jerusalem should be the only place where the Jews offered divine worship (cf. Deut 12:5, 6, 11, 13).

Thus, in the Old Testament divine worship centres mainly on the tabernacle in the early period, and later on the temple.

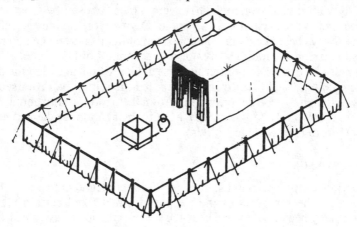

Reconstruction of the tabernacle

1. *The tabernacle* The original tabernacle was a special tent where God frequently manifested himself by descending in a pillar of cloud (cf. Ex 33:9; Num 12:5-10). For this reason the tent itself symbolized the presence of God in the midst of his people. Moses frequently went into this tent to speak to God "face to face" (cf. Ex 33:11; Num 12:8) and to act as mediator between the Most High and his chosen people (cf. Ex 33:7). Sacrifices were offered in the enclosure around the tent.

As described in Exodus 25-27 the tabernacle "complex" consisted of the tent and an elaborate courtyard around it. The courtyard was rectangular, surrounded by wooden posts on bronze bases; linen curtains were hung right round this. Inside this court, between the entrance and the tabernacle, was positioned the altar of holocaust;[1] on this the carcasses of sacrificed animals were burned, and beside it stood a large laver or basin for ablutions.[2]

---

1. This was made of acacia wood and was covered with bronze. It was rectangular and each of the four top corners extended in the form of a bull's horn made of bronze (cf. Ex 27:1-8). These four points played an important part in the sacrificial rite. They were called the "horns" of the altar and were an essential part of it: if they were taken off or were broken it amounted to a profanation of the altar.

The tabernacle in the strict sense, the *Mishkan*, was an area covered by a tent, rectangular in form, made of rich materials and highly adorned; it was entered on the east-facing side, through a curtain. Within, a richly embroidered veil divided it in two, hanging between the "Holy [Place]" (*Qodesh*) and the "Holy of Holies" (*Qodesh qodashim*). The Holy Place contained the altar of the bread of the Presence;[3] the altar of incense;[4] and a golden seven-branched lampstand,[5] provided with oil. The Holy of Holies was empty except for the ark of the covenant (cf. Ex 25:10-22; 37:1-9). This was a rectangular box made of wood overlaid with pure gold inside and out. Its four lower corners had rings of gold; wooden stakes overlaid with gold were positioned in these rings, ready for transporting the ark. The ark was covered with a "mercy seat", a slab of pure gold; this was called the "propitiatory" (*Kapporet*) and on it rested representations of two cherubim made of beaten gold, facing one another and protecting the propitiatory with their outstretched wings.

The ark of the covenant was Israel's most sacred object, for it contained the tablets of the Law, which God had given Moses (cf. Deut 10:1-5; Ex 25:16, 21; 40:20; 1 Kings 8:9), and probably a jar containing manna and Aaron's rod, which had miraculously sprouted buds (cf. Ex 16:32-34 and Num 17:1-11). Above the propitiatory the "glory" of Yahweh appeared, that is, God made himself present: hence it used to be said that he was seated above the propitiatory or "mercy seat", as if on a throne of divine majesty, hidden from view by a bright cloud and with cherubim in attendance. From here God used to speak to the children of Israel through Moses, and tell them what to do.

Only the high priest was permitted to enter the "Holy of Holies", and that only once a year, on the solemn "Day of Atonement", *Yom Kippur*.

The ark of the covenant accompanied the Israelites on their journey in the wilderness and during the settlement of the promised land. It was at Gilgal, Bethel (cf. Judg 20:27) and Shiloh (cf. 1 Sam 4:3). For a short while it fell into the hands of the Philistines after the battle of Aphek (cf. 1 Sam 4:4-11), but it was miraculously recovered and lodged in Kiriath-Jearim (cf. 1 Sam 5:1 - 7:1).

2. The priests were required to wash their hands and feet in the basin before ascending to the altar to perform the sacrifice and before entering the sanctuary; this symbolized the cleanliness and holiness of body and soul needed for engaging in divine worship.

3. The loaves of proposition or bread of the Presence were a grain offering of a special (because permanent) kind. The Hebrew description means "loaves of peace" or "loaves for presentation" because they were presented or designed to remain permanently in the presence of Yahweh. They were twelve in number—symbolizing the twelve tribes of Israel—and were placed in two rows on a table of pure gold. They were replaced each sabbath by fresh loaves and eaten by the priests: only priests were allowed to eat them because they had been offered to God (cf. Mt 12:3ff). This weekly offering of the "shew bread" (as the loaves are also termed) was a symbol of the renewal of Israel's covenant with God (cf. Ex 25:23-30).

4. Every morning and evening aromatic substances were burned here in honour of God. Rectangular in shape, this altar was made of acacia wood covered in gold, with a golden rim to prevent perfume or embers spilling off it. This also had four "horns", one at each corner of the table (cf. Ex. 30:1-10).

5. This was made of pure gold; it had a base in the form of a cup on which a shaft stood and from the shaft six branches stemmed, three on each side rising to the same height as the centre shaft. At the end of each branch was a cup of hammered work in which oil was burned night and day before the Lord (cf. Ex 25:31-40).

When David made Jerusalem his capital, the tabernacle and the ark were set up there (cf. 2 Sam 6). When Solomon built the temple, that became the home of the ark of the covenant (cf. 1 Kings 6:19; 8:1-9) and the rest of the tabernacle was deposited in special rooms designed for sacred objects not in use. Unfortunately when Nebuchadnezzar sacked Jerusalem in the sixth century B.C., everything belonging to the temple—ark, tent, staves, and other cultic objects—disappeared. The Babylonians burned the temple, and carried off the vessels of gold and silver, eventually using them in the royal palace of Babylon (cf. Dan 5:1-3: Belshazzar's feast and his vision).

2. *The temple*   Solomon started work on the temple around 970 B.C. and the building was seven years in the making. The site chosen for it was Mount Moriah, a hill on the northern ridge of Mount Ophel, the site of the highest point of the city in David's time. It was a spot which had been the scene of an important theophany and where David had built an altar (cf. 2 Sam 24:18-24; 1 Chron 21:18-26; 2 Chron 3:1).

The temple of Solomon, built on the Egyptian model with slight changes, consisted of three parts (cf. 1 Kings 5-8)—the vestibule (*Ulam*) which was a covered porch about 11 metres (36 ft) wide by 5.5 metres long; the hall or house (*Hekhal*), also called "the Holy Place", 11 metres wide by 22 metres long; and finally the *Debir* or inner sanctuary, the "most Holy Place" or Holy of Holies, which was closed off from the Holy Place. On each side of the temple, built up against its walls, there was a three-storey building; its rooms were used, among other things, for storing offerings and for the temple treasury. The area immediately around the temple was called the "inner court" and was marked off by a wall. Outside this was the "great" or "outer" court; a second wall surrounded the entire complex of the temple and Solomon's palace.

In the inner court was located the altar of holocausts, a huge bronze table on which sacrificial victims were burned. Near this was "the molten sea", a

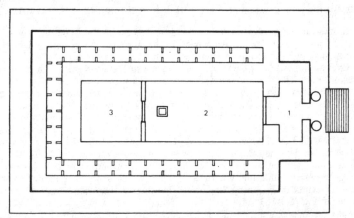

Plan of the temple of Solomon: 1. Vestibule (*Ulam*); 2. Hall (*Hekhal*);
3. Inner sanctuary (or Holy of Holies)

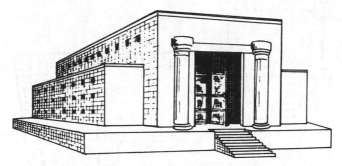

Reconstruction of the temple of Solomon

huge container of water which took the place of the earlier large basin used for ritual ablution. It stood on twelve bronze oxen, three at each corner.

The Holy Place had a golden altar on which incense was stored, and the table of the loaves of proposition and ten golden candelabra. The only thing in the Holy of Holies was the ark of the covenant, and just as with the tabernacle only the high priest might enter there on the Day of Atonement.

The temple of Solomon, which was the pride of the Jewish people, was completely destroyed by the army of Nebuchadnezzar in the year 586 B.C. at the time when the Jews were deported to Babylon (cf. 2 Kings 24:13 and 25:13ff). On their return after the exile, they began the rebuilding of the temple and finished it in 515 B.C. (cf. Ezra 4:24 - 6:22). The new temple was called the "second temple" or the temple of Zerubbabel, the man largely responsible for its construction. It was built on the same general lines as the temple of Solomon, but it was must less elaborate. The Holy of Holies no longer contained the ark. However, the Holy Place still had the table with loaves of proposition and a golden seven-branched candlestick instead of the ten candelabra that had been in the temple of Solomon.

This second temple also had its misfortunes, the worst being when it was sacked (cf. 1 Mac 1:21-24; 2 Mac 5:15-16) and profaned (cf. 1 Mac 1:44-49; 2 Mac 6:1-7; Dan 9:27; 11:31) by Antiochus IV Epiphanes in 169 and 167 B.C. respectively. The temple was cleansed and restored some years later by Judas Maccabeus (cf. 1 Mac 4:41-59), an event which gave rise to the annual feast of the "Dedication".

In 20-19 B.C. Herod the Great, to win favour with the Jews, began work on the rebuilding and embellishing of the temple,[6] a project which took ten years, although some details were not completed until A.D. 62. The temple proper was now almost a replica of Solomon's temple, but the surrounding buildings were considerably different. This third temple or temple of Herod was the one that was sanctified by the presence of Jesus Christ.

6.   Cf. Flavius Josephus, *Jewish Antiquities*, XV, 11, 1.

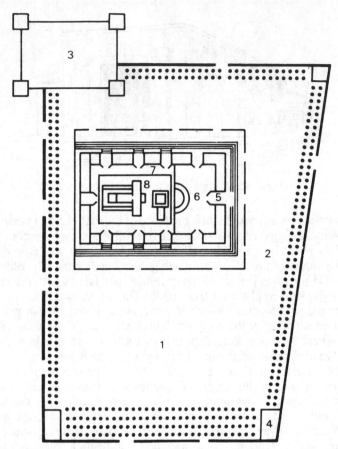

Plan of the temple built by Herod: 1. Court of the Gentiles;
2. Portico of Solomon; 3. Antonia Tower;
4. Pinnacle of the temple; 5 Inner court;
6. Court of the Israelites; 7. Court of the priests

The esplanade around the temple was greatly expanded and divided into three concentric courts, each on a higher level than the one outside it. The outermost court was known as the *court of the Gentiles*. There was no restriction on entry into this court. A porch ran right round it, with either two or three rows of pillars. The porch on the eastern side was known as the *portico of Solomon*.[7] The court of the Gentiles was also the location of the temple market, with booths for money-changers and sellers of victims for sacrifice.[8] On the north-eastern

7. Our Lord and the Apostles used go there (cf. Jn 10:23; Acts 3:11; 5:12).
8. These facilities were made available to suit the faithful who used the temple and wanted to

28

corner was an imposing military fortress known as the Antonia Tower,[9] and there were towers also at the other three corners, of which the most prominent was that on the southeastern corner; this looked down on the Kidron valley; from the base of the tower, known as the "pinnacle of the temple",[10] the ground fell steeply away, a drop of 70 metres.

A flight of steps led up from the court of the Gentiles to the *inner court*. To enter this one had to cross a colonnade which ran round it and which carried inscriptions prohibiting the entry of pagans under pain of death. Within this inner court the first area was the *women's court* from which women assisted at religious worship. The walls of this court contained boxes for the collection of the faithful's alms for the temple. This was known as the "treasury" (cf. Mk 12:41; Lk 21:1-4). From this court a staircase led into the *court of the Israelites*, which immediately led on to the slightly higher *court of the priests*. Here were located the altar of holocausts, the basin for ablutions which took the place of the "molten sea", and everything needed for the sacrificing of victims.

On a slightly higher level still, which meant that it could be seen from any part of the city, was the temple itself with its traditional areas—the porch; the Holy Place, with the seven branch candlestick, the table for the loaves of proposition, and the altar of incense; and the Holy of Holies, whose entrance was closed off by a heavy, ornate curtain;[11] the Holy of Holies was empty.

The temple of Herod was completely razed by the legions of Titus in the year A.D. 70 and never rebuilt. Today a mosque stands on the site of the esplanade—the mosque of Omar. The enormous foundations of the western wall which supported the esplanade on the temple of Herod constitute what is popularly known today as the "wailing wall".

THE PRIESTHOOD

The priest in Israel was called *cohen*, a word whose etymology means "he who is standing", that is, one who stands before God and serves him. Priests in the strict sense of the word only appear after God made the covenant with Moses. Prior to then the priesthood was not formally organized; it was exercised in the same fashion as obtained among other ancient peoples. In the case of nomadic peoples the chief of the clan or tribe acted as its priest as well, offering sacrifice and leading prayers. This explains, for example, why we find Abraham and Jacob offering sacrifice (cf., e.g., Gen 15:9ff; 22:13; 31:54; 46:1) and dedicating altars (cf. Gen 12:7; 13:18; 28:16ff).

offer sacrifices (of cattle, sheep, doves and pigeons) and pay their contributions in shekels, special temple coinage. These sellers and money-changers provoked Christ to anger and he expelled them from the precincts (cf. Mt 21:12-13 and par., and corresponding notes).

9. The praetorium of Pilate was located here. It was in the large courtyard of this fortress, the *Gabbatha* or *Lithostrotos*, that Jesus was presented to the crowd dressed in a purple robe and wearing a crown of thorns; and it was here he was scourged and condemned to death.
10. This seems to have been where Satan brought our Lord during his temptation in the wilderness (cf. Mt 4:5; Lk 4:9).
11. This is the curtain which tore at the same time as Jesus gave up his spirit (cf. Mt 27:51; Heb 9:3).

29

Moses, on God's instruction, entrusted cultic duties to the members of one tribe only, that of Levi (cf. Ex 32:25-29; Num 1:49-53; 3:6-10; Deut 33:8-11), and the priesthood in particular was linked with the descendants of Aaron, whom Moses anointed as high priest (cf. Ex 28:1; 29:7; Lev 8:1-36). The high priesthood passed on from eldest son to eldest son and the other descendants of Aaron were simply priests (cf. Ex 29:9; 30:31; Lev 7:35; 10:7). The other members of the tribe of Levi assisted the priests in ancillary cultic functions—cleaning the tabernacle, acting as watchmen, orderlies, helpers at sacrifice, etc.

In addition to being descendants of Aaron it was a requirement that priests be free from physical mutilation or defects; they had to observe ritual purity in religious ceremonies and lead an unblemished and irreproachable life (cf. Lev 21; 22:1-15). When engaging in religious worship they had also to wear special, very ornate vestments (cf. Ex 28:40ff; 29:4-8ff).

Although the functions of priests underwent changes in the course of the centuries, their role always had to do with offering sacrifice, engaging in temple ritual, instructing the people in the Law and interpreting and applying its prescriptions. Their main source of support was the portion of the sacrifices allotted to them, the money they had to be given by way of tithes in accordance with various precepts of the Law, and donations from the faithful.

SACRIFICE

The priest is the mediator between God and men, and his reason for being is closely connected with sacrifice, for there can be no priesthood without sacrifice. Sacrifice is the principal act of religious worship, the highest form of that adoration which a creature renders his Creator. Thus, sacrifice in one form or another is a feature of all religions. Generally among the other Semitic peoples, as distinct from the Jews, sacrifice—which usually involved the shedding of blood—was connected with the provision of food for the divinity present in an idol. Sacrifice reflected the god's power over living things. The Greeks and Latins had a similar notion of sacrifice, but they spoke not of feeding the deity but of winning his favour or placating his anger.

According to biblical teaching, sacrifice was an offering, a gift, of an animal or product of the soil, made to God in recognition of his sovereignty and in gratitude for gifts received; this offering involved the total or partial destruction of the victim on an altar. Depending on the purpose of the sacrifice, it involved or did not involve the shedding of blood.

Sacrifice involving the shedding of blood took various forms:

a) *Peace offering* or *communion offering* (*zebah shelamim*)   An offering to thank God for benefits received or in supplication for future divine favour (cf. Lev 3:1-17). The purpose of this offering was to bring the offerer closer to God, as symbolized by the feast that followed the sacrifice, at which the priest, the offerer, and his family and perhaps invited guests (provided none was suffering from legal impurity) ate part of the sacrificed victim (cf. Lev 7:19ff; Deut 12:12, 18; 16:11f).

b) *Holocaust* (*ola^c*) This was the most solemn form of sacrifice and involved the total destruction of the victim in honour of God (cf. Lev 1:1-17; 6:8-13; Num 15:3-9). The flesh was burned and the blood sprinkled round the altar; only the victim's pelt was kept; it became the priest's property. The victim had to be male, unblemished, and chosen from "pure" categories—cattle, sheep, goats, or birds such as turtle-doves or pigeons. These victims could be offered by private persons as well as the people as a whole. The practice was to have one morning and one evening sacrifice every day on behalf of the whole people (cf. Ex 29:38-43). Before the victim was put to death, the offerer would put his hand on its head to indicate that it was his property and that he was donating it to the Lord and therefore was deserving of the fruits of the sacrifice; sometimes the imposition of hands meant that the victim was a stand-in for the offerer.

c) *Atonement sacrifices* This type of sacrifice came into special prominence in the post-exilic period; it was designed mainly to reconcile the sinner with God. There were two types of atonement offerings—the sin offering (*hattat*) (cf. Lev 4:1 - 5:13; 6:24-33) and the trespass offering (*asham*) (cf. Lev 5:14-26; 7:1-6). Although the distinction between the two is not very clear, the sin offering was apparently made in atonement for faults which had not encroached on one's neighbour's rights; whereas the trespass offering was designed to make up for faults which involved injustice to God and neighbour. In these sacrifices the victim was burned on the altar of holocausts and the unused portion went to the priests. When the offering was being made to atone for the sin of the people or of the high priest (who represented the community), the unburnt part did not go to the priests: it had to be burned away from the sanctuary, on some waste land.

This offering cleansed people from legal impurity and from various transgressions committed out of frailty or ignorance. Sacrifices could not cancel out voluntary faults, the result of conscious malice.

An important element in these sacrifices was the rite of anointing the horns of the altar with the victim's blood and sprinkling it on the curtain that separated the Holy Place from the Holy of Holies. Atonement offerings were made on the main feasts; they conformed to various rules depending on who the offerer was, but the main event each year in this connexion was the Day of Atonement (*Yom Kippur*).

In addition to bloody sacrifices there were others which usually took the form of offerings of cereals (*minhah*) (cf. Lev 2:1-16; 6:7-16) and other agricultural produce. For example, offerings of finest flour, the high priest's perpetual offering, and the offering of first-fruits; in all these cases the use of leaven was avoided and a little salt was added. A portion of these offerings was burned on the altar and the rest kept for the priests unless the offerer was himself a priest.

Mention might also be made—though it has nothing to do with sacrifice—of a rite of purification mentioned in the Epistle to the Hebrews. This was a rite of individual purification and atonement involving the use of a heifer's ashes (cf. Num 19:1-9). A young red heifer without blemishes and which had never been under the yoke was slaughtered outside the camp as a sacrifice for sin, and then burned. Its ashes, which were kept in a clean place outside the camp, were used for adding to water which was kept for certain purification ceremonies.

FESTIVALS

In early times the Jewish people had three main annual festivals—Passover, Pentecost and the feast of Tabernacles (cf. Ex 12; 23:14-16; 34:18-23; Lev 23; Num 28-29; Deut 16:1ff). Of later origin, but also important, are the Day of Atonement, the Day of the Dedication, and the feast of Purim. The Day of Atonement gradually acquired more and more importance, and because it is particularly relevant to the Epistle to the Hebrews, we shall go into it in some detail; but first we shall briefly describe the other feasts of the Jewish calendar.

a) *The Passover and the Feast of the Azymes*   This was the main feast of the year or, rather, the main festival period, because it lasted eight days. Although these two feasts were probably of different origin, for they were celebrations of different events, in practice, with time, they became a single festival. The Passover commemorated the rescue of the Jewish people from their enslavement in Egypt, when the exterminating angel passed over the houses of the Hebrews and inflicted death on the first-born of the Egyptians only (cf. Ex 12:1-32). The Passover was celebrated every year on a fixed day, in the evening before the fourteenth day of Nisan, that is, the day of the spring full moon. Although the passover rites have their origin in very early customs of nomadic shepherd people, the feast was instituted in response to an explicit divine command. The feast of the Azymes, for its part, was the festival at which the first-fruits of the harvest were dedicated to God (cf. Lev 23:15; Deut 16:9). This indicates that the feast was not established until the Israelites entered the promised land.

According to the official rite laid down after the exile, both feasts had to be celebrated in Jerusalem, beginning with the passover meal on the night before 14 Nisan. The festival lasted for a week, during which it was forbidden to eat leavened bread or even to keep leaven in one's house. The most solemn days were the first and the last days of the festival, and the sabbath which fell between 14 and 21 Nisan.

At the passover meal each family had to eat an entire lamb, which had previously been sacrificed in the temple; the lamb was served with unleavened bread and bitter herbs. The entire supper involved a series of rites such as, for example, the rite of different drinks of wine, very specifically prescribed. In our Lord's time this feastday had enormous importance. On this day all Israelite men had to appear before Yahweh, that is, visit his sanctuary (cf. Ex 23:14-17).

b) *The Feast of Weeks, or Pentecost* This was celebrated seven weeks after the feast of the Azymes and was designed to thank God for the completion of the grain harvest (wheat, barley and rye). The Azymes and Pentecost were closely connected, being celebrated respectively at the start and the finish of the grain harvest, with a gap of fifty days between them (hence its Greek name, Pentecost). As at Passover, so too at this festival every Israelite man had to appear in the temple; this meant that a huge number of pilgrims from all parts of Palestine and from the Jewish communities in the Diaspora flocked to Jerusalem at this time. The atmosphere of Pentecost was very festive and gay; everywhere noisy sacred banquets were held, with the whole family, servants and invited guests taking part (cf. Acts 2:5-13).

c) *The Feast of Tabernacles* This was the third of the great festivals of the year. All Israelite men had to present themselves at the temple of Jerusalem. It was also called the feast of "ingathering" and it was a very joyful affair because it celebrated the happy end of the harvest of all agricultural produce. It took place from the fifteenth to the twenty-second day of the seventh month in the Jewish calendar—more or less our September-October. It was a time of rejoicing and thanksgiving for the fruits of the land God had given the people of Israel. The name probably originated in the tabernacles or tents which the Israelites used to put up in the fields and vineyards as living quarters during the harvesting. As the years went by this custom was given a religious and historical significance by reference to the tents which the Hebrews lived in when they led the nomadic existence of their pilgrimage in the wilderness. The Israelites used to camp out in the open during this seven-day period. This feast has special interest for the New Testament because it was the background to certain episodes in our Lord's life, which are described in chapter 7 of St John's Gospel. It is worth recalling that in Jerusalem on each of the eight days of the festival the high priest sprinkled the altar of holocausts with water in a large cup taken from the Pool of Siloam, in remembrance of the water which sprang up miraculously in the wilderness, and to petition God for the gift of rain (cf. Ex 17:1-7). On the first night the entire city was lit up by the light of four huge lamps in the women's court, a reminder of the bright cloud of the Exodus (cf. Jn 7:37-39; 8:12). This background explains our Lord's reference to the rivers of living water that the spirit would cause to flow out of the hearts of the faithful, and to the fact that he himself was the "light of the world".

d) *The Day of Atonement* Over the course of the history of Israel this feast gradually grew in importance. There are numerous references to it in Hebrews. Its Hebrew name is *Yom Kippur* and it is celebrated on the tenth day of the month of Tishri, the same month in which the feast of Tabernacles is held. It was primarily penitential in character and was known for its austere solemnity. The purpose of the feast was to blot out the sins of the whole nation, including those of the priests and leaders of the people, and to atone for faults and impurities which the ordinary sacrifices had not been able to make up for. The feast was also the occasion for cleansing the sanctuary from any contamination produced by the presence of sinners. The ceremonies in the temple were conducted by the high priest, unaccompanied, and wearing simple priestly vestments made of linen. This was the only day in which he could enter the Holy of Holies.

The high priest first sacrificed a young bull for his own sins and those of the priestly line. After this he entered the Holy of Holies and performed certain rites, particularly that of sprinkling some of the bull's blood in the direction of the mercy seat (cf. Lev 16:11-14). He then came out and performed another ceremony in which a goat, chosen by lot from a pair, was sacrificed for the sins of the people. He then went back into the Holy of Holies with the blood of this animal and sprinkled it likewise at the mercy seat. The he came out again and anointed the altar with some of the blood of the bull and the goat (cf. Lev 16:15-19, 33). Coming out of the temple he then laid his hands on the second of the two goats, the one which had not been sacrificed, symbolizing that the goat was being burdened with all the sins and faults, voluntary and involuntary, of the Israelites. This animal was then led out into the wilderness to fend for itself. The ceremony continued with biblical readings relevant to the feast and the recitation of various prayers. The high priest then put on solemn priestly garments and sacrificed two rams as a burnt offering—one for himself and one for the people—and then carried on the rest of the normal sacrifices and, after blessing the people, dismissed them.

The Day of Atonement was the day on which Israel was reconciled with God. It restored to the Hebrew nation its status of being a holy people, through the forgiveness of everything which could have separated them from their God, that is, whatever sins they had committed in the past year which remained unpardoned.

e) *The Feast of the Dedication* (*Hanukkah*)   This was a celebration of the day when Judas Maccabeus cleansed the temple of Jerusalem (cf. 1 Mac 4:58) three years after it had been profaned (in 167 B.C.) by Antiochus IV Epiphanes (cf. 1 Mac 1:54). Judas determined that this great event should be commemorated every year, on the twenty-fifth of the month of Chislev (December). On that day sacrifices were offered in the temple and processions took place with singing of hymns and psalms. The temple, synagogues and houses displayed so many lights at this festival that it was known as the "Festival of Lights". In our Lord's time it was known by its Greek name of "Feast of Encaenia" (from the Greek *enkainia* = inauguration).

f) *The Feast of Purim*   This was celebrated on 14 and 15 Adar (February-March) and was preceded by a fast on 13 Adar. It commemorated the liberation of the Jews living in Persia from their enemy Haman, minister of King Ahasuerus, thanks to Esther and Mordecai (cf. Esther 8-10). The feast took its name from the way Haman decided on the day on which all the Jews should be massacred: this was done by the casting of "Pur, that is the lot" (Esther 3:7);

the Hebrew word *Purim* means "lots". This feast was the least religious of all the Jewish feasts and it does not seem to have had any special importance in New Testament Palestine.

g) *The sabbath* This was the day of the week dedicated to the Lord in commemoration of his covenant with his people (cf. Ex 34:21) and of the creation of the world (cf. Gen 2:3); its observance is laid down in the third commandment of the decalogue (cf. Ex 20:8-11; Deut 5:12-15). No work was done on the sabbath and in addition to the weekday sacrifices in the temple two lambs were sacrificed along with an offering (cf. Num 28:9-10)—effectively doubling the weekday offering.

h) *The day of the new moon* This was the first day of the month: ancient Israel followed a lunar calendar. It was laid down (cf. Num 28:11-15) that there should be a solemn burnt offering of bulls and lambs, together with a sin offering. As on the sabbath, no work was done and it was a day dedicated to praising the name of God and thanking him for his blessings. Although it was tending to die out, it does get a mention in the New Testament (cf. Col 2:16).

CONCLUSIONS

All these festivals and celebrations show the important part played by divine worship in the life of Israel; this was in preparation for the definitive revelation of the New Testament, where rites are simplified and people's relationship with God goes deeper (since it should be more personal) and at the same time more universal (worship is not concentrated in one specific location).

Both the earlier tabernacle and the temple of Jerusalem, as also the feasts celebrated therein, show not just that the Israelite people offered worship to God: they were also the sign of the Lord's presence among his people. By the Covenant of Sinai God brought into being a people whom he would protect in a singular way. As the chosen people made their way through the wilderness, his presence was a source of help and consolation: God, too, had pitched his tent among theirs. This was the tabernacle, jealously guarding the point where God's presence made itself manifest to the Israelites—the ark of the covenant and more specifically the mercy seat. The Jews called this presence *Shekinah* (a word derived from a verb meaning "to stay under a tent"), and it was seen as the equivalent of the very "glory of God". Initially the *Shekinah* manifested itself around the ark and also in the temple of Jerusalem in a physical form, as a pillar of cloud or of fire. Later this special presence of God in the midst of the people lost these physical attributes and became something interior and spiritual—disengaged from that worldly, triumphalist tendency of the Jews to see themselves as invincible simply because they had the ark of the covenant. After the destruction of the temple by Nebuchadnezzar and the loss of the ark (cf., e.g., Is 6; Ez 8-9; Zech 8:1-18), the Jews, thanks to the part played by the prophets, came more to realize that God's presence was, above all, spiritual and personal; in this way the chosen people were being prepared for the fulness of the presence of God in the world through the Incarnation of his Son (cf. Jn 1:14).

At the same time it came to be seen that the temple, like the tabernacle, was or had been only a symbol of the heavenly temple, that is, the dwelling-place of God and the ultimate home that awaits us. As the Epistle to the Hebrews makes clear, entry thereto has been opened up by the sacrifice of Christ, which has established a new, eternal and universal covenant with mankind. Thus, the Letter to the Hebrew is a stage in the Revelation process, showing as it does that the true sanctuary is to be found in heaven, and that it is, at the same time, the body of Christ; and that the time has come "when the true worshippers will worship the Father in spirit and truth" (Jn 4:23).

Introduction to
the Epistle to the Hebrews

The content of the Epistle to the Hebrews makes it one of the most imposing and important books in the New Testament. It is very accurately reflected in its title, even though that title probably only goes back to the second century. It is very likely that the "Hebrews" to whom this epistle was addressed were in the first instance Christians of Jewish background who were very familiar both with the Greek language and with Hebraic culture, particularly the ceremonies of Mosaic worship.

The Epistle to the Hebrews is of a type which falls between a letter and a written address or sermon (cf. 13:22, where it is described as a "word of consolation"). Its structure and presentation are reminiscent of a short theological treatise. This is perhaps why some scholars have described it as a "literary letter", although the literary letter proper is addressed to a fictitious reader, which is not the case here. By using the letter form the writer was able to produce a text which would appeal to a wider readership than an essay would.

Be that as it may, historically and doctrinally this epistle is connected, via its content, with the corpus of Pauline letters, for it faithfully echoes the preaching of St Paul. And yet it has characteristic features of its own which point to its obvious originality.

The main purpose of the letter is to show the superiority of Christianity over the Old Covenant; yet its style and purpose are not polemical. It is designed to show that the New Law is the perfection, the fulfilment, of the Old Law, which it supersedes. To do this it focuses on the idea that Christ's priesthood and sacrifice are superior to those of the Levitical priesthood. The writer uses this teaching as the basis for exhorting his readers to persevere in the faith: this pastoral purpose is also a primordial aim of the epistle.

CANONICITY

The epistle forms part of the canon of the Bible and therefore it must be taken as divinely inspired: certain early councils—for example, the Council of Carthage in 397—put it in this category, as did all the Fathers of the Church.

The Epistle to the Hebrews was solemnly pronounced to be canonical by the Councils of Florence (1442) and Trent (Session IV, 1546).[1]

1. *Reply* of the Pontifical Biblical Commission, 24 June 1914, *Dz-Sch* 2176.

Many Christian writers of the East regarded the Letter to the Hebrews as having been written by St Paul himself. These included, for example, St John Chrysostom, a great admirer of the writings of the Teacher of the Gentiles and one deeply versed in them.

If St Paul did write this letter, it would mean that there is a total of fourteen letters in the canon written by the Apostle. However, the tradition of the western Church is not quite unanimous on this point. "Ambrosiaster", the anonymous author of the first complete Latin commentary on St Paul, does not include this letter in his work. St Jerome himself touches on the question and expresses some doubts, as does St Augustine from 409 onwards. However, as to whether it can be directly attributed to St Paul, both Augustine and Jerome (later on and under the influence of tradition), came to accept not only that this is an inspired letter—which was never in doubt—but also that it is by Paul. Thus St Jerome, for example, quoting a passage from Hebrews, writes: "thus speaks St Paul in his letter, the letter he writes to the Hebrews, although many Latin authors doubt (his authorship)" (*In Mt* IV, 26). The Muratorian Fragment or "Muratorian Canon", a Roman papyrus of the end of the second century containing an official listing of inspired books, does not explicitly include this letter among the Pauline writings, whereas the others are listed in detail. Some Renaissance theologians, among them Erasmus and Cajetan, also held the view that St Paul was not the author of this letter—and this is the opinion of most twentieth-century exegetes. According to these scholars the main arguments against St Paul's authorship are—the absence of his name at the heading of the letter; the absence also of St Paul's usual form of signing off, as of other typical features of Pauline letters; the marked difference in syntax and other aspects of literary style between this and the other Pauline letters; the diversity of doctrinal themes; and the letter's particular way of quoting the Old Testament.

The sacred writer and his personality stay very much in the background (cf. Heb 13:18b), as if he were deliberately hiding behind the sublimity of his subject-matter. At the same time it is quite clear that he was an educated Christian, deeply versed in Sacred Scripture and very familiar with the main theological issues of the day. The person who actually wrote the letter must have been someone very close to St Paul, familiar with his thinking and with his apostolic work. The content of the letter clearly shows the writer to have been someone of Hellenist culture and a person with much pastoral zeal, who had a deep knowledge of the religious life of the Jews and of the religious worship conducted in the temple of Jerusalem.

Origen, in the second century, spoke of the possibility of an "editor" of Paul's ideas being the direct author of the letter. "The ideas of the epistle", the Alexandrian exegete writes, "certainly belong to the Apostle; however, the language and composition seem to belong to someone else, who wished to record Paul's thinking, writing down the words of the Master."

Origen's theory has been widely followed in the tradition of the Church and has been indirectly supported by the Pontifical Biblical Commission in its reply of 24 June 1914.[2] However, attempts are still made to identify the author-editor, and among the names put forward as possible editors are those of St Barnabas, St Luke, St Clement of Rome and the disciple Apollos (cf. Acts 18:24f). However, all these suggestions are pure conjecture.

Most of the Fathers and early commentators were of the opinion that the letter was written in Rome or in some part of Italy—given the reference in Heb 13:24, "Those who come from Italy send you greetings." However, that sentence could also be taken as a greeting from a group of Italian Christians now living in some other (unidentified) place from which the letter is being sent. In fact, one manuscript gives Athens as its place of composition; others say it was written in Rome or in Italy; basically we do not know for sure where it was written.

It is less difficult to establish the approximate time of writing. Hebrews 1:3-13 appears as a quotation in chapter 36, 2-5 of St Clement of Rome's letter to the Corinthians, which was written around the year 95. If the letter was already quite widely known by that date, then it could not have been written later than the start of the 90s.

The internal evidence of the letter allows us to push the date back much further and to say that there is every likelihood that it was written prior to the destruction of Jerusalem in the year 70. At no point is there any reference to the fall of the city; whereas many references clearly imply that the temple and Mosaic worship are still active (cf. Heb 8:4; 9:7, 13, 25).

Moreover, the text refers repeatedly (cf. Heb 10:25; 10:37; 12:26f; 13:13) to difficult times for the Jews. This might suggest that we are on the eve of the Jewish-Roman war, which was declared in the year 67. Quite a number of scholars opt for 67 as the date of composition.

ADDRESSEES

The content of the letter allows us to state that it was undoubtedly addressed to converts from Judaism, that is, Christians of Jewish origin. They seem to be people well-known to the writer, for he confidently asks them to pray for him and tells them to expect him soon (cf. Heb 13:18-19, 23). They are Christians who are familiar with the sacred books, especially the Book of Exodus and the Psalms, and they are very familiar with standard Jewish interpretation. They know the temple well and are familiar with the details of divine worship as performed there; they have attended the ceremonies of the great "Day of Atonement", and the daily sacrifices (cf. Heb 8:1-10, 18) and understand the terminology connected with those rites.

Furthermore, they are not recent converts. The letter refers to their having already received initiation catechesis (cf. Heb 5:12); and they may even have been teachers, because they were converted a long time back (cf. Heb 10:32) and saw for themselves the miracles and supernatural gifts which accompanied the early preaching of the Apostles (cf. Heb 6:4-5; 10:26). They may even have

2. Cf. *Dz-Sch* 2178.

heard the preaching of Stephen (cf. Heb 2:4; Acts 6:8). However, in addition to this, they have earned merit by their service to the saints (cf. Heb 6:10) and have bravely and patiently borne overt persecution involving public opprobrium, confiscation of property, imprisonment and, in some cases, even capital punishment (cf. Heb 10:32-34; 12:4).

The central purpose of the epistle is to encourage these brethren to stay loyal in the face of persecution—because they were showing signs of weakening (cf. Heb 10:25; 12:25; 13:10)—and ultimately to protect them from the danger of apostasy. This explains the way in which the sacred writer prudently combines warm encouragement with straight talk (cf. Heb 6:4-6; 10:26-31; 12:15-29).

From early on commentators have asked whether the author of Hebrews was addressing a specific local church, as in the case of the letters to the Romans, Corinthians, Galatians etc; or whether he was writing to a small group of people within a wider Christian community—what we might call a "domestic church" or perhaps a group of faithful who used to meet in the house of some particular family. The writer seems to be addressing a group of people who are cut off from their background—perhaps refugees or exiles.

Certainly, the specialized subject and focus of the letter suggest that the sacred writer is addressing a definite group which forms part of a wider Christian community. Some scholars even think that it is addressed to former Levitical priests, converts to the Gospel, who, harassed by persecutions, feel tempted to revert to Judaism (cf. Acts 6:7; Heb 3:12-14; 6:4-6; 10:39; 12:12-13; 13:5-6).

STRUCTURE

The literary structure of Hebrews has been the subject of detailed study; nevertheless, it is difficult to come to grips with, for various reasons. Firstly, the rules of rhetoric in the ancient Greek and Latin world did not require a rigorously developed composition, with paragraphs of more or less equal length: the writer was free to digress, develop, go back, anticipate himself, etc. Secondly, although the literary form chosen by the writer, that of a letter, approaches that of a sermon or theological essay, it does not really lend itself to a very systematic exposition; and thirdly, the writer's Semitic mind is not concerned with the harmonious arranging of parts (of the letter) but rather focuses on certain basic ideas. All this helps to explain why, throughout his exposition, he is constantly changing from a doctrinal vein to an exhortative one and back again. He purposely mixes moral and dogmatic elements, presenting the truths of faith as the basis for the line of conduct he is recommending. From this point of view the letter is a very good example of the unity that should obtain between doctrine and life, a unity which is so proper to the New Testament; it is a model for the best sort of Christian religious writing.

Hebrews does not, therefore, contain a doctrinal section followed by a moral section. Its doctrinal content is spread throughout the letter and liable to appear at any moment. Drawing on earlier exegetical tradition, St Thomas Aquinas rightly says that the central theme of the epistle is Christ; in which case the letter can be divided into four sections. The first three would aim at showing Christ's superiority over the most prominent figures in the Old Testament—angels, Moses and the priests of the Levitical order. The fourth and last section would be mainly moral and exhortative in character. Hugh of St-Cher proposes a similar division of the letter: 1) Christ's superiority over all creation; 2) the superiority of Christ's priesthood over the priesthood of the Old Testament; 3) an exhortation to faith, which brings us closer to Christ; and 4) moral teaching.

Modern scholarship proposes a division into five parts (individual scholars would propose minor variations on this). Obviously there is nothing hard and fast about this division; it is essentially tentative.

It is fairly easy to identify five doctrinal sections in the letter:

1) Christ's pre-existence, his divine condition and his activity as Creator (1:1-4);
2) Christ's superiority over angels (1:5 - 2:18);
3) his superiority over Moses (3:1 - 4:13);
4) Christ's priesthood is on a higher level than the Levitical priesthood (4:14 - 7:28);
5) Christ's sacrifice is greater than all the sacrifices of the Old Law (8:1 - 10:18).

The ascetic, exhortatory and moral content of the letter, which is interlayered with the theological parts, deals with the following themes:

a) to attain salvation it is essential to follow Jesus (2:1-4);
b) to enter God's "rest" one must imitate those faithful souls who accepted Revelation (3:7 - 4:13);
c) the prospect of everlasting joy; criteria for Christian living (5:11 - 6:20);
d) reasons why a believer should persevere in the faith despite difficulties; and the good example set by those who have gone before (10:19 - 12:29);
e) final advice (13:1-19).

Verses 7-17 of chapter 13 seem to summarize the main themes of the epistle and contain a concluding exhortation to that right living and spiritual vitality which should characterize Christian life.

LANGUAGE AND STYLE OF ARGUMENT

The language of the Epistle to the Hebrews is notable for its singular clarity; this gives it an important place in literature and it also makes it a well argued theological treatise. Its majestic flow and the sublimity of its subject-matter explain why the Church uses it so extensively in the Liturgy.

The author, who must have had a good Hellenist education, writes very correct and elegant Greek; his vocabulary is rich and he manages to express his thought very graphically by employing many stylistic devices, such as contrasts, comparisons, parallelisms, and use of quotations and examples from Scripture. He is particularly good at linking phrases and clauses to form elaborate, formal sentences, in line with the style of the best writers of Hellenist Greek prose. The letter does not have the limpid, transparent and agile Greek of St Luke, but from a literary point of view it undoubtedly comes next in line in the New Testament after Luke.

We might refer in particular to how, in the midst of the generally precise and sober style of the letter, certain passages stand out for their deep religious emotion—for example, its evocation of Christ's agony in Gethsemane (cf. Heb 5:7-8), his passion and death on the Cross (cf. Heb 6:6; 12:2; 13:22), and the faith and steadfastness of the Patriarchs (cf. Heb 11:1-40).

The author, who was deeply versed in Sacred Scripture, uses for the most part the Greek translation (the "Septuagint"), which was what all the Apostles used in their preaching. When he quotes a passage of the Old Testament he does so with an introductory formula which shows his conviction that the Bible is divinely inspired: the passage being quoted is seen as something said directly by God the Father or by the Son, or, in some instances, by the Holy Spirit (cf. Heb 3:7; 10:15). Also, the author of Hebrews almost always interprets Sacred Scripture in its literal sense, that is, he focuses on what the text seems to be saying directly. A distinguishing feature of Hebrews is the way it "actualizes" the Old Testament texts by applying them to Christ. In the Psalms and the Prophets it is God the Father who is addressing his Son, or God the Son his Father.

INTERPRETATION OF THE OLD TESTAMENT

To understand the way the author of Hebrews uses Sacred Scripture, it is useful to bear in mind that in many instances he is applying rabbinical rules of biblical interpretation. This type of exegesis is called *derash* in Hebrew (deriving from the verb meaning "to seek", "to interpret").[3]

Derash is to be found in many documents—translations of biblical texts with short explanations built into them; ascetical or moral commentaries; and lists of rules and regulations derived from the Law (for example, marriage rites, regulations about the celebration of feasts, etc.).[4] It is essentially a form of

---

3. In Jewish culture we find three main types of biblical interpretation. The first is *derash*, used in the synagogue, this uses a series of seven fixed criteria, laid down—as tradition has it—by Rabbi Hillel; the second is the form of exegesis known as *pesher* (= explanation), widely used in the Qumran community on the shores of the Dead Sea in the period from the second century B.C. to the first century A.D. and found in the famous Dead Sea Scrolls; the third is exegesis of an allegorical-moral type popularized by the famous Jewish scholar Alexander of Philo (*d.* A.D. 40).

4. Particularly the *targumim*, the *midrashim*, the *Mishnah* and the *Talmud*. The targums are translations of the Hebrew Old Testament into Aramaic, with explanatory notes. These are of

exegesis which sticks to the letter of the text and uses certain procedures from logic—analogies, reflections on the text, parallel passages, moving from the general to the particular, etc. However, in the course of its development this type of exegesis tended more and more to become a search for a religious meaning which went beyond the obvious or immediate meaning, towards "actualization" of the texts, in other words, applying it to new situations in history. *Derash* gradually liberated itself from purely literal and linguistic explanations and tended to take on the main features of spiritual or allegorical interpretation.

An example might show more clearly what we mean. Heb 1:5-14 quotes a number of Old Testament text to show the superiority of Christ, the Son of God over the angels (cf. 2 Sam, 7:14; Deut 32:43; Ps 45:7-8; 97:7; 102:256ff; 104:4; 110:1); in addition to the number of references given, the interesting thing to note is that some of the Psalms are read as words of God the Father addressed to his Son, even though in their original context these psalms were addressed to God in praise of his omnipotence (cf. Ps 97:7; 102:26; 104:4) or, in some instances, were prayers or petitions to the Messiah King (cf. Ps 45:7-8; 110:1).

What the author of Hebrews, under divine inspiration, has done is to "actualize" the psalm by interpreting it as referring to Jesus Christ (whom he implicitly sees as Author of creation and true King of the chosen people).

There are many other examples[5] that might be given of the same type of exegesis. One very important one has to do with the figure of Melchizedek, without father, mother or genealogy; another concerns the sprinkling of the tablets of the Law with the blood and ashes of a cow, using a swab of scarlet wool: they are important because they refer to the priesthood and sacrifice, respectively, of Christ.

The compilation of sequences of scriptural passages and the application of texts to current situations were methods frequently used in derashic interpretation. There is every reason, therefore, for saying that Hebrews was written by a Jew steeped in rabbinical ways, a qualified "doctor of the Law" or scribe, or perhaps a rabbi. The intellectual or cultural background, then, of the writer, is that of a rabbi, a Pharisee; whereas its literary form is appropriate to a Hellenist Jew of Alexandrian background. This is compatible with seeing St

great importance, on account both of their antiquity (they go back to the first century B.C., but use material of an earlier date) and of their content; and they reflect common rabbinical interpretation of difficult passages. The *midrashim* (from *midrash* = research, search) are explanations of the Bible, of an exhortatory or edifying character, sourced in synagogal preaching, that is, in the homilies of rabbis. The *Mishnah* (= repetition) is a collection of short legal and ethical treatises based on rabbinical sayings and decisions. It began to be compiled as a text in the second century A.D. and was finished around the fifth century A.D. It reflects the Law or Torah and the interpretations of numerous oral prescriptions. Its exegesis is called *halakic* (from *halak* = walking, in both the physical and moral sense); it is legal and ethical in character and has to do with providing answers to particular questions and situations. The *Talmud* (= teaching) is a commentary on the Mishnah in line with traditional Jewish religious teaching. It has only a distant connexion with Sacred Scripture but it does provide information useful to understanding Jewish customs during the period of our Lord's life on earth.

5. Other examples of "actualization" are to be found in the case of Ps 40:7 and 95:8, applied to the situation of Christians or to the sacrifice of the Cross.

Paul as responsible for the ideas of the letter: Paul was a Pharisee, a zealous upholder of the Law, a member of the tribe of Benjamin, proud of his background, in his youth a student of Gamaliel.[6]

The *derash* of the Letter to the Hebrews, however, parts company with rabbinical exegesis on one fundamental point: it is centred on Jesus, the climax of the Law. In this respect it is very different from rabbinical exegesis, which confined itself to explaining obscure or difficult points and attended only to Mosaic precepts.

In Hebrews the Old Testament is not quoted to "prove" the excellence and superiority of Jesus; rather, the truths concerning Jesus throw light on and enable us to understand what the Old Testament is all about. The Old Testament is not used to interpret the New: on the contrary, the opposite is the case. The Old Testament text is "actualized" in the light of the New, or, as the Fathers often put it, the New Testament is to be found latent in the Old, and the Old is made manifest in the New. In line with this approach, the first Christians delved in the Old Testament to discover predictions about Christ's birth and his role. As they saw it, it was not possible to understand the Old Testament without reference to the New; however, using the Old Testament as a basis, they felt they could demonstrate that everything to do with Christ occurred in line with a pre-ordained divine plan.

THEOLOGY

The theological teaching contained in the Letter to the Hebrews is essentially Christological. Its view of Christ, God and man and High Priest of the New Law, provides the structure of the letter, linking all its parts together and giving the whole letter a remarkable cohesion.

In connexion with this Christological purpose the letter has extremely important things to say on the relationship between Judaism and Christianity, on faith and revelation, on the last things and on Christian life in the world as the way to eternal life.

a) *Judaism and Christianity*   The relationship between the two religions— Judaism and Christianity—which contain supernatural Revelation, being, respectively, the foundation and the culmination of God's saving designs, is not viewed only from the standpoint of defence of the Christian faith. In a non-polemical spirit and with a serenity befitting one who is writing with a vision of eternity and in the presence of God, the sacred author shows that the objective superiority of Christianity is the key factor in salvation history. The thrust of the letter is not designed to discredit the Jewish religion but rather to assign it its proper place as a preparatory stage in God's plan of salvation.

The central idea of the epistle is that the Mosaic Law is incapable of saving mankind which finds itself in a fallen state because of Adam's sin. In line with this it proclaims the religious impermanence of the Old Law, which Christ has

6.   Cf. Phil 3:5-6; Acts 8:13; 21:40; 22:3; 23:6; Rom 9:3-5; 10:1-2; 2 Cor 11:22.

abolished and replaced with the Law of the Gospel, which is the law of grace, freedom and interior challenge. This is in fact a basic principle in the thinking which imbues the letters of the Apostle of the Gentiles. This was the great dogmatic point clarified by the Council of Jerusalem. As recounted in Acts 15, that first assembly laid down that it is not necessary for salvation to observe the rites of the Mosaic Law, and that therefore people of Gentile background who become Christians are not obliged to observe those regulations. The letter is very mindful of this teaching and in a sense develops it.

The superiority of the New Testament over the Old—which comes across clearly not only from the letter's teaching about Christ but also from what is has to say about the sacraments and about sacrifice, and from the unvarying testimony of the Apostles—does not, however, affect the *unity*, the continuum, of the two Testaments. The letter evidences this unity, which the Second Vatican Council solemnly reminded the Church about;[7] it does this mainly by its use of Old Testament figures or "types". All the key figures in the Old Covenant look forward to Christ and place their hope in him. Moses and Melchizedek are, respectively, "types" of the Messiah and High Priest of the New Law.

Christianity is therefore the culmination of Judaism, with the result that the Mosaic religion cannot be understood without reference to the Gospel. Logically, the dogmatic principle enunciated here has many implications for properly understanding the history of salvation and Judaism; and it also is very relevant to the life of the converts to whom the letter seems to be addressed.

b) *Faith and Revelation* The Letter to the Hebrews is a "word of exhortation" (Heb 13:22) to steadfastness in the faith. The letter frequently makes reference to this virtue, but Heb 11:1 offers a particularly rich and concise definition of faith, one which has become classical in the commentaries of the Fathers and Doctors of the Church. St Thomas Aquinas studies it at length in his treatise on faith and says that it meets all the conditions necessary to make it an exact and adequate definition. In as many words, he defines faith as "that habit of mind whereby we attain to an initial grasp of eternal life, leading the understanding to assent to things unseen."[8] Faith, as described in the epistle, is seen as a habit,[9] a disposition which moves a person to adhere firmly to what God has revealed. The characters and situations of the Old Testament whom the epistle refer to are always cited in connexion with fidelity to God's promises. But the content of these promises was Jesus Christ himself and the benefits he would provide to men through his redemptive sacrifice. Faith, therefore, is anchored in Jesus, "the pioneer and perfecter of our faith" (Heb 12:2): He is the cause of our faith, and it is in him that we believe in the first instance. He it is, as author of grace, who infuses this virtue into us. We start out from faith

7. Cf. *Dei Verbum*, 16.
8. *Summa theologiae*, II, q. 4, a. 1.
9. Faith as an act is dealt with particularly in Rom 4, when St Paul comments on the faith of Abraham who "believed against (all) hope" (Rom 4:18).

in Jesus, and in our ultimate homeland we shall see him face to face. In heaven faith is transformed into glory—hence its close connexion with hope. Faith in Christ, in his sacrifice, in his resurrection and glorification is the foundation of Christian hope. Christ has entered into heaven, thereby opening the way for all mankind. That is why suffering makes sense, that is why it is worth the effort to endure affliction (cf. Heb 10:19ff).

But faith in Christ is faith in Revelation, because Christ is the fulness of the revelation of the Father. God has made himself manifest to us in his own Son, the perfect Word of the Father spoken to mankind.[10] Faith in Christ requires, therefore, that we should not only believe in him, in his person, but also believe in his precepts and teachings. Hence the letter's numerous exhortations to Christian living interwoven with its dogmatic teaching: these exhortations are consequences which arise from faith in the Son of God and in what he has revealed to us.

c) *Christology* The teaching about Jesus Christ which is the predominant feature of the letter is extremely rich and at the same time has a remarkable simplicity and directness. The subject of Christ's priesthood, tying in naturally with discussion of the Mosaic Law and the Levitical priesthood, is central to the letter.

The sacred author explores the subject of the universal Redemption brought about by Christ the mediator through the sacrifice of the Cross and the shedding of his blood. Christ is at one and the same time the perfect Victim atoning for all the sins of mankind and the true High Priest offering to God the Father a worship which is acceptable and everlasting; this is another basic idea of Pauline theology. However, prior to dealing with the subject of Redemption and priesthood, in its opening verses the letter gives a brief but solemn proclamation of the eternal pre-existence of the Word, his role as creator and his equality with the Father (cf. Heb 1:1-3)—verses which are reminiscent of what the prologue to St John's Gospel reveals about the Word.

The letter's teaching about Christ is given against the backdrop of the fact that Christ is true God and true man—as he must be if he is to bring about Redemption. It never juxtaposes the divine and the human: these are inseparable dimensions of our Lord's being. What alone appears is the unique person of the Word Incarnate, the Son of God: everything he does on earth reveals who he is—God made man.

In line with the general subject of the letter, which is the salvation wrought by Christ, the sacred writer concentrates on our Lord's priesthood, which makes him higher than the angels, superior to the lawgiver of the Old Law and to the Levitical priesthood and superabundantly fitted to redeem mankind. The Redemption wrought by Christ is a universal remedy for a universal need.

Christ alone is the true High Priest and his is the only true priesthood, that is, the mediation of his priesthood alone is capable of blotting out men's sins. From now on no one can be a true priest unless he be called by and receive

10. Cf. Heb 1:1-2; *Dei Verbum*, 4.

priestly anointing from Jesus. The priesthood cannot result from inheritance or birth into a particular tribe; it stems from a vocation, a call, from our Lord, who is the only Priest of the New Testament.

Christ's sacrifice, which does not consist—as Old Testament sacrifices did—in ritual shedding of the blood of animals, is something unrepeatable; its saving effects have been produced once for all, for it is infinite in its effectiveness. What happens in the Mass is that the sacrifice of the Cross is made present in an unbloody manner: Jesus Christ "renews" the offering he made to the Father "once for all".

The intercession of Christ the Priest on our behalf is effective, definitive and enduring. What redeemed man must do is to apply to himself, through faith, the effects of Christ's sacrifice and grow in that charity which saves him.

Jesus Christ manifests who he is and his priestly function both in his self-abasement and in his glorification. Both were necessary to the performance of his priestly and redemptive role. Christ's self-abasement and humiliation demonstrate his absolute obedience to the Father's will; they also show the strength of the temptations which overtook his human nature, and the extraordinary sufferings he experienced in the mortal flesh he chose to assume (cf. Heb 5:7).

The sacred writer's reflections, which are so full of emotion and pathos, come to a head in the statement which is the very core of the letter: "we have such a high priest, one who is seated at the right hand of the throne of the Majesty in heaven" (Heb 8:1). This central truth of Christian dogma is also, as the letter makes clear, a moving exhortation to hope.

In addition to showing Jesus and his work from the viewpoint of his eternal priesthood and exploring what flows from his being Priest and Mediator, the epistle applies to Christ four main titles—Son, Messiah, Jesus and Lord. Each of these reveals different aspects of Christ. The letter also refers to him elsewhere as Sanctifier, Heir, Mediator, Shepherd and Apostle (this being the only place in the New Testament where he is described as Apostle).

Thus, the sacred writer emphasizes the fact that Christ is always, for each and every Christian, his Priest and Mediator: "Jesus Christ is the same yesterday and today and forever" (Heb 13:8).

d) *Eschatology*   The letter's teaching on the subject of the last things takes an apparently secondary place in the sense that it occurs apropos of other themes. Eschatology, however, imbues the entire letter. It provides the key to interpreting the relationship between the provisional covenant of Judaism and the definitive covenant of Christianity. Judaism was a preparation for Christianity, and Christianity is the perfection of the Mosaic religion. At the same time, Christianity has two dimensions: it is something which begins here on earth but it will find its full expression only in heaven. It is true that the land promised to Abraham was Palestine; but it was much more than that. It was the grace of Christ, which guarantees heaven. The promised land, which we are all called to enter, is heaven. In this sense the Exodus whereby Moses led the people to take possession of the promised land, is a prefigurement of the Christian life: Jesus, the new Moses, will lead his people into the definitive Fatherland. And so the exhortation addressed to the followers of Moses, "Today, when you hear his voice, do not harden your hearts" (Heb 3:7; 4:7), means a number of things: it is an invitation to make an act of faith, similar to Abraham's, that is, to enjoy, through faith, the peace which grace brings; but it also is an invitation to stay faithful until the last moment of our life, and so enter into eternal rest. This focus on the future life runs right through the letter. It is a way of presenting the Christian life as a journey from the salvation which has already been brought about but which has yet to take its final form, towards the Kingdom of the future city, whose builder is God (cf. Heb 11:10; 12:8) and whose head is Christ.

The letter speaks often of the second coming of Christ, the Parousia, when he will judge the living and the dead (cf. Heb 10:25). It also announces the future judgment (cf. Heb 10:27; Acts 24:25) and refers to the final re-creation of the world (cf. Heb 12:26-28).

e) *The Christian's life on earth*   The letter sees Christian life in the world as a pilgrimage to the heavenly Fatherland, where one will "rest" in God. In keeping with this perspective, it frequently emphasizes the virtues of faith and hope, virtues necessary to pilgrim man. Despite the difficulties and obstacles encountered, he will reach the end of the journey if he has Christ as his guide. This is in fact an "exodus" theology, seen from a Christian or New Testament perspective. Christians are engaged in a new exodus, leaving Judaism and sin behind them, and they are convinced and fully assured of reaching the true promised land (cf. Heb 4:11; 9:11; 11:8-10; 13:13).

The Epistle to the Hebrews

ENGLISH AND LATIN VERSIONS, WITH NOTES

1

PROLOGUE

The greatness of the incarnate Son of God

¹In many and various ways God spoke of old to our fathers Lk 1:55

---

¹Multifariam et multis modis olim Deus locutus patribus in prophetis, ²in

---

1-4. The first four verses are a kind of prologue to the letter, which does not carry the greetings and words of thanksgiving to God normally found in letters of St Paul. Like the prologue of St John's Gospel, the letter moves immediately into its main subject—the divinity of Jesus Christ, our Redeemer. It speaks of Christ as a Son whose sonship is eternal, prior to the creation of the world and to his Incarnation; it speaks also of Christ's mission to save all men, a mission appropriate to the Word who created all things. This exposition culminates in the affirmation of Christ's absolute superiority over angels, a theme dealt with, in different ways, up to the end of the second chapter.

The entire epistle in fact develops the subject entered on in the prologue—the sublimity of Christ, the natural and eternal Son of God, the universal Mediator, the eternal Priest. This is why St Thomas Aquinas says that the subject matter of this epistle is the "excellence" of Christ. In this respect the Letter to the Hebrews is different from the other letters in the Pauline corpus: in some letters (the "Great Epistles" and the Captivity Letters) the Apostle deals with the grace which imbues the entire mystical body of the Church; others (the Pastoral Letters) deal with the grace bestowed on certain members of the Church (such as Timothy and Titus); whereas the Letter to the Hebrews looks at grace as it is found in the Head of the mystical body, Christ. This "excellence" of Christ, the Angelic Doctor adds, is examined by St Paul from four points of view: the first is that of Christ's origin, which the sacred writer identifies by calling him the true (natural, metaphysical) Son of God, when he says that God has spoken to us by a Son; the second is that of his power, for he depicts him as being made the heir of all things; the third is that of his activity, when he affirms that he created the world; the fourth, his sublime dignity, when he says that Christ reflects the glory of God (cf. *Commentary on Heb*, prologue and 1:1).

Christ is thus presented as the pinnacle and fulness of salvific Revelation, as the Second Vatican Council reminds us: "After God had spoken many times and in various ways through the prophets 'in these last days he has spoken to us by a Son' (Heb 1:1-2). For he sent his Son, the eternal Word who enlightens all men, to dwell among men and to tell them about the inner life of God [. . .]. He did this by the total fact of his presence and self-manifestation—by words and works, signs and miracles, but above all by his death and glorious resurrection from the dead, and finally by sending the Spirit of truth. He revealed that God was with us, to deliver us from the darkness of sin and death, and to raise us up to eternal life" (*Dei Verbum*, 4).

by the prophets; 2 but in these last days he has spoken to us by a Son, whom he appointed the heir of all things, through

novissimis his diebus locutus est nobis in Filio, quem constituit heredem

1. Divine Revelation, which is rightly called "the Word of God", develops in stages in the course of the Old and New Testaments. "By this Revelation," Vatican II teaches, "the invisible God (cf. Col 1:15; 1 Tim 1:17), from the fulness of his love, addresses men as his friends (cf. Ex 33:11; Jn 15:14-15), and moves among men (cf. Bar 3:38), in order to invite and receive them into his own company. This economy of Revelation is realized by deeds and words, which are intrinsically bound up with each other. As a result, the works performed by God in the history of salvation show forth and bear out the doctrine and realities signified by the words; the words, for their part, proclaim the works, and bring to light the mystery they contain" (*Dei Verbum*, 3). Revelation is, then, a gradual opening up of God's mysteries whereby little by little, like a wise teacher, it makes known who he is and what his plans are concerning the salvation of all mankind. For, although there is only one God and one way of salvation, man needs to be educated by means of many precepts and to progress by stages on his way to God and so advance in faith towards complete salvation in Christ. God in his mercy reveals his mysteries to man in this way in order that the whole world experiencing "this saving proclamation, on hearing it should believe, on believing it hope, on hoping in it love" (St Augustine, *De catechizandis rudibus*, 4, 8).

When speaking of Revelation, the First Vatican Council recalled that although "God, the origin and end of all things, can be known with certainty by the natural light of human reason from the things that he created, [. . .] it was, nevertheless, the good pleasure of his wisdom and goodness to reveal himself and the eternal decrees of his will to the human race in another and supernatural way" (*Dei Filius*, chap. 2). This supernatural revelation, as it says (reaffirming the teaching of the Council of Trent), is contained in books and in oral traditions which the Apostles received from Christ or from the Holy Spirit and passed on to us. Christ's Gospel had earlier been promised by the prophets and, more generally, by the entire Old Testament. The epistle refers to this when it says that God spoke in the past through the mouth of the prophets "in many ways", that is, at various stages in the history of the chosen people, and "in various ways", that is, by means of visions, words, actions and historical events.

2. "The most intimate truth which this revelation gives us about God and the salvation of man shines forth in Christ, who is himself both the mediator and the sum total of Revelation" (*Dei Verbum*, 2).

St John of the Cross comments on this passage in a very beautiful and profound way: "And this is as if he had said: That which God spoke of old in the prophets to our fathers in sundry ways and divers manners, he has now, at last, in these days, spoken to us once and for all in the Son. Herein the Apostle declares that God has become, as it were, dumb, and has no more to say, since that which he spoke before, in part, to the prophets, he has now spoken altogether in him, giving us the All, which is his Son.

"And so he who would now enquire of God, or seek any vision or revelation, would not only be acting foolishly, but would be committing an offence against God, by not setting his eyes altogether upon Christ, and seeking no new thing or aught beside. And God might answer him after this manner, saying: 'If I have spoken all things to you in my Word, which is my Son, and I have no other word, what answer can I now make to you, or what can I reveal to you which is greater than this? Set your eyes on him alone, for in him I have spoken and revealed to you all things'" (*Ascent of Mount Carmel*, book 2, chap. 22).

The "last days" refer to the period of time between the first coming of Christ and the second coming, or Parousia. These days have begun because the definitive "Word" of God, Jesus Christ, can be seen and heard. Mankind already finds itself in the "last age", in the "end of the ages" (cf. 1 Cor 10:11; Gal 4:4; Eph 1:10).

By speaking to us through his Son, God reveals to us his saving will from the moment of the Incarnation onwards, for the second person of the Blessed Trinity has come into the world to redeem us by dying for us and to open for us the way to heaven by his glorification. Therefore, Jesus Christ is the "prophet" par excellence (cf. note on Jn 7:40-43), for he perfects and completes God's merciful revelation. The Incarnation and the subsequent events of our Lord's life are, like his teaching, a source of salvation.

It was appropriate that the Son who perfectly revealed God the Father should also be the divine Word, the Creator of the world (cf. Jn 1:3). The creative action of the divine *Logos* or Word is not contradicted by the statement that Creation is the work of God the Father, for everything done by God outside himself (*ad extra*) is an action common to the three divine persons; nor is it correct to see the Word as merely an instrument used by the Father, for he is one in substance with him.

"It is the good Father's own, unique Word who has ordered this universe. Being the good Word he has arranged the order of all things [. . .]. He was with God as Wisdom; as Word he contemplated the Father and created the universe, giving it substance, order and beauty" (St Athanasius, *Oratio contra gentes*, 40 and 46). Not only did the Word make the Father manifest by creation; he, together with the Father and the Holy Spirit, acted in the revelation of the Old Testament: in fact, many patristic writers attributed to the Son—as "angel" or "messenger of Yahweh"—the divine epiphanies witnessed by Moses and the prophets. St Irenaeus writes, for example, that Christ prefigured and proclaimed future events through his "Patriarchs and prophets", thereby acting in his role as Teacher, promulgating the divine commandments and rules and training his people to obey God the Father (cf. *Against Heresies*, XIV, 21). A profound harmony links God's revelation in Creation, in the Old Testament and in the New Testament: in each case it is the same God who is manifesting himself and the Word is ever actively involved. This activity of the Word is hidden and happens through the prophets in the Old Testament; whereas in the New the

Col 1:15-17
Wis 7:25
Heb 9:14, 26
whom also he created the world. ³He reflects the glory of God and bears the very stamp of his nature, upholding the

---

universorum, per quem fecit et saecula; ³qui, cum sit splendor gloriae et figura substantiae eius et portet omnia verbo virtutis suae, purgatione peccatorum

---

Word becomes flesh and acts directly. This passage in Hebrews combines the revelation of Jesus Christ as Mediator and maker of the universe (cf. Col 1:15-18; 1 Cor 8:6) with the idea that God has at last spoken to us in his Son, who "is in the bosom of the Father", and has made known to us the invisible mysteries of the Godhead (cf. Jn 1:18).

3a. These words, which describe Christ's divinity and eternity, recall the passage in the Book of Wisdom which reads, "For she is a reflection of eternal light, a spotless mirror of the working of God" (Wis 7:26). What the Old Testament described as an attribute of God is now revealed as a personal being, the second person of the Trinity, the incarnate Word, Jesus Christ.

Using three images, the text teaches that Jesus Christ is perfect God, identical to the Father. By saying that he "reflects" the glory of the Father it means that he and the Father share the same nature—which is what we profess in the Creed when we say that Jesus Christ, the only-begotten Son of God, is "light from light, true God from true God" (Nicene-Constantinopolitan Creed). "The author means", St John Chrysostom writes, "that Christ has this glory in his own right; it can suffer no eclipse nor can it either increase or diminish" (*Hom. on Heb*, 2).

The Son is also "stamped" with the nature of the Father; "stamp" is a translation of the Greek word *character*, which means the mark left by a tool used to engrave or seal (for example, the impression of a seal on wax, or the seal affixed to a document, or the brand used to identify livestock). This word indicates two things—first, the perfect equality between the mark and the seal which makes it, and second, the permanence of the mark.

"Upholding the universe by his word of power": the Son, through whom all things have been created, is also maintaining them in existence. God the Father not only creates but, through the Son, maintains a continual, direct influence on his creation; if he did not do so, as St Thomas Aquinas explains, the world would revert into non-being: "If the divine power ceased to operate, existence would cease, the being and subsistence of every created thing would end: (the Word) therefore upholds all things in respect of their existence, and he sustains them also by virtue of being the first cause of everything he has created" (*Commentary on Heb*, 1, 2). It makes sense that God the Father should wish to keep the world in existence by means of the same Word by whom he created it.

3b. This is the central message of the Epistle to the Hebrews: Christ, the consubstantial Son of the Father, the perfect reflection of his substance, who created all things and maintains them in existence, by becoming man brought

54

universe by his word of power. When he had made purification for sins, he sat down at the right hand of the Majesty
on high, [4]having become as much superior to angels as the
name he has obtained is more excellent than theirs.

Mk 16:19
Ps 110:1

Phil 2:9
Eph 1:20f
1 Pet 3:22
Ps 113:5

facta, consedit ad dexteram maiestatis in excelsis, [4]tanto melior angelis effectus,

about purification for sins and by his sacrifice was glorified and put at the right
hand of the Father, receiving "the name which is above every name" (cf. Phil
2:6-11; Jn 1:1, 3, 14). The actions of Jesus Christ are a continuum of mercy and
salvation which extends from the creation of the world and mankind to the point
where he is seated in heaven at the right hand of the Father. Creation and
Redemption are mysteries intimately linked to each other. The Son, the divine
Word, is both Creator and Redeemer. "It is appropriate to speak in the first
instance", St Athanasius writes, "of the creation of the universe and of God its
Creator, in order correctly to appreciate the fact that the new creation of this
universe has been brought about by the Word who originally created it. For
there is no contradiction in the Father's effecting the salvation of creatures by
him through whom they were created" (*De Incarnatione contra arianos*, 1).
This is why the tradition of the Church, echoing certain references in the New
Testament (cf. Gal 6:15; 2 Cor 5:17; Eph 4:24; Col 3:10), describes the
Redemption as a "new creation".

To "sit down at the right hand of the Majesty" is equivalent to saying "has
the status of God": "Majesty" is a term of reverence used to refer to God without
naming him; thus, Jewish rabbis would refer to God as "Lord", "the most High",
"the Power", "Glory", etc. Sitting in the presence of God was a prerogative of
the Davidic kings (cf. 2 Sam 7:18; Ezek 44:3), and the person at the right hand
was seen as occupying the place of honour (cf. Ps 45:10). Psalm 110 proclaims
that God will have the Messiah sit at his right hand, and at various times Christ
referred to that prophecy to assert that he was the Messiah and God (cf. Mt
22:44; 26:63-65; Jn 5:17-18; 10:30-33). The exaltation of the Son to the right
hand of the Father was a constant theme of apostolic preaching (cf. Acts 2:33;
Rom 8:34; 1 Pet 3:22; Rev 3:21; Eph 1:20). As St John Chrysostom comments,
when St Paul says that the Son sat down at the right hand of the Majesty he
means principally to refer to the status of the Son as equal to that of the Father.
And when he says that he is on high, in heaven, far from meaning to confine
God within spatial limits, he wants us to see God the Son, as Lord of the
universe, raised up to the very throne of his Father (cf. *Hom. on Heb*, 2).

4. The prologue ends with a very important statement, which introduces the
theme of the rest of the first chapter: Christ is superior to the angels. To
understand this comparison of Christ with the angels, one needs to bear in mind
the outlook of the Jews at the time. The period immediately prior to the New
Testament had seen a considerable development of devotion to angels among
the ordinary religious Jews; with the result that this was the danger of Jesus,

THE EXCELLENCE OF THE RELIGION REVEALED BY CHRIST

CHRIST IS GREATER THAN THE ANGELS

Ps 2:7, LXX
2 Sam 7:14
Acts 13:33

Proof from Sacred Scripture

⁵For to what angel did God ever say,

---

quanto differentius prae illis nomen hereditavit. ⁵Cui enim dixit aliquando angelorum: *"Filius meus es tu; ego hodie genui te"* et rursum: *"Ego ero illi in*

---

because he was a man, in some way being seen as on a lower level than angels, who, created beings though they are, are pure spirits. In the Acts of the Apostles (cf. Act 23:9), we find the Pharisees in the Sanhedrin surmising that St Paul's preaching may result from revelation given him by an angel; and belief in the existence of angels was a point of contention between Pharisees and Sadducees (cf. Acts 23:7). For this reason the author of Hebrews wants to make it quite clear to Christians of Jewish origin that Jesus is much more than an angelic being.

Christ is superior to angels, the inspired writer says, because he has the title of Son, which is his by natural right. This name demonstrates his divine nature, a nature superior to that of any visible or invisible created being, whether material or spiritual, whether earthly or angelic: something's name describes its essence and, particularly in Sacred Scripture, name and essence are at times one and the same. Thus, for example, the phrase "in the name of" (cf. Mt 28:19; Acts 3:6; 4:7; 4:12; etc.) refers not just to the authority or power of the person named, but to the person himself. Jesus Christ, because he is the very Son of God, is superior to angels by virtue of the glory due to his eternal oneness with the Father. As eternal Son of God, to him belonged, by right of inheritance, the title of Son and Lord. Moreover, after his passion and resurrection he has "become" superior to angels by a new title through his exaltation on high (cf. 1 Cor 15:24-27; Phil 2:9-11). This passage refers primarily to Jesus' glorification as man; for the words "having become as much superior to angels . . ." cannot refer, St John Chrysostom points out, to his divine essence: by virtue of his divinity the Son is equal to the Father and cannot be subject to change, cannot "become" anything: he is eternally what he is by generation from the Father: "Eternal Word by nature, he did not receive his divine essence by way of inheritance. These words, which manifest his superiority over the angels, can only refer to the human nature with which he has been clothed: for it is that nature that is a created one" (*Hom. on Heb*, 1).

On the essence of angels and what they are, see the note on Lk 1:11.

5. Ancient Hebrew exegesis of this verse of Psalm 2 took it in a messianic sense: the Messiah or Anointed would be king of Israel and would enjoy God's

"Thou art my Son,
today I have begotten thee"?

patrem, et ipse erit mihi in filium"? [6]Cum autem iterum introducit primo-

special protection. Therefore he merited being called "Son of God", in the same kind of way, though more eminently, as other kings and just men of Israel deserved the title. But in Hebrews 1:5 the verse is given a much more profound interpretation: the Messiah, Jesus Christ, is the eternal Son of God, begotten "today", that is, in the continuous present of the eternal Godhead. It is affirming the generation of the Son by the Father in the bosom of the Trinity, whereby the Son proceeds eternally from the Father and is his mirror image. This form of generation is radically different from physical generation, whereby one living being physically begets another like unto himself; and it is also quite different from Creation, whereby God makes everything out of nothing. It is different from physical generation because, in the Holy Trinity, Father and Son co-exist eternally and are one and the same and only God, not two gods. It is different from Creation because the Son has not been made from nothing but proceeds eternally from the Father.

God created angels in the context of time, as the Fourth Lateran Council says in its profession of faith: "We firmly believe and profess without qualification that there is only one true God [. . .], Creator of all things visible and invisible, spiritual and corporeal, who, by his almighty power, from the very beginning of time, has created both orders of creatures in the same way out of nothing, the spiritual or angelic world and the corporeal or visible universe. And afterwards he formed the creature man, who in a way belongs to both orders, as he is composed of spirit and matter" (*De fide catholica*, chap. 1).

The Son, on the other hand, proceeds from the Father eternally as light rays come constantly from the sun or as water forms one single thing with the spring from which it flows.

"These words have never been addressed to an angel," St Thomas Aquinas comments, "but to Christ alone. In them three things may be observed. First, the mode of origin, expressed in the word 'say'. It refers to a type of generation which is not of the flesh but rather of a spiritual and intellectual kind. Second, this generation has an altogether singular character, for he says, 'Thou art my Son', as if saying that although many others are called sons, being [God's] natural son is proper to Him alone; others are called sons of God because they partake of the Word of God. Third, this is not a temporal but an eternal generation" (*Commentary on Heb*, 1, 3).

The quotation from Psalm 2 is completed by Nathan's prophecy to David (2 Sam 7:14: "I will be his father, and he shall be my son"), which announces that a descendant of David will be the Messiah and will ever enjoy God's favour. But the Hebrews text also makes it much clearer that the Messiah is the Son of God in the proper sense of the word—a son by nature, and not by adoption (cf. Lk 1:32-33). In Christ, therefore, two things combine: he is the Son of God and he is the Messiah King.

Or again,
"I will be to him a father,

Deut 32:43, LXX
1 Chron 17:13
Ps 97:7
Rom 8:29
Col 1:18

and he shall be to me a son"?
⁶And again, when he brings the first-born into the world, he says,
"Let all God's angels worship him."

Ps 104:4, LXX

⁷Of the angels he says,
"Who makes his angels winds,
and his servants flames of fire."

---

genitum in orbem terrae, dicit: *"Et adorent eum omnes angeli Dei."* ⁷Et ad angelos quidem dicit: *"Qui facit angelos suos spiritus et ministros suos flammam ignis"*; ⁸ad Filium autem: *"Thronus tuus, Deus, in saeculum saeculi,*

6. Here the words of Deuteronomy 32:43, identical with those of Psalm 97:7 as given in the Septuagint, are used to convey, as a divine commandment addressed to spiritual beings, a directive to adore the Son. This is a further proof of Christ's superiority: the angels are to worship him. "This adoration shows his absolute superiority over angels: it is the superiority of the master over his servants and his slaves. When Jesus Christ left the bosom of his Father to enter this world, God required his angels to worship him. This is what a monarch does when he brings some great personage into his palace and wishes to have him honoured: he orders his dignitaries to bow in his presence" (*Hom. on Heb*, 3).

This reference to "bringing the first-born into the world" is consistently interpreted by the Fathers of the Church and by ancient writers as a reference to the Incarnation. Some authors also see this verse as referring to the second coming of Christ, when the world to come, unlike the present world, will be totally subject to the Redeemer. This interpretation connected with the end of time may explain why the text of Deuteronomy 32:43 is used: that passage is followed by reference to the last judgment by God.

Christ's human nature should be worshipped now and always by angels and men alike, for by doing so they adore Jesus, who is one person—which is divine—with two natures, one divine and one human; he is worshipped as one: his divinity and his humanity are worshipped at one and the same time.

This worship due to Christ over every created being is reminiscent of what St Paul says in Philippians 2:10: "at the name of Jesus every knee should bow, in heaven and on earth and under the earth", referring to the glorified human nature of Christ. "It is fitting that the sacred humanity of Christ should receive the homage, praise and adoration of all the hierarchies of the angels and of all the legions of the blessed in heaven" (Blessed J. Escrivá, *Holy Rosary*, second glorious mystery).

7-8. Unlike the Son, who is divinely unchangeable like the Father, angels are on a lower level of being, although a spiritual one; words of Psalm 104:4

[8]But of the Son he says,
"Thy throne, O God,[a] is for ever and ever,
the righteous sceptre is the sceptre of thy[b] kingdom.
[9]Thou hast loved righteousness and hated lawlessness;

---

et virga aequitatis virga regni tui. [9]Dilexisti iustitiam et odisti iniquitatem, propterea unxit te Deus, Deus tuus, oleo exsultationis prae participibus tuis"

used here convey this idea: winds often change direction and flames constantly change shape. St Thomas Aquinas says that this double comparison fits in very well with what angels are: they are messengers and ministers. "The air can receive light and in a similar way any image perfectly reflects what it receives and it moves with speed. These are qualities which a good messenger should also have [. . .] and they are very appropriate to angels because angels receive divine illuminations perfectly, for they are the purest of mirrors [. . .]. Similarly they are excellent transmitters of what is said to them [. . .] and are also very swift [. . .]. As ministers they are flames of fire, for of all the elements fire is the most active and most effective. Therefore in Psalm 104 where it says that angels are ministers of God it adds that he makes his ministers 'fire and flame'" (*Commentary on Heb*, 1, 3).

V. 8 of Psalm 45 is taken in Hebrews 1:8 as words spoken by God the Father to his Son, whose throne is established for ever and ever. The term "God" is expressly applied to Jesus Christ. Although the New Testament normally uses "Lord" when referring to the divinity of the Son, it does not systematically refrain from calling him "God" (cf. Jn 1:1; 20:28; Rom 9:5; Tit 2:13; 2 Pet 1:1); but it usually keeps that word for the person of the Father. The "throne" is Christ's and expresses his majesty, because, as St Thomas comments, a throne is a royal seat but it is also a teacher's chair and a judgment seat, all of which are very appropriate to Christ, who is our King by virtue of his Godhead, and also, as man, he has merited the kingship by virtue of his passion, victory and resurrection (cf. *Commentary on Heb*, 1, 4). It is stressed that this throne will remain for ever, in keeping with Nathan's prophecy (cf. note on Heb 1:5) and the announcement made to the Blessed Virgin (cf. Lk 1:33) and another prophecy in the Book of Daniel: "their kingdom shall be an everlasting kingdom, and all dominions shall serve and obey them" (Dan 7:27).

9. Through the author of Hebrews God himself is revealing to us the deeper meaning of this psalm. The psalmist, who was also divinely inspired, addresses the people's king on his wedding-day; he extols him and praises him, emphasizing his beauty, the fact that he is fully endowed with spiritual gifts, virtues and power. Praise on this scale goes far beyond what any human being could deserve. It shows the king of Israel as an eternal king, a king of righteousness who hates lawlessness, and it says that he has not been anointed

[a]Or *God is thy throne*
[b]Other ancient authorities read *his*

therefore God, thy God, has anointed thee
with the oil of gladness beyond thy comrades."

Ps 102:26-28, LXX

[10]And,

"Thou, Lord, didst found the earth in the beginning,
and the heavens are the work of thy hands;
[11]they will perish, but thou remainest;
they will all grow old like a garment,

---

[10]et: *"Tu in principio, Domine, terram fundasti; et opera manuum tuarum sunt caeli. [11]Ipsi peribunt, tu autem permanes; et omnes ut vestimentum veterascent,*

---

just with ordinary oil but the oil "of gladness", a distinction not given to other princes and kings. All these prerogatives, particulary joy and gladness, are proper to the advent of the Messiah (cf. Ps 21:6; 72:1-7; Song 5:10-16; Is 44:23; 51:1; 52:9; 54:1; etc.). The Messiah King, therefore, as portrayed in the Old Testament and definitively confirmed by Hebrews, has divine authority. He is Christ who, through the anointing he has received, has been put over all his "comrades", that is, over all creatures, whose "comrade" or fellow he has become through the Incarnation: by becoming man, the eternal Son of the Father has, as man, the fulness of grace and divine gifts; and thanks to him everyone can obtain these graces and gifts, but not to the same, full, extent. Some Fathers were of the view that this anointing refers directly to the eternal generation of the Word; others applied it to the Incarnation. Certainly, Christ's exaltation is entirely due to his being God; however, because anointing is here linked with love of righteousness and hatred of evil-doing, it seems more likely that it refers to the divine favour shown to Jesus throughout his life, especially at his Baptism (cf. Lk 4:18; Acts 10:38) and in his glorification after the Resurrection (cf. 1 Tim 3:16). Of course, the very name "Christ", meaning "anointed", refers to the fact that he had the fulness of the Holy Spirit. "These words", St Thomas writes, "refer to the spiritual anointing which makes Christ full of the Holy Spirit" (*Commentary on Heb*, 1, 4). St John says as much when he describes the Word as being "full of grace and truth" (Jn 1:14). "To the name *Jesus* is added that of *Christ*, which signifies *the anointed*. [. . .] Jesus Christ was anointed for the discharge of these functions, not by mortal hand or with earthly ointment, but by the power of his heavenly Father and with a spiritual oil; for the plenitude of the Holy Spirit and a more copious effusion of all gifts than any other created being is capable of receiving were poured into his soul. This the Prophet clearly indicates when he addresses the Redeemer in these words: 'You love justice, and hate iniquity. Therefore God, your God, has anointed you with the oil of gladness above your fellows" (*St Pius V Catechism*, I, 3, 7).

10-12. To the arguments previously given (vv. 5-9) in support of Christ's superiority over angels, a further factor is now added—his power to create the world; 1:10 links up with 1:2 (cf. *Commentary on Heb*, 1, 5). This passage is

¹²like a mantle thou wilt roll them up,
and they will be changed.^c
But thou art the same,
and thy years will never end."
¹³But to what angel has he ever said,
"Sit at my right hand,
till I make thy enemies
a stool for thy feet"?

Rev 6:14

Ps 110:1, LXX
Mt 22:44

---

¹²*et velut amictum involves eos,* sicut vestimentum *et mutabuntur. Tu autem idem es, et anni tui non deficient.*" ¹³Ad quem autem angelorum dixit aliquando: *"Sede a dextris meis, donec ponam inimicos tuos scabellum pedum tuorum"*?

---

taken from Psalm 102:25-27, a psalm of lamentation in which a just man in affliction confidently asks God to hear his prayer because God is forever, whereas all created things are transitory. This is an idea which occurs very often in the Old Testament and is very much part of Jewish piety (cf., e.g., Ps 119:88-90; Is 40:8; 51:6-8; Sir 43:26-32). All these passages stress the everlasting nature of God's "Word" in contrast with the changeability of created things. In Hebrews 1:10-12 the words of Psalm 102:25-27, which were addressed to Yahweh, are applied to Christ: that is, he is regarded as being God, the Father's equal.

12. To show the difference between Creator and creature the epistle uses the words of Psalm 102, mentioning two attributes of the Creator: he is eternal, and he is unchanging. The visible world, on the contrary, had a beginning and it will come to an end. The comparison with a mantle and a garment reminds us that the material world will ultimately disintegrate; it is a passing thing despite its beauty and apparent solidity.

This basic truth of revelation is directly at odds with the notion that the universe is eternal and the world and matter are in some way divine. The Magisterium of the Church has often rejected theories which say that "God is identical with nature [. . .], God is actually in the process of becoming, in man and in the world; all things are God and have the very substance of God himself; God and the world are one and the same thing" (Pius IX, *Syllabus of Errors*, 1). As Christians understand it, the created universe not only will not retain its present form but at the end of time will undergo a transformation which will turn it into "a new heaven and a new earth" (Rev 21:1; cf. Rom 8:19; Is 65:17; 2 Pet 3:13). Only God is eternal.

14. "Ministering spirits sent to serve" is a very accurate definition of angels: they are spiritual creatures whose role is to serve and worship God. In the New Testament the angels, good and bad, are given various names such as "powers",

---

^cOther ancient authorities add *like a garment*

¹⁴Are they not all ministering spirits sent forth to serve, for the sake of those who are to obtain salvation?

---

¹⁴Nonne omnes sunt administratorii spiritus, qui in ministerium mittuntur propter eos, qui hereditatem capient salutis?

"principalities", "thrones", "dominions" (cf. Rom 8:38; 1 Cor 15:24; Eph 1:21; Col 1:16). In the Old Testament angels served God by bearing messages to men (cf. Gen 16:7f; Judg 2:1; 6:11; 1 Kings 13:18; 40:3; Dan 8:16-26; 9:21-27; etc.), by protecting them and on occasions by imposing divine punishment on them. From the time of Christ's coming, angels "ministered" to him on earth (cf. Mt 4:11; Lk 22:43) and they helped the early Church to develop (cf. Acts 5:19; 12:7-10). Hebrews 1:14 underlines the role of angels in the salvation of men; in the Gospel we are told that children have angels of their own in heaven (cf. Mt 18:10); and indeed everyone has a guardian angel (cf. Acts 12:15). This ministerial role of angels is a consequence of their state of blessedness, because, as St Thomas Aquinas explains, there is no difference between angels who contemplate God and angels who have service functions, for "all are ministers or administrators, in that the higher ones convey the will of God to those in the middle rank; and the latter to those of lower rank, and these last-mentioned to us" (*Commentary on Heb*, 1, 6). Ministerial angels have the specific task of helping us to reach heaven; "by God's providence angels have been entrusted with the office of guarding the human race and of accompanying every human being so as to preserve him from any serious danger. Just as parents, whose children are about to travel a dangerous and infested road, appoint guardians and helpers for them, so also in the journey we are making towards our heavenly country our heavenly Father has placed over each of us an angel under whose protection and vigilance we may be enabled to escape the snares secretly prepared by our enemy [. . .] and thus be secure against all false steps which the wiles of the evil one might cause us to make in order to draw us aside from the path that leads to heaven" (*St Pius V Catechism*, XIV, 9, 4). In addition to giving personal help to every human being, the Church teaches that angels echo the prayer of the faithful and carry their petitions to God. Origen, a very early ecclesiastical writer and in this matter a faithful representative of orthodox teaching, says in this connexion: "We say that the angels ascend to bear men's prayers to the purest parts of the world, that is, the heavenly regions [. . .]. And from there they descend in turn to bear to everyone, according to his merits, such benefits as God entrusts to them [. . .]. Given that they have this role, we have learned to call them angels or messengers" (*Against Celsus*, V, 4). Devotion to angels and to one's own guardian angel is an important and ancient teaching: "You are amazed that your guardian Angel has done you such obvious favours. And you should not be amazed: that's why our Lord has placed him beside you" (Blessed J. Escrivá, *The Way*, 565).

An appeal for faith

¹Therefore we must pay the closer attention to what we have

---

¹Propterea abundantius oportet observare nos ea, quae audivimus, ne forte praeterfluamus. ²Si enim, qui per angelos dictus est, sermo factus est firmus, et

---

1-4. At this point the epistle makes an earnest appeal for prudence and fidelity. The direct style and confident tone of personal exhortation which runs right through the letter indicates that the author knew his readers very well, as they did him. He has no inhibitions about showing that he is somewhat worried that some of them may not appreciate the wonderful gift they have received. They should all remember that apostasy can come about not only through a conscious, clear rejection of faith but also through continuous neglect of God's teaching. This exhortation reminds us of 2 Corinthians 6:1: "We entreat you not to accept the grace of God in vain". Christians should absorb God's word as much as possible and strive to put it into practice, thereby becoming ever holier. Also, the practice of Christian life is the best way to obtain a deeper understanding of the faith.

2-3. "The Apostle has previously explained, in various ways, Christ's superiority over angels. Here he concludes by stating that greater obedience is due to Christ's teaching, that is, to the New Testament, than to the Old Testament [. . .]. Thus, by obeying the command of the angel through whom the Law was given, they obtained entry into the promised land (Ex 23:20- 22). Therefore, it is said in Mt 19:17, 'If you would enter life, keep the command-ments.' So, if it was necessary to obey the commandments of Moses, now it is even more necessary to obey the commandments of Him who is higher than the angels by whom the Law was promulgated" (St Thomas, *Commentary on Heb*, 2, 1).

The Law of Moses is not being viewed as something at odds with the redemption and grace won by Christ, but as a first stage on the way of salvation and a kind of foretaste of eternal beatitude. The Law also is a manifestation of God's mercy. "This Law", Tertullian writes, "was not promulgated out of the severity of its author but out of that supreme generosity which decided to teach a rebellious people and to make easier (by stipulating with exact duties) a faith which they were as yet unable to obey" (*Against Marcion*, 2, 19).

In the Old Covenant God backed up his word by imposing just punishment for prevarication and disobedience—as happened, for example, in the case of Dathan, Korah, Abiram (cf. Num 16:1-35), Moses' sister Miriam (cf. Num 12:1-9) and later Saul (1 Sam 15:9-23) and unfaithful kings of Judah and Israel. We should, therefore, have a holy fear of being unfaithful to the New Covenant established in Jesus Christ, for the divine word of salvation which Jesus promulgated is infinitely precious. It is the greatest gift a human being can be

Acts 7:38, 53
Gal 3:19
Heb 10:28f

Acts 10:37

2 Cor 12:12
1 Cor 12:4, 11
Mk 16:20

heard, lest we drift away from it. [2]For if the message declared by angels was valid and every transgression or disobedience received a just retribution, [3]how shall we escape if we neglect such a great salvation? It was declared at first by the Lord, and it was attested to us by those who heard him, [4]while God also bore witness by signs and

---

omnis praevaricatio et inoboedientia accepit iustam mercedis retributionem, [3]quomodo nos effugiemus si tantam neglexerimus salutem? Quae, cum initium accepisset enarrari per Dominum, ab eis, qui audierunt, in nos confirmata est, [4]contestante Deo signis et portentis et variis virtutibus et Spiritus Sancti

---

given, because it equips one to know and to praise God and at the same time attain one's own temporal and eternal happiness.

"It was attested to us by those who heard him": an explicit reference to the preaching of the Apostles, which confirms and transmits the proclamation of salvation initiated by Christ's preaching (cf. 1 Cor 11:23; 15:3).

2. The *a fortiori* kind of argument used here was very popular in rabbinical exegesis at that time. The argument is this: if transgression of the Old Covenant commandments promulgated by angels was severely punished, so much more respect is due to the commandments of the New Testament, established by the Son of God. The same form of argument is used in Heb 7:21-22; 9:13-14; 10:28-29 and 12:25.

The "message declared by angels" is the Mosaic Law. According to some Jewish traditions, the Law was given to Moses on Mount Sinai by an angel or by a number of angels. The New Testament reflects this tradition in Acts 7:38, 53 and Gal 3:19.

4. "Signs", "wonders" and "miracles" are to a certain extent all the same—things which bear witness to supernatural Revelation. "Signs" may be natural events which, occurring as they do at a special time, carry a supernatural meaning and manifest God's power. "Wonders" and "miracles", on the other hand, exceed in various degrees, the possibilities of nature; "wonders" seems to refer to signs in the heavens (cf. Acts 2:19), whereas miracles are any type of special demonstration of divine power, like the sudden cure of paralysis or the raising of a person from the dead.

The miracles Jesus worked help us see him as bringing God's salvation to men. They are, as it were, credentials the Father gives the Son (Acts 2:22; Jn 3:2). From the start, signs and wonders also accompanied apostolic preaching to attest to its divine origin (cf. Mk 16:20; Acts 2:43; 4:30; 5:12; etc.). Thus, we are told that Stephen "did great wonders and signs among the people" (Acts 6:8) and that St Paul's preaching was confirmed by signs and miracles (cf. Acts 14:3; Rom 15:19; 2 Cor 12:12).

St John Chrysostom asked: "Could it happen that those who made out they were God's witnesses were nothing but imposters? No!, St Paul replies. This

wonders and various miracles and by gifts of the Holy Spirit distributed according to his own will.

Jesus, man's brother, was crowned with glory and honour above the angels

⁵For it was not to angels that God subjected the world to

---

distributionibus secundum suam voluntatem. ⁵Non enim angelis subiecit orbem

revelation was not the invention of the human mind. If men had thought up these truths and these mysteries, how could God's omnipotence have supported this lie with supernatural actions? So, God intervenes, through the wonders worked by the Apostles, to support the testimony they bear [. . .]. He supports it not by speech (which would have been enough, for God is trustworthy) but by 'various miracles', the greatest type of testimony he can provide. The Apostle speaks of diverse miracles to show the greater abundance of spiritual gifts given Christians as compared with the ancient Jewish people who were given few wonders and less marvellous signs" (*Hom. on Heb*, 3).

The early years of the Church were indeed marked by an exceptional number of miracles and signs of the Holy Spirit (cf. Acts 4:31; 10:44; 1 Cor 12:4-11). Once apostolic preaching became consolidated, the incidence of signs diminished but there remained and still remains the greatest of these signs, charity (cf. 1 Cor 13:1).

5-9. The saving dimension of the Incarnation is being explored here with the help of quotations from Psalm 2 and other psalms. Christians should stay true to Christ, because in addition to his being the cause and beginning of salvation he has been made Lord of the universe; everything is subject to him. God the Father, in other words, has established Christ—not the angels—as Lord of "the world to come".

God has put everything under Christ *as man*. The words of Psalm 8 are quoted as applying to Christ as man, for he is the perfection of manhood, the perfect man, and he merited being crowned with glory and honour because of his obedience, humility, and passion and death (cf. Phil 2:6-11; 1 Pet 2:21-25); even death itself has become subject to him (cf. 1 Cor 15:22-28). His enemies have been made his footstool (cf. Ps 8:6; 110:1; Mt 22:44); he will channel everything back to God, and God will be all in all.

5. "The world to come" was a term the Jews used to refer to the period immediately following the coming of the Messiah. The rabbis distinguished three periods in the history of the world—the "present world", the time when they were waiting for the Messiah; the "day of the Messiah", the point at which his kingdom would be established; and the "world to come", which would begin with the Resurrection of the dead and the judging of the nations. Many teachers of the Law tended to confuse the "world to come" in some way with the "day of the Messiah", which was its initial stage.

65

Ps 8:5-7, LXX come, of which we are speaking. [6]It has been testified
somewhere,

> "What is man that thou art mindful of him,
> or the son of man, that thou carest for him?
> [7]Thou didst make him for a little while lower than the
> angels,
> thou hast crowned him with glory and honour,[d]
> [8]putting everything in subjection under his feet."

1 Cor 15:25-27
Eph 1:20-23
Phil 3:21

---

terrae futurum, de quo loquimur. *[6]Testatus est autem in quodam loco quis
dicens: "Quid est homo, quod memor es eius, aut filius hominis, quoniam visitas
eum? [7]Minuisti eum paulo minus ab angelis, gloria et honore coronasti eum,
[8]omnia subiecisti sub pedibus eius." In eo enim quod ei omnia subiecit, nihil
dimisit non subiectibile ei. Nunc autem necdum videmus omnia subiecta ei;*

The author of the epistle seems to be saying that the government of the
present world is entrusted by God to angels (cf. Deut 32:8; Dan 10:13f), but
that in the world to come—that is, in the definitive Kingdom—God the
Creator's original plan will be implemented: Christ, true God and true man,
with his glorified manhood, will be the King of Creation and the holy angels
and the blessed will reign with him. The "world to come", although it has begun
with the Resurrection and glorification of Jesus, will not reach its fulness until
the second coming of Christ and the resurrection of the dead. Until then, there
exists a tension between "this world" and the "world to come": the former has
received a mortal wound but it is still alive; the latter has begun to exist but it
has not yet attained its final full expression.

6. Psalm 8 is a hymn praising God for creating all things; particularly man,
whom he has made master of all creation. The words of the Psalm quoted here
are those which praise God's caring love, as shown by his making man, despite
his limitations, lord of Creation.

However, the text of the epistle shows us that the words of the Psalm have
a deeper meaning: they refer to Jesus (cf. 1 Cor 15:27; Eph 1:22) and particularly to his degradation. "Although these words can be applied to every man,"
St John Chrysostom comments "they do however most properly apply to Christ.
For the words 'thou hast put everything in subjection under his feet' (v. 8) are
more suitable to him than to us, for the Son of God visited us who were of no
account and having taken and loved our condition, he became higher than us
all" (*Hom. on Heb*, 4).

The author of Hebrews uses Psalm 8 to demonstrate Christ's superiority over
angels by giving it a deeply messianic interpretation. Thus, the man "crowned
with glory and honour" is the risen Christ, now seated at the right hand of the
Father; and the one to whom everything has been subjected is also the same
Christ (cf. 1:13), as St Paul proclaims in 1 Cor 15:27; Eph 1:22; Phil 3:21.

[d]Other ancient authorities insert *and didst set him over the works of thy hands*

Now in putting everything in subjection to him, he left
nothing outside his control. As it is, we do not yet see
everything in subjection to him. ⁹But we see Jesus, who for   Phil 2:6-11

---

⁹eum autem, qui *paulo minus ab angelis minoratus est*, videmus Iesum propter
passionem mortis *gloria et honore coronatum*, ut gratia Dei pro omnibus

---

8. In keeping with its application to Christ of the words of Psalm 8:4-6, the
epistle says that God the Father has subjected everything to him. This does not
mean that there is inequality or difference in power or nature between Father
and Son, as if the Son himself were subject to the Father, and the Father had
given him, as he would a subordinate, authority over the world. "Arius argued
in this way," writes St Thomas: "the Father subjected everything to the Son;
therefore, the Son is less than the Father. I reply that it is true that the Father
subjected everything to the Son according to his human nature, in respect of
which he is less than the Father, as St John says, 'the Father is greater than I'
(14:28). But according to his divine nature, Christ himself subjected all things
to himself" (*Commentary on Heb*, 2, 2).

Christ's dominion over the universe is something which men cannot see and
it will not become manifest until his second coming as Lord and Judge of the
living and the dead. "Christ, true God and true man, lives and reigns. He is the
Lord of the universe. Everything that lives is kept in existence only through
him. Why, then, does he not appear to us in all his glory? Because his kingdom
is 'not of this world' (Jn 18:36), though it is *in* this world [. . .]. Those who
expected the Messiah to have visible temporal power were mistaken. [. . .] When
Christ began to preach on earth he did not put forward a political programme.
He said, 'Repent, for the kingdom of God is at hand' (Mt 3:2; 4:17). He
commissioned his disciples to proclaim this good news (cf. Lk 10:9) and he
taught them to pray for the coming of the Kingdom (cf. Mt 6:10)" (Blessed J.
Escrivá, *Christ is passing by*, 180).

9. The words "who for a little while was made lower than the angels" refer
to Jesus in the crisis of his Passion and Death, when he freely humbled himself
and lowered himself to suffer punishment and death—sufferings to which
angels are not subject.

"For a little while" is a translation of the Greek word which the New Vulgate
renders as "paulo minus" (a little less than), and which also occurs in Hebrews
2:7 in the quotation from Psalm 8. The RSV translation in both instances is "for
a little while".

Every human creature, including Christ as man, can be seen in some sense
as lower than the angels. This inferiority basically has to do with the fact that
human knowledge is inferior to that of angels because it is dependent on sense
experience, and also because angels cannot experience suffering and death.
"The angels cannot suffer and are immortal by nature, so that when Christ
deigned to submit to his passion and death he made himself lower than them,
not because he lost his sublimity or in any way was diminished, but because he

67

a little while was made lower than the angels, crowned with glory and honour because of the suffering of death, so that by the grace of God he might taste death for every one.

gustaverit mortem. [10]Decebat enim eum, propter quem omnia et per quem omnia, qui multos filios in gloriam adduxit, auctorem salutis eorum per

took on our weakness. He made himself lower than the angels, not as far as his divinity or his soul were concerned but only in respect of his body" (*Commentary on Heb*, 2, 2).

Christ's self-abasement is a permanent example to us to strive to respond to his love. St John Chrysostom suggests that we draw from it this practical lesson: "If he whom the angels worship consented, out of love for us, to become for a time lower than them, you for your part should endure everything out of love for him" (*Hom. on Heb*, 4).

One of the results of Christ's passion was his exaltation and glorification. Because Christ attained victory on the Cross, to the benefit of all mankind, the Cross is the only route to heaven: "The holy cross is shining upon us", the Church says. "In the cross is victory, in the cross is power. By the cross every sin is overcome" (*Liturgy of the Hours*, Exaltation of the Cross, morning prayer, Ant. 3). By virtue of Christ's passion, the Cross is no longer an ignominious scaffold; it is a glorious throne. Tradition attributes to St Andrew the Apostle these words in praise of the cross on which he was going to die: "O goodly Cross, glorified by the limbs of our Lord, O Cross so long desired, so ardently loved, so tirelessly sought and now offered to me: take me to my Master so that he who redeemed me through thee, may welcome me through thee" (*Ex passione S. Andreae*, reading).

Through his death, Christ has been crowned with glory and honour; moreover he has died on our behalf. His death and glorification are the cause and model of our salvation and glorification. Sacrifice, atonement and merit are indissolubly linked to the redemptive work of Christ and constitute a "grace of God", that is, a gratuitous gift from God. St Thomas Aquinas explains that "the passion of Christ is here alluded to in three ways. Firstly, its cause is referred to, for the text says 'by the grace of God'; then, its usefulness, when it says 'for every one'; thirdly, its outcome, when it says 'might taste'" (*Commentary on Heb*, 2, 3): Jesus did indeed, by the will of the Father, experience or "taste" death. His death is described as being like a bitter drink which he chose to take in sips, as if savouring it. The "cup" or chalice of the agony in the garden comes immediately to mind (cf. Mt 26:39; Mk 14:26; Lk 22:42; Jn 18:11; cf. also Mt 20:22f and Mk 10:38f).

Christian tradition has seen these words about "tasting death" as underlining that Christ underwent a most severe passion voluntarily, accepting it to atone for all the sins of mankind. These words also show that he accepted death without ceasing to be Lord of life: "This expression", St John Chrysostom states, "is very precise. It does not say 'that by the grace of God he might die', for the Lord once he tasted death delayed there only for a moment and

^{10}For it was fitting that he, for whom and by whom all things exist, in bringing many sons to glory, should make the pioneer of their salvation perfect through suffering. ^{11}For he who sanctifies and those who are sanctified have

Rom 11:36
Heb 5:8f

Jn 17:19

---

passiones consummare. ^{11}Qui enim sanctificat et qui sanctificantur, ex uno omnes; propter quam causam non erubescit fratres eos vocare ^{12}dicens:

---

immediately rose [...]. All men fear death; therefore, to enable us to take death in our stride, he tasted death even though it was not necessary for him to do so" (*Hom. on Heb*, 4).

10. After pointing to the results of Christ's death, the text stresses how appropriate it was that he should be abased in this way: he had to make himself in every way like his brethren in order to help them.

God the Father, who is the beginning and end of all things, desired to bring men to glory by means of his Son. Christ was to be the author of their salvation, and therefore it was fitting that he should be made perfect through suffering. The Father made his Son "perfect" in the sense that by becoming man and therefore being able to suffer and die, he was fully equipped to be mankind's representative. "God has acted in a manner in keeping with his kindness towards us: he has clothed his first-born in a glory greater than that of all mankind and made him outstanding as a champion. Suffering is, therefore, a way to attain perfection and a source of salvation" (*Hom. on Heb*, 4). By perfectly obeying his Father, offering his life and especially his passion and death, Christ offers a perfect and superabundant sacrifice for the forgiveness of the sins of mankind and makes full atonement to the Father. As a reward for his obedience, Christ, as man, is made Head of the Church and King of the universe. It is in that sense that he is made "perfect" by the Father.

Ever since the Redemption, human suffering has become a way to perfection: it acts as expiation for personal sins, it spurs man to assert his spiritual and transcendental dimension, it makes for solidarity with others and links man to Christ's sacrifice. "Suffering must serve for conversion, that is, for the rebuilding of goodness in the subject, who can recognize the divine mercy in this call to repentance [...]. But in order to perceive the true answer to the 'why' of suffering, we must look to the revelation of divine love, the ultimate source of the meaning of everything that exists [...]. Christ causes us to enter into the mystery and to discover the 'why' of suffering, as far as we are capable of grasping the sublimity of divine love" (John Paul II, *Salvifici doloris*, 12-13).

11. To accomplish the salvation of men Christ needed to be one of them—to share, with them, a human nature. This is why Christ is the only "true sanctifier", that is, the priest who performs rites and sacrifices, taking things stained by sin and making them pure and pleasing to God, that is, holy. Our Lord said

Ps 22:23, LXX

all one origin. That is why he is not ashamed to call them brethren, [12]saying,

"I will proclaim thy name to thy brethren,
in the midst of the congregation I will praise thee."

"Nuntiabo nomen tuum fratribus meis, in medio ecclesiae laudabo te"; [13]*et iterum:* "*Ego ero fidens in eum*"; *et iterum:* "*Ecce ego et pueri, quos mihi dedit*

---

something similar in the Gospel: "For their sake I consecrate myself, that they also may be consecrated in truth" (Jn 17:19).

"Have all one origin". Various interpretations have been given to these words. Most have to do with the parallelism between the first man and Christ (cf. Acts 17:26; Rom 5:15-19), seeing this "origin" as Adam—in which case the text would mean that Christ and other men are children of Adam. A more usual interpretation sees the "one" origin as being God, thus stressing that Christ's holy humanity and the humanity of men both stem from the one Creator and derive from the first man. In either case, Christ and the rest of men can rightly be called "brethren". "As to his divine generation he has no brethren or co-heirs, being the only- begotten Son of the Father, while we mortals are the work of his hands. But if we consider his birth as man, he not only calls many by the name of brethren, but treats them as such, since he admits them to share with him the glory of his paternal inheritance" (*St Pius V Catechism*, I, 3, 10).

12. Psalm 22, which begins with the words, "My God, my God, why has thou forsaken me?", speaks of the sufferings and exaltation of the Messiah, as perfect Servant of Yahweh. Christ prayed this psalm on the Cross, applying it to himself and thereby revealing it to be a prophecy of his passion (cf. Mt 27:35, 46; Mk 15:34). For this reason it is a psalm which is highly revered and much used by Christian tradition. It had a special place in divine services in the synagogue and is used by the Church in the liturgical ceremonies of Holy Thursday and Good Friday.

The Servant of Yahweh, after being freed by God from the suffering and abuse inflicted on him, expresses his gratitude to his liberator. That is why he wishes to "proclaim", that is, extol the name of Yahweh before the faithful who meet in the congregation and whom he calls "brethren". The evangelists see this psalm as being fulfilled in our Lord's passion (cf. Mt 27:35 and Jn 19:23-24 compared with Ps 22:18). But in Hebrews 2:12 other words of the same Psalm (Ps 22:23) are applied not so much to our Lord's passion as to Christ's revelation of the Father: he proclaims the name of the true God, that is, his inner life, his mercy and power. This passage of Hebrews echoes the words of Jesus in John 17:6, 26: "I have manifested thy name to the men whom thou gavest me out of the world; thine they are, and thou gavest them to me, and they have kept thy word [. . .]. I have made known to them thy name, and I will make it known, that the love with which thou hast loved me may be in them, and I in them."

¹³And again,
"I will put my trust in him."
And again,
"Here am I, and the children God has given me."
¹⁴Since therefore the children share in flesh and blood,
he himself likewise partook of the same nature, that through

Deus." ¹⁴Quia ergo pueri communicaverunt sanguini et carni, et ipse similiter participavit iisdem, ut per mortem destrueret eum, qui habebat mortis

---

13. Two verses from Isaiah are now quoted, revealing their messianic meaning: what the prophet said centuries earlier anticipated the sentiments of Christ. Isaiah 8:17 shows his trust in God despite the threat of an Assyrian invasion and the unfaithfulness of the people of Israel, who had resorted to superstition and magic instead of turning to God. The same words express Christ's confidence in God the Father.

In Isaiah 8:18 the children of the prophet, whose names symbolize the divine plan of salvation, stand for the Christian people whom the Father has entrusted to Christ, the Saviour and Sanctifier (cf. Jn 6:37, 39; 17:6, 12).

14. As in the prologue of St John's Gospel (Jn 1:12-13), "flesh" and "blood" apply to human nature in its weakened condition. Jesus has assumed man's nature: "He has taken it on without sin but with all its capacity to suffer pain, given that he took a flesh similar to sinful flesh; he 'shared therefore in flesh and blood', that is, he took on a nature in which he could suffer and die—which could not occur in a divine nature" (St Thomas, *Commentary on Heb*, 2, 4).

Christ chose to submit to death, which is a consequence of sin, in order to destroy death and the power of the devil. The Council of Trent teaches that, as a result of original sin, man "incurred the wrath and indignation of God, and consequently incurred death [. . .] and, together with death, bondage in the power of him who from that time had the empire of death" (*De peccato originali*, can. 3; cf. Rom 5:12; 6:12-14; 7:5; etc.). To explain this power of the devil, St Thomas comments: "A judge has one kind of power of death: he can punish people with death; a criminal has a different kind of power of death—a power he usurps by killing another [. . .]. God has the first kind of dominion over death; the devil has the second kind, for he seduces man to sin and leads him to death" (*Commentary on Heb*, 2, 4).

Addressing Christ and his cross, the Church sings, "O altar of our victim raised, / O glorious passion ever praised, / by which our Life to death was rendered, / that death to life might thence be mended" (Hymn *Vexilla Regis*). The death of Christ, the only one who could atone for man's sin, wipes out sin and makes death a way to God. "Jesus destroyed the demon", St Alphonsus writes; "that is, he destroyed his power, for the demon had been lord of death on account of sin, that is, he had power to cause temporal and eternal death to all the children of Adam infected by sin. And this was the victory of the

71

1 Cor 15:56
Rev 12:10
Is 41:8f

death he might destroy him who has the power of death, that is, the devil, [15]and deliver all those who through fear of death were subject to lifelong bondage. [16]For surely it is

---

imperium, id est Diabolum, [15]et liberaret eos, qui timore mortis per totam vitam obnoxii erant servituti. [16]Nusquam enim angelos apprehendit, sed *semen*

Cross—that Jesus, the author of life, by dying obtained Life for us through that death" (*Reflections on the Passion*, chap. 5, 1).

15. Christ has freed men not from physical but from spiritual death and therefore from fear of death, because he has given us certainty of future resurrection. Man's natural fear of death is easily explained by his fear of the unknown and his instinctive aversion to what death involves; but it can also be a sign of excessive attachment to this life. "Because it does not want to renounce its desires, the soul fears death, it fears being separated from the body" (St Athanasius, *Oratio contra gentes*, 3).

The fear of death which some people in the Old Testament had can be explained by their not knowing what fate awaited them, and by the possibility of being completely cut off from God. But physical death is not something to be feared by those who sincerely seek God: "To me to live is Christ, and to die is gain," St Paul explains (Phil 1:21). "Don't be afraid of death. Accept it from now on, generously . . . when God wills it, where God wills it, as God wills it. Don't doubt what I say: it will come in the moment, in the place and in the way that are best: sent by your Father-God. Welcome be our sister death!" (Blessed J. Escrivá, *The Way*, 739).

16. "It is not with angels that he is concerned": the original text says literally "he did not take angels with his hand", " did not catch hold of", "did not take [the nature of angels]"; meaning that Christ took to himself a human nature, not an angelic nature. St John Chrysostom explains the text in this way: "What does he mean by 'take with his hand'; why does he not say 'took on/assumed' but instead uses the expression 'took with his hand'? The reason is this: this verb has to do with those who are in pursuit of their enemies and are doing all they can to catch those who are in flight from them and to seize those who resist. In other words, humankind had fled from him and fled very far, for it says 'we were very far from God and were almost without God in the world' (Eph 2:12). That is why he came in pursuit of us and 'seized us for himself'. The Apostle makes it clear that he did all this entirely out of love for men, in his charity and solicitude for us" (*Hom. on Heb*, 2).

"This single reflection, that he who is true and perfect God became man, supplies sufficient proof of the exalted dignity conferred on the human race by the divine bounty; since we may now glory that the Son of God is bone of our bone, and flesh of our flesh, a privilege not given to angels" (*St Pius V Catechism*, I, 4, 11).

not with angels that he is concerned but with the descendants of Abraham. [17]Therefore he had to be made like his brethren in every respect, so that he might become a merciful and faithful high priest in the service of God, to make expiation for the sins of the people. [18]For because he himself has suffered and been tempted, he is able to help those who are tempted.

Rom 8:3
1 Sam 2:35
Ex 4:16
1 Jn 2:2

Heb 4:15
Mt 4:1-11

Abrahae apprehendit. [17]Unde debuit per omnia fratribus similari, ut misericors fieret et fidelis pontifex in iis, quae sunt ad Deum, ut repropitiaret delicta populi; [18]in quo enim passus est ipse tentatus, potens est eis, qui tentantur, auxiliari.

17. This is the first mention of the central theme of the epistle, the priesthood of Christ. Because he is God and man, Jesus is the only Mediator between God and men, who have lost God's friendship and divine life on account of sin; he exercises this mediation as High Priest; his Love saves men by bridging the abyss which separates the sinful stock of Adam from God whom it has outraged.

It first refers clearly to our Lord's human nature: he is in no way different from men (except that he is not guilty of sin: cf. Heb 4:15). "These words mean that Christ was reared and educated and grew up and suffered all he had to suffer and finally died" (Chrysostom, *Hom. on Heb*, 5). "He partook of the same food as we do," writes Theodoret of Cyrus, "and he endured work; he experienced sadness in his soul and shed tears; he underwent death" (*Interpretatio Ep. ad Haebr.*, II).

Christ the Priest is able perfectly to understand the sinner and make satisfaction to divine Justice. "In a judge what one most desires is mercy," St Thomas writes, "in an advocate, reliability. The Apostle implies that both things were found in Christ by virtue of his Passion. Mankind desires mercy of him as judge, and reliability of him as advocate" (*Commentary on Heb*, 2, 4).

Christ's priesthood consists in making expiation by a sacrifice of atonement and a peace-offering for the sins of men: he takes our place and atones on our behalf: "Christ merited justification for us [. . .] and made satisfaction for us to God the Father" (Council of Trent, *De iustificatione*, chap. 7).

18. Suffering can link a person to Christ in a special and mysterious way. "The Redeemer suffered in place of man and for man. Every man has *his own share in the Redemption*. Each one is also *called to share in that suffering* through which the Redemption was accomplished. He is called to share in that suffering through which all human suffering has also been redeemed. In bringing about the Redemption through suffering, Christ *has* also *raised human suffering to the level of the Redemption*. Thus each man, in his suffering, can also become a sharer in the redemptive suffering of Christ" (John Paul II, *Salvifici doloris*, 19).

Christ's main purpose in undergoing his passion was the Redemption of mankind, but he also suffered in order to strengthen us and give us an example.

73

"By taking our weaknesses upon himself Christ has obtained for us the strength to overcome our natural infirmity. On the night before his passion, by choosing to suffer fear, anguish and sorrow in the garden of Gethsemane he won for us strength to resist harassment by those who seek our downfall; he obtained for us strength to overcome the fatigue we experience in prayer, in mortification and in other acts of devotion, and, finally, the fortitude to bear adversity with peace and joy" (St Alphonsus, *Reflections on the Passion*, chap. 9, 1).

A person who suffers, and even more so a person who does penance, should realize that he is understood by Christ. Christ will then console him and help him bear affliction: "You too some day may feel the loneliness of our Lord on the Cross. If so, seek the support of him who died and rose again. Find yourself a shelter in the wounds in his hands, in his feet, in his side. And your willingness to start again will revive, and you will take up your journey again with greater determination and effectiveness" (Blessed J. Escrivá, *The Way of the Cross*, XII, 2).

Chaps. 2 and 3. This chapter and the following one are a further "word of exhortation". After professing faith in Christ's divinity and showing his superiority over angels, the writer now shows our Lord's superiority over Moses, whom all Jews regarded as the true founder, liberator and lawgiver of the chosen people. This comparing of Christ and Moses is not done in a polemical sort of way: the language is careful and restrained. Conscious that he is addressing Christians of Jewish background, the sacred writer does not try to diminish or gloss over the importance of the first lawgiver and foremost prophet of the Old Testament. His sole purpose is to show the incomparable excellence of Jesus Christ. Our Lord in fact introduced himself as a "new Moses" and that was how those who witnessed his words and actions perceived him (cf. Mt 2:4, recalling Ex 7:11; Mt 2:15, quoting Hos 11:1; Mt 5:21, 27, 31, 33; etc.).

St John Chrysostom points out that the comparison being made here is between Moses and Christ as men, and particularly with Christ as priest, for priesthood in Israel went back to Moses and all the Jews saw Moses as someone of singular importance. By approaching the subject in this way, the sacred writer shows great sensitivity to Christians of Jewish origin: "He starts by laying the foundations of Christ's superiority, beginning with his Incarnation so as to come back later to his divinity; but at that point comparison [of Moses with Christ] is not possible. So he begins by putting them, as *men*, on the same level [. . .]. He does not, to begin with, show Jesus' total superiority, because he was afraid his listeners would rebel and block their ears. Since these people had been devout Jews, the memory of Moses was deeply etched in their hearts" (*Hom. on Heb*, 5).

For the Jews, Moses stands for the entire Law, and for Christians he is a figure of Christ, the new lawgiver. For this reason, tradition has pointed to a certain parallelism between this chapter of the epistle and the episode of the Transfiguration, when our Lord appeared with Moses and Elijah at his side (cf. Mt 17:2-3 and par.). St Ambrose comments that today also Christians can see Moses with Jesus, can see the Law as part of the Gospel; in the Church Moses

3

Moses' ministry and that of Christ compared

¹Therefore, holy brethren, who share in a heavenly call, consider Jesus, the apostle and high priest of our con-

Heb 4:14; 9:15
Eph 1:18
Phil 3:14

---

¹Unde, fratres sancti, vocationis caelestis participes, considerate apostolum et pontificem confessionis nostrae Iesum, ²qui fidelis est ei, qui fecit illum, sicut

---

continues to teach; indeed there he is given greater prominence than he had in the Old Testament (cf. *Expositio Evangelii sec. Lucam*, VII, 10-11). The glory which caused Moses' face to shine now shines from the face of Christ (cf. 2 Cor 3:7-18).

1. "Holy brethren": the faithful are here described as holy because, by virtue of baptismal grace and the sanctification by Jesus which Baptism involves, this is a correct term for them, and one which reminds them of the spiritual perfection they are invited to share in (cf. Rom 1:7 and note; 16:2; 1 Cor 1:2; 2 Cor 1:1; etc.).

Christians have always been conscious of this high calling: "We are not just a people", St Justin writes, "we are a holy people [. . .]. We are not, then, some despicable or barbarous tribe, or nation of [. . .] Phrygians; we have been chosen by God: to us who did not ask about him, he manifested himself" (St Justin, *Dialogue with Trypho*, 119, 3).

The Christian vocation, here described as a "heavenly call" because it comes from heaven and leads towards heaven, is a personal call from God to follow Jesus in the Church: "This is a heavenly call in two senses—because Christians are called not to an earthly kingdom but to a heavenly one; and because the call does not have its source in our merits or any human event: it derives solely from divine grace" (St Thomas, *Commentary on Heb, ad loc.*).

The titles of "apostle" and "high priest", applied here to Christ, convey a very accurate sense of the Son's mission in the world. As "apostle" Jesus is the messenger or envoy of God to men. As "high priest" he is the representative of men before God. Jewish rabbis gave the high priest, in the ceremonies on the Day of Atonement, the title of "Messenger of Justice", that is, God's apostle sent to effect justification. However, Jesus Christ is the only one to whom can be applied the two titles of "apostle" and "high priest". "Christ is called messenger and apostle", St Justin writes, "because he proclaims what must be made known and is sent to reveal what the Father has to tell us. The Lord himself gave us to understand this when he said, 'he who hears me, hears him who sent me'" (*First Apology*, 63, 5).

Num 12:7, LXX

2 Cor 3:7ff

fession. ²He was faithful to him who appointed him, just as Moses also was faithful in[e] God's house. ³Yet Jesus has

et *Moyses in tota domo illius.* ³Amplioris enim gloriae iste prae Moyse dignus est habitus, quanto ampliorem honorem habet quam domus, qui fabricavit

2-6. For the Jews the great prophet and mediator of the Sinai Covenant was vested with such glory that some rabbis ranked him higher than the angels.

Moses can be regarded not only as the founder of the people of Israel and of the Hebrew nation but also as their first prophet. In his religious office, which stemmed from his divine call to be "a servant" of God (v. 5), Moses worked as a priest, teacher and lawgiver, which made him a "type" of Christ. However, Jesus Christ brought to perfection and fulfilment the divine plan of salvation sketched out in the words and actions of Moses, the mediator of the Old Covenant.

The writer of the letter starts out from the faithfulness of Moses and, pre-eminently, of Jesus; he shows the superiority of the latter by using the simile of a house in the sense, sometimes, of a building and, at other times, of a family. Just as the architect is more important than the house he builds, just as God is greater than the universe he created, so Christ is superior to Moses. Similarly, the son or master of a house is on a higher level than its manager; so, although Moses served the house well, Christ is greater than he because he is the Son of God, the master of the house.

2. When it says that "he was faithful to him who appointed him", this refers to Christ's faithfulness to God the Father, who made him the apostle and high priest, the mediator between God and men (cf. Chrysostom, *Hom. on Heb*, 5).

"Moses also was faithful in all God's house": the people of Israel were sometimes described as God's house, and Moses was faithful in "all" God's house because the Lord chose to give him alone the task of governing it and rejected those who tried to put themselves on his level (Num 12:1-9). But Israel, God's house in the Old Testament, has now become the new people of God, the Church, the house of Christ, in the New Testament, as Vatican II says: "Often, too, the Church is called the 'building' of God (1 Cor 3:9). The Lord compared himself to the stone which the builders rejected, but which was made into the cornerstone (Mt 21:42). On this foundation the Church is built by the Apostles and from it the Church receives solidity and unity. This edifice has many names to describe it—the house of God in which his family dwells (1 Tim 3:15); the household of God in the Spirit (Eph 2:19, 22); the dwelling-place of God among men (Rev 21:3), and, especially, the holy temple" (*Lumen gentium*, 6).

3-4. The comparison between Christ and Moses begins by noting that both were faithful to God (v. 2). God himself described Moses as faithful (cf. Num 12:7) and Christ showed his faithfulness, St Thomas comments, firstly by

[e]Other ancient authorities insert *all*

been counted worthy of as much more glory than Moses as the builder of a house has more honour than the house. ⁴(For every house is built by some one, but the builder of all things is God.) ⁵Now Moses was faithful in all God's house as a servant, to testify to the things that were to be spoken later, ⁶but Christ was faithful over God'sᶠ house as a son.

Eph 2:19
1 Cor 3:9
1 Tim 3:15
Heb 4:16; 10:23

illam. ⁴Omnis namque domus fabricatur ab aliquo; qui autem omnia fabricavit, Deus est. ⁵Et *Moyses* quidem *fidelis erat in tota domo eius* tamquam *famulus* in testimonium eorum, quae dicenda erant, ⁶Christus vero tamquam Filius super

attributing his preaching not to himself but to the Father who sent him (cf. Jn 5:41; 7:18); secondly, because he sought the Father's glory and not his own (cf. Jn 8:50); and finally, because he was completely obedient, becoming "obedient unto death, even death on a cross" (Phil 2:8): cf. *Commentary on Heb, ad loc*. Christ's faithfulness, moreover, extended over all nations and not just the people of Israel, which was the case with Moses.

Christ takes precedence over the Prophet not only because he is God's Son but also because he has much more authority. The comparison of the builder of a house and the house itself (connecting with the image of the people of God as God's house) gives the writer a further opportunity to exalt the figure of Christ. Moses and the Law come under Christ by virtue of a sovereign divine disposition establishing Christ as true high priest and new lawgiver. "Christ built the house, that is, the Church. For Christ himself, the author of grace and truth, built the Church: he gave it its laws whereas Moses only built it in the sense of transmitting the Law" (St Thomas, *Commentary on Heb*, 3, 1).

But it goes further than that: the Father who built all things (cf. v. 4) created all things through the Son, and therefore Christ is greater than Moses because he is also the Creator of the universe.

6b. "This house is the faithful", St Thomas writes; "they are Christ's house because they believe in Christ, and also because Christ dwells in them. So, this house is us, the Christian faithful" (*Commentary on Heb*, 3, 1). "The material, the physical structure, of a church should always remind you", John Paul II told the faithful in a suburb of Madrid, "that you are 'living stones' (1 Pet 2:5), that you should always be building yourselves into Christ, to the measure and example of Christ, in all your personal, family and social activities" (*Homily at Orcasitas*, 3 November 1982).

This is the ground on which the author invites his readers to hope and trust in God—a very appropriate exhortation, given the difficult circumstances in which his original readers found themselves. Hope is always an essential virtue, particularly when one is in a difficult situation, for it enables a person to focus on things eternal and thereby helps him stay true to his course. "One needs not only to be able to hold out but to have a stable, solid confidence, which is firmly

ᶠGreek *his*

77

And we are his house if we hold fast our confidence and pride in our hope.[g]

The need for faith; the bad example given by the chosen people

Ps 95:7-11

[7]Therefore, as the Holy Spirit says,
"Today, when you hear his voice,

---

domum illius; cuius domus sumus nos, si fiduciam et gloriationem spei retineamus. [7]Quapropter, sicut dicit Spiritus Sanctus: *"Hodie, si vocem eius*

---

grounded on faith, so as never to be overwhelmed by difficulties" (Chrysostom, *Hom. on Heb*, 5).

The writer boldly speaks of the joyful pride which comes from an awareness of divine filiation. "You are discouraged, why? Is it your sins and miseries? Is it your defeats, at times coming one after the other? A really big fall, which you didn't expect? [...] Take refuge in your divine sonship: God is your most loving father. In this lies your security, a haven where you can drop anchor no matter what is happening on the surface of the sea of life. And you will find joy, strength, optimism: victory!" (Bl. J. Escrivá, *The Way of the Cross*, VII, 2).

7-11. A long quotation from Psalm 95 introduces the theme of that "rest" which the people of the promise will attain at the end of their wayfaring.

In the Book of Genesis we are told that when God finished his work of creation, he "rested". The "rest" prescribed in the Mosaic Law was a kind of imitation of what God did, sharing God's happiness, receiving the reward merited by a life of fidelity and hard work. The Jews had gradually come to a more spiritual understanding of "rest" or, as they termed it, "the place of rest". This idea reaches its highest form of expression in the apocryphal book of Esdras (IV Esdras), where the prayer is raised to God to grant the faithful departed "eternal rest", *Requiem aeternam dona eis, Domine*. The chosen people were helped to arrive at this notion of rest by reflecting on the spiritual meaning of the Exodus and the pilgrimage to the promised land. The Exodus was also seen as a new creation, with God "creating" his people. Like the first creation, this second creation would be followed by "rest"—entry into the promised land. The Epistle to the Hebrews shares this interpretation of the Exodus but it gives it a Christian perspective by seeing the Exodus as the Redemption whereby Christ, a new Moses, leads us to eternal rest.

7. The author of the letter reaffirms that Sacred Scripture—in this case Psalm 95—is the work of the Holy Spirit. As such it always carries a contemporary message; it is a form God uses to speak to all men in all periods of history. Readiness to listen to God and do his will *today* and *now* is an important part of Christian living (cf. 3:13). A Christian should be docile to God speaking in his heart; he should be quick to respond to all the little invitations God gives

[g]Other ancient authorities insert *firm to the end*

⁸do not harden your hearts as in the rebellion,
on the day of testing in the wilderness,
⁹where your fathers put me to the test and saw my works
for forty years.

---

audieritis, ⁸nolite obdurare corda vestra sicut in exacerbatione, secundum
diem tentationis in deserto, ⁹ubi tentaverunt me patres vestri in probatione et

---

him to deny himself and advance in holiness. No excuse is ever valid for delaying to give a positive response to grace. "Do your duty 'now', without looking back on 'yesterday', which has already passed, or worrying over 'tomorrow', which may never come for you" (Blessed J. Escrivá, *The Way*, 253). "Now! Return to your noble life now. Don't let yourself be fooled: 'now' is not too soon . . . nor too late" (*ibid.*, 254).

8. Man is free; he can resist grace, and unfortunately often does. "It is not God's goodness that is to blame for faith not coming to birth in men, but the inadequate dispositions of those who hear the preaching of the word" (St Gregory Nazianzen, *Oratio catechetica magna*, 31). Scripture calls this resistance to grace "hardness of heart" (cf., e.g., Ex 4:21; Rom 9:18; Deut 15:7; Jer 7:26; Acts 19:6).

When withholding belief or resisting conversion, people sometimes claim to have intellectual difficulties, but, very often, the real problem has to do with their dispositions, with not *wanting* to respond to grace. The disobedience and "hardness of heart" or stubbornness of the chosen people is a recurring subject in the Old Testament (cf., e.g., Ex 32:9; Deut 9:13; 2 Kings 17:14; Is 46:12; Jer 5:3; Ezek 2:4; etc.). Their rebellion against God's commands was due to pride, which turned them into a people whose forehead was as hard as brass, whose neck was "an iron sinew" (Is 48:4; cf. Acts 7:51), a people uncircumcised in heart, with uncircumcised ears (cf. Jer 9:26; 6:10). Conversion cannot operate if someone has that attitude. For this reason our Lord, and later his Apostles, referred to the Jews' rejection of him, in order to make Christians steadfast in faith (cf. Is 6:9; Mt 13:13; Jn 12:40; Acts 28:26).

9. Psalm 95 contains a reference to the Israelites' rebellion when God put them to the test in the wilderness. The episode took place in Rephidim, on the border of the wilderness of Zin, in the south-east of the Sinai peninsula. Having made their way out of Egypt, the people grew impatient; they complained about how Yahweh was treating them, and put him to the test by asking him to work a miracle (Ex 17:1-7). God did work a miracle: at Horeb he ordered Moses to strike the rock with his rod, and out of it flowed water to relieve the people's thirst. The place was therefore given the name of Massah (meaning temptation) and Meribah (meaning fault-finding or exasperation). This episode in Jewish history came to symbolize the disgruntlement which typified the Jews in the desert, an attitude which even affected Moses in Kadesh (cf. Num 20:1-13).

¹⁰Therefore I was provoked with that generation,
and said, 'They always go astray in their hearts;
they have not known my ways.'

Num 14:21-23 ¹¹As I swore in my wrath,
'They shall never enter my rest.'"

2 Thess 2:3 ¹²Take care, brethren, lest there be in any of you an evil,

---

viderunt opera mea ¹⁰*quadraginta annos. Propter quod infensus fui generationi huic et dixi: Semper errant corde. Ipsi autem non cognoverunt vias meas.* ¹¹*Sicut iuravi in ira mea: Non introibunt in requiem meam!"* ¹²Videte, fratres, ne forte sit in aliquo vestrum cor malum incredulitatis discedendi a Deo vivo,

---

The leader of the chosen people, in circumstances similar to those of the earlier incident, struck the rock twice, not expecting anything to happen. On account of this he did not merit to enter the promised land: he was only allowed to see it from Mount Nebo, where he died (Deut 34:1-8).

"Putting God to the test", "tempting" him, is a sin of presumption. It involves exposing oneself imprudently and needlessly to physical or spiritual risk from which God's ordinary providence does not provide protection (cf. Mt 4:5-7).

In this passage, "putting God to the test" means demanding more proof than necessary that God is steadfast in his will and continues to protect his chosen people. "God should not be asked to account for his activities", St John Chrysostom comments; "if one asks him to prove his power, his providence, his solicitude, it is the same as not yet being fully convinced of his power and goodness and mercy" (*Hom. on Heb*, 6).

11. There are three kinds of rest. The first is the "sabbath", when God rested after creating the world; then there is the rest provided by the promised land of Canaan after countless afflictions and difficulties; and "finally there is the true rest which belongs to the Kingdom of heaven, where the elect rest from their labours and afflictions: the sabbath is a reflection and symbol of that rest" (*Hom. on Heb*, 6).

St Thomas Aquinas applies the term "rest" to peace of body and soul and says that there are different kinds of peace—physical ease (cf. Lk 12:19); the peace of conscience a person has who does right in the sight of God; and the peace of eternal happiness in heaven (cf. *Commentary on Heb, ad loc.*).

12. "Falling away from the living God" seems to be something more serious than reverting to Judaism; it implies the sad possibility of total loss of belief in God. Thus, in the case of those to whom the epistle was written, a reversion from the Gospel to Judaism would not be simply a matter of returning to a previous religious position but rather a deliberate act involving voluntary resistance to grace and a complete break with God. For people who had not received the Revelation of Jesus Christ, the Jewish religion certainly did

unbelieving heart, leading you to fall away from the living
God. ¹³But exhort one another every day, as long as it is
called "today", that none of you may be hardened by the

1 Thess 5:11

---

¹³sed adhortamini vosmetipsos per singulos dies, donec illud *"hodie"* vocatur,

---

provide access to God; but for those who by embracing Christianity had thereby
received the fulness of Revelation, renunciation of Christ would mean a
virtually irreparable sin (cf. Heb 6:4-6). There is never a valid excuse for giving
up the faith.

The Church teaches and prescribes to its children the need to be true to the
faith even at the cost of life itself. From the very beginning this was the kind
of fidelity practised by the martyrs and confessors of the faith."They cut our
hands off, they nail us to crosses, they throw us to wild beasts, imprison us and
burn us, and we submit to every kind of torture; yet everyone knows that we
do not betray our faith. Rather, the worse our sufferings, the more there are who
embrace faith and devotion in the name of Jesus" (St Justin, *Dialogue with
Trypho*, 110, 4).

Some Christians today are called to stay true in the face of violent
persecution; they and others also have to overcome fear of ridicule, and the
temptation to hide their convictions from unbelievers. The words of the letter
remind us that there is a danger that whereas in earlier times force failed to
achieve its objective, nowadays fear of ridicule could cause us to be ashamed
of Christ or to deny him. "'And in a paganized or pagan environment when my
life clashes with its surroundings, won't my naturalness seem artificial?' you
ask me. And I reply: 'Undoubtedly your life will clash with theirs; and that
contrast—faith confirmed by works!—is exactly the naturalness I ask of you'"
(Blessed J. Escrivá, *The Way*, 380).

13. The more Christians practise charity, the easier it is for them to be
steadfast in the faith. Fraternity, mutual brotherly support, helps provide
protection from the devil's efforts to make us sin: "'*Frater qui adiuvatur a
fratre quasi civitas firma*. Brother helped by brother is a fortress.' Think for a
moment and make up your mind to live the fraternal spirit that I have always
asked of you" (Blessed J. Escrivá, *The Way*, 460).

Aware of his personal weakness and of the need to help others and to let
himself be helped, the Christian keeps striving to practise this fraternity. He
loves the good he sees in others, and he tries to uproot in himself and others
anything that implies a defect. Fraternity, therefore, leads to "fraternal cor-
rection", a word of advice which is always full of understanding, being the
outcome of a desire to live in harmony with others and to remove divisions and
barriers. Christian fraternity binds the Church together.

"Not in vain is there in the depths of man's being a strong longing for peace,
for union with his fellow man, for mutual respect for personal rights, so strong

Heb 6:11; 11:1
Mk 4:19
Rom 7:11
2 Cor 9:4
Ps 95:7f

Ex 17:1ff

deceitfulness of sin. ¹⁴For we share in Christ, if only we hold our first confidence firm to the end, ¹⁵while it is said, "Today, when you hear his voice, do not harden your hearts as in the rebellion."

¹⁶Who were they that heard and yet were rebellious? Was

---

ut non obduretur quis ex vobis fallacia peccati; ¹⁴participes enim Christi effecti sumus, si tamen initium substantiae usque ad finem firmum retineamus, ¹⁵dum dicitur: "*Hodie, si vocem eius audieritis, nolite obdurare corda vestra quemadmodum in illa exacerbatione.*" ¹⁶Qui sunt enim qui audientes exacerbaverunt?

that it seeks to transform human relations into fraternity. This longing reflects something which is most deeply imprinted upon our human condition: since we are all children of God, our fraternity is not a cliché or an empty dream; it beckons as a goal which, though difficult, is really ours to achieve" (Blessed J. Escrivá, *Friends of God*, 233).

14. This is a repetition of the exhortation in v. 6 to remain true to the end.

"Firm confidence" is the very opposite of the "falling away" mentioned in v. 12. From the very beginning of his calling, a Christian is already sharing in Christ's life and in his glory, but he will not share in it fully until after death, when he will be able actually to see the Lord.

This sharing in Christ's grace is a treasure which we carry in "earthen vessels" (2 Cor 4:7) and can lose at any time through sin. We need to nurture this grace and protect our faith by being watchful and active right through our life: "We have shared in Chirst's death through holy Baptism and we have been buried with him; we have shared in his resurrection provided we keep our faith intact" (Theodoret of Cyrus, *Interpretatio Ep. ad Haebreos*, III).

The Christian life is a matter of constantly returning to God, beginning anew, and humbly and decisively correcting our course when we go astray through weakness or indifference.

"What does it matter that we stumble on the way, if we find in the pain of our fall the energy to pick ourselves up and go on with renewed vigour? Don't forget that the saint is not the person who never falls, but rather the one who never fails to get up again, humbly and with a holy stubbornness. If the Book of Proverbs says that the just man falls seven times a day (cf. Prov 24:16), who are we poor creatures, you and I, to be surprised or discouraged by our own weaknesses and falls! We will be able to keep going ahead, if only we seek our fortitude in him who says: 'Come to me, all you who labour and are heavy laden and I will give you rest' (Mt 11:28). Thank you, Lord, *quia tu es, Deus, fortitudo mea* (Ps 42:2), because you, and you alone, my God, have always been my strength, my refuge and my support" (Blessed J. Escrivá, *Friends of God*, 131).

16-19. The Book of Exodus tells how the Israelites left Egypt under the leadership of Moses (cf. Ex 12:35-39), but their unbelief and infidelity

it not all those who left Egypt under the leadership of Moses? [17]And with whom was he provoked forty years? Was it not with those who sinned, whose bodies fell in the wilderness? [18]And to whom did he swear that they should never enter his rest, but to those who were disobedient? [19]So we see that they were unable to enter because of unbelief.

1 Cor 10:5, 10
Num 14:29

Num 14:22

4

Through faith we can attain God's 'rest'

[1]Therefore, while the promise of entering his rest remains,

---

Nonne universi, qui profecti sunt ab Aegypto per Moysen? [17]Quibus autem *infensus fuit quadraginta annos*? Nonne illis, qui peccaverunt, quorum *membra ceciderunt in deserto*? [18]Quibus autem *iuravit non introire in requiem ipsius,* nisi illis, qui increduli fuerunt? [19]Et videmus quia non potuerunt introire propter incredulitatem.

[1]Timeamus ergo, ne forte, relicta pollicitatione introeundi in requiem eius,

---

prevented them, that particular generation, from taking possession of the promised land (cf. Num 14:20-23, 27-30, 36-37; 20:12). Their lack of faith in God and in Moses, their fault-finding and disobedience, which caused God to punish them in this way, are mentioned by the sacred writer because Christians also, through unfaithfulness, can fail to attain eternal life.

Unbelief leads to the temptation to disobey, and disobedience is a sign of unbelief. If a Christian makes a habit of not listening to God's calls, he is in danger of resisting grace more and more, and can end up losing his faith. Unbelief is normally not something which happens all of a sudden; it is usually the outcome of a process of interior disobedience.

1-11. This chapter is a further exhortation to fidelity and develops the theme of that "rest" which the people of Israel failed to attain. The comparison between Moses and Jesus (cf. 3:1ff) is now extended to Jews and Christians. Moses had tried to get the people of Israel to stay true to God and so enter their place of rest (cf. Deut 12:9-10). He laid down the precept of sabbath rest (Deut 5:12-15; Ex 20:8-11; 35:1-3; Num 15:32-36) in memory of God's resting after the Creation, and as a sign of the Covenant and a symbol of eternal rest. In the Gospel Christ promises a new kind of rest, an eternal one, in the house of the Father (cf. Jn 14:1-3, 27).

The history of the chosen people is not, then, a mere chronicle of past events. It is something meaningful to us today and full of lessons for Christian living. To Christians also, as members of the new Israel, God offers a "rest", one which is richer than the temporal rest the Jews obtained when they took possession of

Gal 5:2
1 Cor 10:1-13 let us fear lest any of you be judged to have failed to reach it. ²For good news came to us just as to them; but the

existimetur aliquis ex vobis deesse; ²etenim et nobis evangelizatum est quemadmodum et illis, sed non profuit illis sermo auditus, non commixtis fide

the promised land, for the rest promised to Christians is rest in heaven.

However, the Jews disobeyed God's commandments; they soiled them-selves by worshipping idols and failed to grasp the significance of their own history. And they confused God's rest, their true destiny, with the sabbath rest—a physical rest which they practised in an almost exclusively external way (cf. Mk 3:1-6; Lk 13:10-17). Christians also can run a similar risk if they fail to hold on to everything which Jesus Christ, the mediator of the New Covenant, has won for them.

1. God's promise of rest remains valid, but to attain it one needs to be faithful and obedient—to have a vigilance which comes from holy fear of God, a fear of being excluded from eternal blessedness. The text can also be interpreted as meaning "Let us fear, lest any one of you despair because he thinks he has been excluded permanently"; that is, "let us fear despair".

In this context "rest" refers to all the supernatural graces we obtain through grace, particularly that of seeing and enjoying God in the future life. This rest, which will reach its perfection in heaven and which begins in this life with faith and grace, is man's true end or destiny. "God works with creative power by sustaining in existence the world that he called into being from nothing, and he works with salvific power in the hearts of those whom from the beginning he has destined for 'rest'" (John Paul II, *Laborem exercens*, 25).

The saints have often liked to describe the joy which heaven gives, that eternal rest which God deigns to grant souls who depart this world. "Who can measure the happiness of heaven, where no evil at all can touch us, no good will be out of reach; where life is to be one long laud extolling God, who will be all in all [. . .]. This, indeed, will be that ultimate Sabbath that has no evening and which the Lord foreshadowed in the account of his creation [. . .]. Only when we are remade by God and perfected by a greater grace shall we have the eternal stillness of that rest in which we shall see that he is God. Then only shall we be filled with him when he will be all in all" (St Augustine, *The City of God*, XXII, 30).

Losing this "rest" is the only thing one should really fear.

2. The good news was proclaimed to the Jews in the sense that they also heard the preaching of Moses which aimed at preparing the chosen people to be generous in their fidelity to the Lord's promises. The Israelites, however, rebelled against those who were the first to hear the divine message—Abraham, Isaac, Jacob, Moses himself, Joshua and the prophets.

The preaching of the Word can actually harden a person's heart if he does not listen to it with the right dispositions. "To obtain salvation it is not enough

message which they heard did not benefit them, because it did not meet with faith in the hearers.[h] ³For we who have believed enter that rest, as he has said,

"As I swore in my wrath,
'They shall never enter my rest,'"

Heb 3:11; 12:15
Ps 95:11

although his works were finished from the foundation of the world. ⁴For he has somewhere spoken of the seventh day in this way, "And God rested on the seventh day from all his works." ⁵And again in this place he said,

Gen 2:2, LXX

Ps 95:11

"They shall never enter my rest."

⁶Since therefore it remains for some to enter it, and those who formerly received the good news failed to enter because of disobedience, ⁷again he sets a certain day, "Today," saying through David so long afterward, in the words already quoted,

Heb 3:7f
Ps 95:7f

cum iis, qui audierant. ³Ingredimur enim in requiem, qui credidimus, quemadmodum dixit: *"Sicut iuravi in ira mea: Non introibunt in requiem meam"*, et quidem operibus ab institutione mundi factis. ⁴Dixit enim quodam loco de die septima sic: *"Et requievit Deus die septima ab omnibus operibus suis"*; ⁵et in isto rursum: *"Non introibunt in requiem meam."* ⁶Quoniam ergo superest quosdam introire in illam, et hi, quibus prioribus evangelizatum est, non introierunt propter inoboedientiam, ⁷iterum terminat diem quendam, "Hodie", in David dicendo post tantum temporis, sicut supra dictum est: *"Hodie, si vocem*

to hear the words. One needs to take them in with faith and keep a firm hold on them. What good was God's promise to those who received it if they did not receive it faithfully or failed to put their trust in his power—if they did not, so to speak, fuse with, become one with, the divine words?" (Theodoret of Cyrus, *Interpretatio Ep. ad Haebreos*, IV). What proves a person's true obedience to God's word is his solidarity with those to whom God had given the authority to proclaim it.

3-8. The believer can be said to "enter God's rest" because in this life he already begins to be intimate with the three divine Persons. In biblical terms the "rest" is connected with the Covenant which God establishes with men. "Rest" is the reward for faithfulness to the Covenant; it begins in this life in the form of serenity and interior peace and the enjoyment of material things (such as the promised land), but will reach its perfection only in heaven. In this sense, as Psalm 95 reminds us, God promised his people rest repeatedly: the psalm speaks of a "today" when they will enter his "rest": everyone can begin to enjoy "today" the rest of divine friendship, provided he does not harden his heart, provided he repents and becomes faithful again.

[h]Other manuscripts read *they were not united in faith with the hearers*

"Today, when you hear his voice,
do not harden your hearts."

Deut 31:7
Josh 22:4
[8]For if Joshua had given them rest, God[i] would not speak later of another day. [9]So then, there remains a sabbath rest for the people of God; [10]for whoever enters God's rest also ceases from his labours as God did from his.

Rev 14:13

eius audieritis, nolite obdurare corda vestra." [8]Nam si eis Iesus requiem praestitisset, non de alio loqueretur post hac die. [9]Itaque relinquitur sabbatismus populo Dei; [10]qui enim ingressus est in requiem eius, etiam ipse requievit ab operibus suis, sicut a suis Deus. [11]Festinemus ergo ingredi in illam requiem, ut ne in idipsum quis incidat inoboedientiae exemplum. [12]Vivus est enim Dei sermo et efficax et penetrabilior omni gladio ancipiti et pertingens usque ad divisionem animae ac spiritus, compagum quoque et medullarum, et discretor cogitationum et intentionum cordis; [13]et non est creatura invisibilis in conspectu eius, omnia autem nuda et aperta sunt oculis eius, ad quem nobis sermo.

Christians have received a further invitation from God to enter his rest: because many Jews proved to be unfaithful, a new people of God was established. This marks a new "today", a new point when one can opt for fidelity and enter the promised land. This "today" has two characteristics: it requires our free response to God's decision to call us; and it does not happen immediately: for the new people of God, also, there is a future "sabbath", that is, heaven.

To appreciate the subtle play on words, one should remember that the same term is used in Hebrew for the word "rest" and for the sabbath as a day of the week.

9-10. The peace and serenity of a Christian who has dominion over sin is described as "sabbath rest", a pledge and symbol of the "heavenly sabbath" of the blessed. "The spiritual sabbath consists in a holy and mystical rest, wherein the 'old man', being buried with Christ, is renewed to life and carefully applies himself to act in accordance with the spirit of Christian piety" (*St Pius V Catechism*, III, 4, 15). This has been the experience of many holy people who have enjoyed peace of soul: St John of the Cross expresses it poetically in these words: "On a dark night, / afire with yearnings full of love / —O moment of delight!— / I slipped out unnoticed / while all my household slept" (*Poems*, I).

In this life a person's interior peace is dependent on his effort to control his passions.

"Let us remember that our life is a form of combat; let us never seek repose; let us never see affliction as something exceptional. We must be like the athlete who is always ready for the test. The time for rest has not yet come: we still need to be made perfect by suffering" (Chrysostom, *Hom. on Heb*, 5).

[i]Greek *he*

¹¹Let us therefore strive to enter that rest, that no one fall by the same sort of disobedience. ¹²For the word of God is living and active, sharper than any two-edged sword, piercing to the division of soul and spirit, of joints and marrow, and discerning the thoughts and intentions of the heart. ¹³And before him no creature is hidden, but all are open and laid bare to the eyes of him with whom we have to do.

Is 49:2
Wis 7:22-30
Eph 6:17
1 Pet 1:23
Rev 1:16

---

¹⁴Habentes ergo pontificem magnum, qui penetravit caelos, Iesum Filium Dei,

11. The sacred writer ends his commentary on Psalm 95 with a short, concise exhortation summing up what he has been saying and inviting his readers to enter God's rest without delay.

"There are a number of reasons why the text speaks of striving to enter (God's) rest," St Thomas comments. "First, because, there is a long road ahead. Then because time is short— and we do not know how much time we have. Third, because ours is a pressing interior call which urges us on with the stimulus of love. Finally, because of the danger of delaying, as happened in the case of the foolish virgins (Mt 25:1-13), who arrived late and failed to gain entry" (*Commentary on Heb*, 4, 2).

The central idea is not only urgency and eagerness but also dogged perseverance with the help of grace.

12-13. The "word of God", which the text speaks about, probably refers to Revelation taken as a whole, particularly Sacred Scripture; but it may also refer to the *Logos* or Word, the second person of the Holy Trinity. The "word" of God is presented as an expression of God's power: it is that active word (Gen 1:3ff; Ps 33:9) which creates everything out of nothing. In the Wisdom books we find this word personified (Sir 42:15; 43:26; Wis 9:1; 18:15; Ps 148:1-5). But this living and active word of God is also to be seen in the New Testament (Gal 3:8, 22) and in its full and perfect form in Christ himself (Jn 1:1; Rev 9:13).

God's word is also very much at work in Revelation: "In the sacred books the Father who is in heaven comes lovingly to meet his children, and talks to them. And such is the force and power of the Word of God that it serves the Church as her support and vigour, and the children of the Church as strength for their faith, food for the soul, and a pure and lasting fount of spiritual life" (Vatican II, *Dei Verbum*, 21).

God's word is consoling and life-giving, but it also inspires fear in those who try to ignore it. "The word of his truth is hotter and brighter than the sun, and pierces the very depths of hearts and minds" (St Justin, *Dialogue with Trypho*, 121, 2). The depths of a person's heart, his deepest thoughts, attitudes and intentions, lie open to God's all-seeing eye. "What a person does or thinks is expressed in his actions, but one can never be sure of what motivates his actions. That, however, is never hidden from God" (St Thomas, *Commentary on Heb*, 4, 2).

CHRIST, OUR HIGH PRIEST, IS GREATER THAN THE PRIESTS OF THE MOSAIC LAW

Our confidence is based on Christ's priesthood

Heb 5:5-10; 7:26;
9:11, 24; 10:21
Eph 4:10

Heb 2:17f
Rom 8:3

¹⁴Since then we have a great high priest who has passed through the heavens, Jesus, the Son of God, let us hold fast our confession. ¹⁵For we have not a high priest who is unable to sympathize with our weaknesses, but one who in

---

teneamus confessionem; ¹⁵non enim habemus pontificem, qui non possit compati infirmitatibus nostris, tentatum autem per omnia secundum similitudinem

---

The last judgment, which is a hidden backdrop to these words of the sacred text, calls us to present conversion. "The Apostle of God wrote this not only for his [immediate] readers but also for us. It behoves us therefore always to keep that divine judgment before our minds, and to be full of fear and trembling and to keep God's commandments faithfully and be ever hopeful of that rest promised us which we shall attain in Christ" (Theodoret of Cyrus, *Interpretatio Ep. ad Haebreos, ad loc.*).

14-16. The text now reverts to its main theme (cf. 2:17), that is, the priesthood of Christ. It highlights the dignity of the new high priest, who has passed through the heavens; and his mercy, too, for he sympathizes with our weaknesses. We have, therefore, every reason to approach him with confidence. "The believers were at that time in a storm of temptation; that is why the Apostle is consoling them, saying that our high priest not only knows, as God, the weakness of our nature: as man, he has also experienced the sufferings that affect us, although he was free from sin. Since he knows our weakness so well, he can give us the help we need, and when he comes to judge us, he will take that weakness into account in his sentence" (*Interpretatio Ep. ad Haebreos, ad loc.*).

We should respond to the Lord's goodness by staying true to our profession of faith. The confession or profession of faith referred to here is not simply an external declaration: external confession is necessary but there must also be commitment and a spirit of fidelity. A Christian needs to live up to all the demands of his calling; he should be single-minded and free from doubts.

15. "If we should some time find ourselves sorely tempted by our enemies, it will greatly help us to remember that we have on our side a high priest who is most compassionate, for he chose to experience all kinds of temptation" (*St Pius V Catechism*, IV, 15, 14). In order to understand and help a sinner to get over his falls and cope with temptation, one does not oneself need to have

every respect has been tempted as we are, yet without
sinning. ¹⁶Let us then with confidence draw near to the
throne of grace, that we may receive mercy and find grace
to help in time of need.

Rom 3:25
2 Cor 5:21
1 Jn 3:21

---

absque peccato. ¹⁶Adeamus ergo cum fiducia ad thronum gratiae, ut miseri-
cordiam consequamur et gratiam inveniamus in auxilium opportunum.

---

experience of being tempted; in fact, only one who does not sin knows the full
force of temptation, because the sinner gives in prior to resisting to the end.
Christ never yielded to temptation. He therefore experienced much more than
we do (because we are often defeated by temptation) the full rigour and violence
of those temptations which he chose to undergo as man at particular points in
his life. Our Lord, then, allowed himself to be tempted, in order to set us an
example and prevent us from ever losing confidence in our ability to resist
temptation with the help of grace (cf. notes on Mt 4:1-11 and par.).

"There is no man", St Jerome comments, "who can resist all tests except he
who, made in our likeness, has experienced everything but sin" (*Comm. in
Ionam*, II, 46). Christ's sinlessness, often affirmed in Sacred Scripture (Rom
8:3; 2 Cor 5:21; Jn 8:46; 1 Pet 1.19, 2.21-24), follows logically from his being
God and from his human integrity and holiness. At the same time Christ's
weakness, which he chose to experience out of love for us, is a kind of invitation
from God to pray for strength to resist sin. "Let us adore Christ who emptied
himself to assume the condition of a slave. He was tempted in every way that
we are, but did not sin. Let us turn in prayer to him, saying, 'You took on our
human weakness. Be the eyes of the blind, the strength of the weak, the friend
of the lonely'" (*Liturgy of the Hours*, Christmas Day, evening prayer I).

16. The "throne" is the symbol of Christ's authority; he is King of the living
and the dead. But here it speaks of a "throne of grace": through the salvation
worked by Christ, the compassionate Priest and intercessor, God's throne has
become a judgment seat from which mercy flows. Christ has initiated for
mankind a time of forgiveness and sanctification in which he does not yet
manifest his position as sovereign Judge. Christ's priesthood did not cease to
operate with his death; it continues in heaven, where he forever pleads on our
behalf, and therefore we should have confident recourse to him.

"What security should be ours in considering the mercy of the Lord! 'He
has but to cry for redress, and I, the ever merciful, will listen to him' (Ex 22:27).
It is an invitation, a promise that he will not fail to fulfill. 'Let us then with
confidence draw near to the throne of grace, and we may receive mercy and
find grace to help in time of need'. The enemies of our sanctification will be
rendered powerless if the mercy of God goes before us. And if through our own
fault and human weakness we should fall, the Lord comes to our aid and raises
us up" (Blessed J. Escrivá, *Christ is passing by*, 7).

5

Christ has been made high priest by God the Father

Heb 2:17; 7:28 ¹For every high priest chosen from among men is appointed

---

¹Omnis namque pontifex ex hominibus assumptus pro hominibus constituitur

---

1-10. The central theme of the epistle, broached in 2:17 and taken up again in 4:14-15, is discussed from here up to the start of chapter 10—the theme of Christ as high priest, the high priest who really can free us from all sin. In fact, Christ is the only perfect Priest: other priests— in both natural religions and the Jewish religion—are only prefigurements of Christ. The first thing to be emphasized, because the writer is addressing people of Jewish background, is that Christ's priesthood is on a higher plane than that of the priests of the Old Law. However, the argument applies not only to the priesthood of Aaron, to whose family all Israelite priests belonged, but also, indirectly, to all forms of priesthood before Christ. But there is a basic difference, in that whereas other priests were chosen by men, Aaron was chosen by God. Sacred Scripture introduces him as Moses' brother (cf. Ex 6:20), acting as his interpreter to Pharaoh (because Moses was "slow of speech": Ex 4:10; cf. 7:1-2) and joining him to lead the people out of Egypt (cf. Ex 4:27-30). After the Israelites left Egypt, God himself instituted the priesthood of Aaron to minister and carry out divine worship at the tabernacle and later at the temple in Jerusalem (cf. Ex 28:1-5).

Divine intervention, therefore, brought to a close the period when sacrifice was offered by the head of the family or the chief of the tribe and when no specific calling or external ordination rite was connected with priesthood. Thus, for example, in the Book of Genesis we read that Cain, and Abel, themselves offered sacrifices (cf. Gen 4:35), as did Noah after coming safely through the flood (cf. Gen 8:20); and the patriarchs often offered sacrifices to God in adoration or thanksgiving or to renew their Covenant—for example, Abraham (cf. Gen 12:8; 15:8-17; 22:1-13) and Jacob (cf. Gen 26:25; 33:20), etc.

Although for a considerable time after the institution of the Aaron priesthood, sacrifices continued to be offered also by private individuals—for example, in the period of the Judges, the sacrifice of Gideon (Judg 6:18, 25-26) or that of Samson's parents (Judg 13:15-20)—gradually the convictions grew that to be a priest a person had to have a specific vocation, one which was not given to anyone outside males of the line of Aaron (cf. Judg 17:7-13), whom God had chosen from out of all the people of Israel, identifying him by the sign of his rod sprouting buds (Num 17:16-24). God himself meted out severe punishment to Korah and his sons when they tried to set themselves up as rivals of Aaron: they were devoured by fire from heaven (cf. Num 16); and it was specified in Mosaic legislation time and time again that only the sons of Aaron could act as priests (cf. Num 3:10; 17:5; 18:7). This priesthood offered the sacrifices of Mosaic worship—the burnt offerings, cereal offerings, sin offerings and peace offerings (cf. Lev 6). To the descendants of Aaron, assisted by the Levites, was entrusted also the care of the tabernacle and the protection of the ark of the Covenant. They received their ministry and had it confirmed by the offering of sacrifice and by anointing of the man's head and hands with oil (Ex 29; Lev 8-9; Num 3:3). For all these reasons Hebrew priests were honoured and revered by the people and regarded (not without reason, because God had ordained them) as on a much higher plane than other priests, particularly those of the peoples of Canaan, the priests of Baal, for example. In Christ's time the high priest was the highest religious authority in Israel; his words were regarded as oracular statements, and his decisions could have important political repercussions.

However, Christ came with the very purpose of taking this ancient institution and transforming it into a new, eternal priesthood. Every Christian priest is, as it were, Christ's instrument or an extension of his sacred humanity. Christian priests do not act in their own name, nor are they mere representatives of the people: they act in the name of God. "Here we have the priest's identity: he is direct and daily instrument of the saving grace which Christ has won for us" (Blessed J. Escrivá, *In Love with the Church*, 39). It is really Christ who is acting through them by means of their words, gestures etc. All of this means that Christian priesthood cannot be separated from the eternal priesthood of Christ. This extension of God's providence (in the form of the Old Testament priesthood and the priesthood instituted by Christ in the New Testament and the mission entrusted to New Testament priests) should lead us to love and honour the priesthood irrespective of the human defects and shortcomings of these ministers of God: "To love God and not venerate his Priests . . . is not possible" (Blessed J. Escrivá, *The Way*, 74).

1a. These words provide a very good short definition of what every priest is.

"The office proper to a priest", St Thomas Aquinas points out, "is to be a mediator between God and the people, inasmuch as he bestows divine things on the people (he is called *sacerdos* (priest), which means 'a giver of sacred things', *sacra dans* [. . .]), and again inasmuch as he offers the people's prayer to God and in some way makes satisfaction to God for their sins" (*Summa theologiae*, III, q.22, a.1).

In this passage of the letter we can detect an echo of the description of Aaron in the Book of Sirach: "He chose him out of all the living to offer sacrifice to the Lord, incense and a pleasing odour as a memorial portion, to make atonement for the people" (Sir 45:16). Four elements characterize the office of the high priest (the text speaks of the "high" priest in the strict sense, but it is applicable to all priests)—1) his special dignity, because although he is a man he has been specially chosen by God; 2) the purpose of his mission, which is the good of mankind ("to act on behalf of men"); 3) the "material" side of his office, that is, public divine worship; 4) the specific acts he must perform, the offering of sacrifice at appropriate times.

In the specific case of priesthood instituted by God—such as that of Aaron or the new priesthood instituted by Christ—the calling ("taken" or "chosen" from among men) is not simply an influence the person feels interiorly, or a desire to be a priest: its divine origin is confirmed by nomination by the proper authority, and by official consecration.

1b. A priest is "chosen from among men", that is, he should possess a human nature. This is a further sign of God's mercy: to bring about our salvation he uses someone accessible to us, one who shares our human condition, "so that man might have someone like himself to have recourse to" (St Thomas, *Commentary on Heb, ad loc.*). These words also indicate the extent of God's kindness because they remind us that the divine Redeemer not only offered himself and made satisfaction for the sins of all, but desired that "the priestly life which the divine Redeemer had begun in his mortal body by his prayers and sacrifice (should not cease). He willed it to continue unceasingly through the ages in his mystical body, which is the Church; and therefore he instituted a visible priesthood to offer everywhere a clean oblation (Mal 1:11), so that all men all over the world, being diverted from sin, might serve God con-scientiously, and of their own free will" (Pius XII, *Mediator Dei*, 1).

He is "chosen from among men" also in the sense that he is given special consecration which in some way marks him off from the rest of the people of God. St John Chrysostom comments, recalling Jesus triple question to Peter after the Resurrection (cf. Jn 21:15-17): "When he asked Peter if he loved him, he did not do so because he needed to know whether his disciple loved him, but because he wanted to show how great his own love was; thus, when he says, 'Who then is the faithful and prudent servant', he does not say this because he does not know the answer, but in order to show us how unique and wonderful an honour it is, as can be deduced from the rewards: 'he will place him over all his goods.' And he concludes that the priest ought to be outstanding in holiness (*De sacerdotio*, II, 1-2).

"The priests of the New Testament", Vatican II reminds us, "are, by their vocation to ordination, set apart in some way in the midst of the people of God, but this is not in order that they should be separated from that people or from anyone, but that they should be completely consecrated to the task for which God chose them" (*Presbyterorum ordinis*, 3). This calling, then, constitutes a distinction but not a separation because it is indissolubly linked to a specific mission: a priest is "chosen from among men" but for the purpose of acting "on behalf of men in relation to God". In this delicate balance between divine call and spiritual mission to men lies the essence of priesthood. Christians, there-fore, should never view a priest as "just another person". "They want to find in the priest the virtues appropriate to any Christian and even any upright man—understanding, justice, commitment to work (priestly work, in this case), charity, good manners, social refinement. But the faithful also want to be able to recognize clearly the priestly character: they expect the priest to pray, not to refuse to administer the sacraments; they expect him to be open to everyone

to act on behalf of men in relation to God, to offer gifts and sacrifices for sins. ²He can deal gently with the ignorant and wayward, since he himself is beset with weakness. ³Because of this he is bound to offer sacrifice for his own sins

---

in his, quae sunt ad Deum, ut offerat dona et sacrificia pro peccatis, ²qui aeque condolere possit his, qui ignorant et errant, quoniam et ipse circumdatus est

---

and not set himself up to take charge of people or become an aggressive leader of human factions, of whatever shade (cf. *Presbyterorum ordinis*, 6). They expect him to bring love and devotion to the celebration of Mass, to sit in the confessional, to console the sick and the troubled; to teach sound doctrine to children and adults, to preach the Word of God and no mere human science which—no matter how well he may know it—is not the knowledge that saves and brings eternal life; they expect him to give counsel and be charitable to those in need" (Blessed J. Escrivá, *In Love with the Church*, 42).

Priests "could not be the servants of Christ unless they were witnesses and dispensers of a life other than that of this earth. On the other hand, they would be powerless to serve men if they remained aloof from their life and circumstances" (*Presbyterorum ordinis*, 3). In this connexion, Pope John Paul II has made the following appeal: "Yes, you are chosen from among men, given to Christ by the Father, to be in the world, *in the heart of society*. You are appointed to act on behalf of men (Heb 5:1). The priesthood is the sacrament whereby the Church is to be seen as the society of the people of God; it is the 'social' sacrament. Priests should 'convoke' each of the communities of the people of God, around them but not for themselves—*for Christ!*" (*Homily at an ordination of priests*, 15 June 1980).

The specific function of the priest has, then, been clearly identified: he is concerned about his brethren but he is not here to solve temporal problems; his role is only "in relation to God". "Christian ministerial priesthood is different from any other priesthood in that it is not an office to which someone is appointed by others to intercede with God on their behalf; it is a mission to which a man is called by God (Heb 5:1-10; 7:24; 9:11-28) to be towards others a living sign of the presence of Christ, the only Mediator (1 Tim 2:5), Head and Shepherd of his people [. . .]. In other words, Christian priesthood is essentially (this is the only possible way it can be understood) an eminently sacred mission, both in its origin (Christ) and in its content (the divine mystery) and by the very manner in which it is conferred (a sacrament)" (A. del Portillo, *On Priesthood*, pp. 59f).

2-3. From the moral qualities a priest needs, these verses single out mercy and compassion, which lead him, on the one hand, to be gentle to sinners and, at the same time, to desire to make personal reparation for their sins. The Latin translation of v. 2a puts the emphasis on the fact that the priest shares in suffering for sin: he can "suffer along with" (*aeque condolere*) but in just measure on seeing those who go astray, and, imitating Christ, he can himself perform some of the penance those sinners should be doing. The original word translated here as "deal gently" recalls the profound, but serene, sorrow which Abraham felt when Sarah died (cf. Gen 23:2) and at the same time it alludes to the need for forbearance, generosity and understanding: a priest must be a person who, while rejecting sin, is understanding to the sinner and conscious that it may take him time to mend his ways. He is also inclined to put the sinner's intentions in the best light (cf. Gal 6:1): people do not always sin deliberately; they can sin out of ignorance (that is, not realizing the gravity of their actions) and, more often than not, out of weakness.

The Old Testament makes a clear distinction between sin committed unwittingly (cf. Lev 4:2-27; Num 14:24, 27-29) and sins of rebelliousness (cf. Num 15:22-31; Deut 17:12). Further on (cf. Heb 6:4-6; 10:26-27; 12:17), the letter will again refer to the gravity of sins committed out of malice. Here, however, it is referring to sin, whether grave or not, committed out of weakness. "Ignorant" and "wayward" are almost synonymous, for a person who sins out of ignorance is described in Hebrews by a word which means "he who goes astray, he who does not know the way". The basic reason why a priest should be understanding and compassionate is his awareness of his own weakness. Thus, the Church puts these words on his lips in Eucharistic Prayer I: "nobis quoque peccatoribus—for ourselves, too, sinners" (cf. Wis 9:5- 6). A priest is compassionate and understanding because "he himself is beset with weakness". The word translated as "beset" contains the idea of surrounded or covered by or wrapped as if in a cloak. Pope Pius XI wrote: "When we see a man exercising this faculty (of forgiving sins), we cannot but repeat (not out of pharisaical scandal, but with reverent amazement) those words, 'Who is this, who even forgives sins?' (Lk 7:49). It is the Man-God, who had and has 'authority on earth to forgive sins' (Lk 5:24), and has chosen to communicate it to his priests, and thereby with the generosity of divine mercy to meet the human conscience's need of purification. Hence the great consolation the guilty man receives who experiences remorse and contritely hears the priest tell him in God's name, 'I absolve you from your sins.' The fact that he hears this said by someone who himself will need to ask another priest to speak the same words to him, does not debase God's merciful gift: it enhances it, for the hand of God who works this wonder is seen (as operating) by means of a frail creature" (Pius XII, *Ad Catholici sacerdotii*).

3. Everyone, including the priest, is a sinner. In the Old Testament rites for the Day of Atonement (*Yom Kippur*), the high priest, before entering the Holy of Holies, offered a sin-offering for his own sins (cf. Lev 16:3, 6, 11; Heb 9:6-14); so too the priests of the New Testament have a duty to be holy, to reject sin, to ask for forgiveness of their own sins, and to intercede for sinners.

The model the priest should always have before him is Jesus Christ, the eternal high priest. "The main motive force actuating a priest should be the determination to attain the closest union with the divine Redeemer [. . .]. He

as well as for those of the people. [4]And one does not take the honour upon himself, but he is called by God, just as Aaron was.

Ex 28:1
Jn 3:27

[5]So also Christ did not exalt himself to be made a high priest, but was appointed by him who said to him,

Ps 2:7, LXX
Heb 4:14

"Thou art my Son,
today I have begotten thee";

---

infirmitate [3]et propter eam debet, quemadmodum et pro populo, ita etiam pro semetipso offere pro peccatis. [4]Nec quisquam sumit sibi illum honorem, sed qui vocatur a Deo tamquam et Aaron. [5]Sicut et Christus non semetipsum glorificavit, ut pontifex fieret, sed qui locutus est ad eum: *"Filius meus es tu;*

---

should continually keep Christ before his eyes. Christ's commands, actions and example he should follow most assiduously, in the conviction that it is not enough for him to submit to the duties by which the faithful are bound, but that he must at a daily increasing pace pursue the perfection of life which the high dignity of a priest demands" (Pius XII, *Menti nostrae*, 7). But, one might object, Christ never had any defect, never sinned, because his human nature was perfect and totally holy: is he not therefore too perfect a model for men who when it comes down to it are sinners? The answer is, No, not at all, for he himself said, "I have given you an example, that you also should do as I have done to you" (Jn 13:15). Besides, when the text (v. 2) refers to "weakness" this may refer to two things—the weakness of human nature (of man as creature), and the imperfection resulting from his faults and his passions. The former kind of defect is one Christ shares with us; the second is one he does not. For this very reason, in the case of the priest, consciousness of his sins, plus his conviction that he has been called by Christ, moves him to be very committed to his apostolic ministry of reconciliation and penance; and in the first instance priests perform this ministry for one another. "Priests, who are consecrated by the anointing of the Holy Spirit and sent by Christ, mortify the works of the flesh in themselves and dedicate themselves completely to the service of people" (Vatican II, *Presbyterorum ordinis*, 12). As Pope John Paul II has stressed, "the priest's celebration of the Eucharist and administration of the other sacraments, his pastoral zeal, his relationship with the faithful, his communion with his brother priests, his collaboration with his bishop, his life of prayer—in a word, the whole of his priestly existence—suffers an inexorable decline if by negligence or for some other reason he fails to receive the sacrament of Penance at regular intervals and in a spirit of genuine faith and devotion. If a priest were no longer to go to confession or properly confess his sins, his *priestly being* and his *priestly action* would feel the effect of this very soon, and it would also be noticed by the community of which he was the pastor.

"But I also add that even in order to be a good and effective minister of Penance the priest needs to have recourse to the source of grace and holiness present in this sacrament. We priests, on the basis of our personal experience,

Ps 110:4
Heb 7:1-28

Mt 26:39f
Ps 22:25

⁶as he says also in another place,
"Thou art a priest for ever,
   after the order of Melchizedek."
⁷In the days of his flesh, Jesusʲ offered up prayers and

---

ego hodie genui te"; ⁶quemadmodum et in alio dicit: *"Tu es sacerdos in aeternum secundum ordinem Melchisedech."* ⁷Qui in diebus carnis suae, preces

---

can certainly say that, the more careful we are to receive the sacrament of Penance and to approach it frequently and with good dispositions, the better we fulfil our own ministry as confessors and ensure that our penitents benefit from it. And on the other hand this ministry would lose much of its effectiveness if in some way we were to stop being good penitents. Such is the *internal logic* of this great sacrament. It invites all of us priests of Christ to pay renewed attention to our personal confession" (*Reconciliatio et paenitentia*, 31).

What the Pope says here ultimately stems from the fact that " as ministers of the sacred mysteries, especially in the sacrifice of the Mass, priests act in a special way in the person of Christ who gave himself as a victim to sanctify men" (*Presbyterorum ordinis*, 13).

In this way, "Christ the shepherd is present in the priest so as continually to actualize the universal call to conversion and repentance which prepares for the coming of the Kingdom of heaven (cf. Mt 4:17). He is present in order to make men understand that forgiveness of sins, the reconciliation of the soul and God, cannot be the outcome of a monologue, no matter how keen a person's capacity for reflection and self-criticism. He reminds us that no one, alone, can calm his own conscience; that the contrite heart must submit its sins to the Church-institution, to the man-priest, who in the sacrament of Penance is a permanent objective witness to the radical need which fallen humanity has of the man-God, the only Just One, the only Justifier" (A. del Portillo, *On Priesthood*, p. 62).

7-9. This brief summary of Christ's life stresses his perfect obedience to the Father's will, his intense prayer and his sufferings and redemptive death. As in the hymn to Christ in Philippians 2:6-11, the point is made that Christ set his power aside and, despite his being the only-begotten Son of God, out of obedience chose to die on the cross. His death was a true self-offering expressed in that "loud voice" when he cried out to the Father just before he died, "into thy hands I commit my spirit" (Lk 23:46). But although Jesus' obedience was most obvious on Calvary, it was a constant feature of "the days of his flesh": he obeyed Mary and Joseph, seeing in them the authority of the heavenly Father; he was obedient to political and religious authorities; and he always obeyed the Father, identifying himself with him to such a degree that he could say, "I have glorified thee on earth, having accomplished the work which thou gavest me to do [. . .]. All mine are thine, and thine are mine" (Jn 17:4, 10).

The passage also points to Jesus' prayer, the high point of which occurred

ʲGreek *he*

in Gethsemane on the eve of his passion. The reference to "loud cries and supplications" recalls the Gospel account of his suffering: "And being in an agony he prayed more earnestly; and his sweat became like great drops of blood falling down upon the ground" (Lk 22:44).

Hebrews 5:7-9 is probably referring not so much to his prayer in the Garden, still less to any prayer of Christ asking to be delivered from death, but to our Lord's constant prayer for the salvation of mankind. "When the Apostle speaks of these supplications and cries of Jesus," St John Chrysostom comments, "he does not mean prayers which he made on his own behalf but prayers for those who would later believe in him. And, due to the fact that the Jews did not yet have the elevated concept of Christ that they ought to have had, St Paul says that 'he was heard', just as the Lord himself told his disciples, to console them, 'If you loved me, you would have rejoiced, because I go to the Father; for the Father is greater than I' [. . .]. Such was the respect and reverence shown by the Son, that God the Father could not but take note and heed his Son and his prayers" (*Hom. on Heb*, 11).

7. "In the days of his flesh", a reference to the Incarnation. "Flesh" is synonymous with mortal life; this is a reference to Christ's human nature—as in the prologue to St John's Gospel (cf. Jn 1:14) and many other places (Heb 2:14; Gal 2:20; Phil 1:22-24; 1 Pet 4:1-2) including where mention is made of Jesus being a servant and capable of suffering (cf. Phil 2:8; Mt 20:27-28). Jesus' human nature "in the days of his flesh" is quite different from his divine nature and also from his human nature after its glorification (cf. 1 Cor 15:50). "It must be said that the word 'flesh' is occasionally used to refer to the weakness of the flesh, as it says in 1 Cor 15:50: 'flesh and blood cannot inherit the kingdom of God'. Christ had a weak and mortal flesh. Therefore it says in the text, 'In the days of his flesh', referring to when he was living in a flesh which seemed to be like sinful flesh, but which was sinless" (St Thomas Aquinas, *Commentary on Heb*, 5, 1). So, this text underlines our Lord's being both Victim and Priest.

"Prayers and supplications": very fitting in a priest. The two words mean much the same; together they are a form of words which used to be employed in petitions to the king or some important official. The plural tells us that there were lots of these petitions. The writer seems to have in mind the picture of the Redeemer who "going a little farther fell on his face and prayed, 'My Father, if it be possible, let this cup pass from me; nevertheless, not as I will, but as thou wilt" (Mt 26:39). St Thomas comments on this description of Christ's prayer as follows: "His action was indeed one of offering prayers and supplications, that is, a spiritual sacrifice: that was what Christ offered. It speaks of prayers in the sense of petitions because 'The prayer of a righteous man has great power' (Jas 5:16); and it speaks of supplications to emphasize the humility of the one who is praying, who falls on his knees, as we see happening in the case of him who 'fell on his face and prayed' (Mt 26:39)" (*Commentary on Heb*, 5, 1).

To emphasize the force of Christ's prayer, the writer adds, "with loud cries

Lk 22:41-44;
23:46
supplications, with loud cries and tears, to him who was
able to save him from death, and he was heard for his godly
Phil 2:8 fear. [8]Although he was a Son, he learned obedience through

---

supplicationesque ad eum, qui possit salvum illum a morte facere, cum clamore
valido et lacrimis offerens et exauditus pro sua reverentia, [8]et quidem cum esset

---

and tears". According to rabbinical teaching, there were three degrees of prayer,
each stronger than the last—supplications, cries and tears. Christian tradition
has always been touched by the humanity of the Redeemer as revealed in the
way he prays. "Everything that is being said here may be summed up in one
word—humility: that stops the mouths of those who blaspheme against Christ's
divinity saying that it is completely inappropriate for a God to act like this. For,
on the contrary, the Godhead laid it down that [Christ's] human nature should
suffer all this, in order to show us the extreme to which he truly became
incarnate and assumed a human nature, and to show us that the mystery of
salvation was accomplished in a real and not an apparent or fictitious manner"
(Theodoret of Cyrus, *Interpretatio Ep. ad Haebreos, ad loc.*). Christ's prayer,
moreover, teaches us that prayer must 1) be fervent and 2) involve interior pain.
"Christ had both [fervour and pain], for the Apostle by mentioning 'tears'
intends to show the interior groaning of him who weeps in this way [. . .]. But
he did not weep on his own account: he wept for us, who receive the fruit of
his passion" (St Thomas, *Commentary on Heb, ad loc.*).

"He was heard for his godly fear." St John Chrysostom's commentary is
very apposite: "'He gave himself up for our sins', he says in Gal 1:4; and
elsewhere (cf. 1 Tim 2:6) he adds, 'He gave himself as a ransom for all'. What
does he mean by this? Do you not see that he is speaking with humility of
himself, because of his mortal flesh? And, nevertheless, because he is the Son,
it says that he was heard for his godly fear" (*Hom. on Heb*, 8). It is like a loving
contention between Father and Son. The Son wins the Father's admiration, so
generous is his self-surrender.

And yet Christ's prayer did not seem to be heeded, for his Father God did
not save him from ignominious death—the cup he had to drink—nor were all
the Jews, for whom he prayed, converted. But it was only apparently so: in fact
Christ's prayer *was* heard. It is true that, like every one, the idea of dying was
repugnant to him, because he had a natural instinct to live; but, on the other
hand, he wished to die through a deliberate and rational act of his will; hence
in the course of the prayer, he said, "not my will, but thine, be done" (Lk 22:42).
Similarly Christ wanted to save all mankind—but he wanted them to accept
salvation freely (cf. *Commentary on Heb, ad loc.*).

8. In Christ there are two perfect and complete natures and therefore two
different levels of knowledge—divine knowledge and human knowledge.
Christ's human knowledge includes 1) the knowledge that the blessed in heaven
have, that is, the knowledge that comes from direct vision of the divine essence;

what he suffered; [9]and being made perfect he became the

Filius, didicit ex his, quae passus est, oboedientiam; [9]et, consummatus, factus

---

2) the knowledge with which God endowed man before original sin (infused knowledge); and 3) the knowledge which man acquires through experience. This last-mentioned knowledge could and in fact did increase (cf. Lk 2:52) in Christ's case. Christ's painful experience of the passion, for example, increased this last type of knowledge, which is why the verse says that Christ learned obedience through suffering. There was a Greek proverb which said, "Sufferings are lessons." Christ's teaching and example raise this positive view of suffering onto the supernatural level. "In *suffering there is concealed* a particular *power that draws a person interiorly close to Christ*, a special grace [. . .]. A result of such a conversion is not only that the individual discovers the salvific meaning of suffering but above all that he becomes a completely new person. He discovers a new dimension, as it were, of *his entire life and vocation*" (John Paul II, *Salvifici doloris*, 26)

In our Lord's case, his experience of suffering was connected with his generosity in obedience. He freely chose to obey even unto death (cf Heb 10:5-9; Rom 5:19; Phil 2:8), consciously atoning for the first sin, a sin of disobedience. "In his suffering, sins are cancelled out precisely because he alone as the only-begotten Son could take them upon himself, accept them *with that love for the Father which overcomes* the evil of every sin; in a certain sense he annihilates this evil in the spiritual space of the relationship between God and humanity, and fills this space with good" (*Salvifici doloris*, 17). Christ "learned obedience" not in the sense that this virtue developed in him, for his human nature was perfect in its holiness, but in the sense that he put into operation the infused virtue his human soul already possessed. "Christ knew what obedience was from all eternity, but he learned obedience in practice through the severities he underwent particularly in his passion and death" (St Thomas Aquinas, *Commentary on Heb, ad loc.*).

Christ's example of obedience is something we should copy. A Christian writer of the fifth century, Diadochus of Photike, wrote: "The Lord loved (obedience) because it was the way to bring about man's salvation and he obeyed his Father unto the cross and unto death; however, his obedience did not in any sense diminish his majesty. And so, having—by his obedience— dissolved man's disobedience, he chose to lead to blessed and immortal life those who followed the way of obedience" (*Chapters on Spiritual Perfection*, 41).

9. Obviously Christ as God could not increase in perfection. Nor could his sacred humanity become any holier, for from the moment of his Incarnation he received the fulness of grace, that is, he had the maximum degree of holiness a man could have. In this connexion Thomas Aquinas points out that Christ had grace to an infinite degree. In Christ there is a dual grace: one is the grace of

source of eternal salvation to all who obey him, [10]being designated by God a high priest after the order of Melchizedek.

est omnibus oboedientibus sibi auctor salutis aeternae, [10]appellatus a Deo

union (that is, the personal union to the Son of God gratuitously bestowed on human nature): clearly this grace is infinite as the person of the Word is infinite. The other grace is habitual grace which, although it is received in a limited human nature, is yet infinite in its perfection because grace was conferred on Christ as the universal source of the justification of human nature (cf. *Summa theologiae*, III, q. 7, a. 11). In what sense, then, could Christ be "made perfect"? St Thomas provides the answer: Christ, through his passion, achieved a special glory—the impassibility and glorification of his body. Moreover, he attained the same perfections as we shall participate in when we are raised from the dead in glory, those of us who believe in him (cf. *Commentary on Heb, ad loc.*). For this reason our Redeemer could exclaim before his death, "It is finished" (Jn 19:30)—referring not only to his own sacrifice but also to the fact that he had completely accomplished the redeeming atonement. Christ triumphed on the cross and attained perfection for himself and for others. In Hebrews the same verb is used for what is translated into English as "to be made perfect" and "to finish". Christ, moreover, by obeying and becoming a perfect victim, truly pleasing to the Father, is more perfectly positioned to perfect others. "Obedience" is essentially docility to what God asks of us and readiness to listen to him (cf. Rom 1:5; 16:26; 2 Cor 10:5; Heb 4:3). Christ's obedience is a source of salvation for us; if we imitate him we will truly form one body with him and he will be able to pass on to us the fulness of his grace.

"Now, when you find it hard to obey, remember your Lord: '*factus obediens usque ad mortem, mortem autem crucis:* obedient even to accepting death, death on a cross!'" (Blessed J. Escrivá, *The Way*, 628).

10. As the epistle repeatedly teaches, Christ is a high priest "after the order of Melchizedek". Two essential characteristics come together here: he is the eternal Son of God, as announced in the messianic Psalm 2:7: "You are my Son, today I have begotten you"; and he is at the same time high priest not according to the order which God instituted with Aaron but according to the order of Melchizedek, also established by God. Further on the letter explains in what sense this "order of Melchizedek" is superior to that of Levi and Aaron. What it stresses at this point is the connexion between Christ's priesthood and his divine sonship. Christ, the Son of God, was sent by the Father as Redeemer and mediator, and the mediation of Christ, who is God and true man, is exercised by way of priesthood. So, in the last analysis Christ is Priest both by virtue of being the Son of God and by virtue of his Incarnation as man. "The abyss of malice which sin opens up has been bridged by his infinite charity. God did not abandon men. His plans foresaw that the sacrifices of the Old Law would be insufficient to repair our faults and re-establish the unity which had been lost.

The need for religious instruction

1 Cor 3:1-3
Heb 6:1
1 Pet 2:2

¹¹About this we have much to say which is hard to explain, since you have become dull of hearing. ¹²For

---

pontifex *iuxta ordine Melchisedech.* ¹¹De quo grandis nobis sermo et in-interpretabilis ad dicendum, quoniam segnes facti estis ad audiendum. ¹²Etenim cum deberetis magistri esse propter tempus, rursum indigetis, ut vos doceat

A man who was God would have to offer himself up. To help us grasp in some measure this unfathomable mystery, we might imagine the Blessed Trinity taking counsel together in their uninterrupted intimate relationship of intimate love. As a result of their eternal decision, the only-begotten Son of God the Father takes on our human condition and bears the burden of our wretchedness and sorrow, to end up sewn with nails to a piece of wood" (Blessed J. Escrivá, *Christ is passing by,* 95).

It was appropriate that the divine person who became incarnate should be the Son or Word, for "the Word has a kind of essential kinship not only with rational nature but also universally with the whole of creation, since the Word contains the essences of all things created by God, just as man the artist in the conception of his intellect comprehends the essences of all the products of art [. . .]. Wherefore all things are said to be made by the Word. Therefore, it was appropriate for Word to be joined to creature, that is, to human nature" (St Thomas, *Summa contra Gentiles,* IV, 42). Finally, it was fitting that Redemption from sin should be brought about by way of a sacrifice offered by the same divine person.

So it is that Christ, the only-begotten Son, to whom God said, "You are my son, today I have begotten you", is also the priest to whom God swears, "Thou art a priest for ever, after the order of Melchizedek".

11-14. The writer explains in what sense Christ is called a "priest for ever, after the order of Melchizedek", because he is afraid his readers will not understand, despite their being Jews and therefore familiar with Melchizedek. This is a very important subject, calling for an extensive and complex explanation, and therefore it needs to be followed carefully. The people to whom the letter is addressed would have been very familiar with Sacred Scripture and would have received catechesis prior to and subsequent to Baptism. By rights, at this stage they should be teachers of other Christians, well able to give them a clear exposition of the truths of faith. And yet they need to be told again about the rudiments of Christianity in the same sort of way as children need to be taught the basics of language—the alphabet and pronunciation. The Jewish Christians to whom the letter is addressed, have become, because of their doubts and wavering, rather like those first Christians in Corinth, recent converts and already divided into separate parties, whom the Apostle calls "babes" and "men of the flesh" (cf. 1 Cor 3:1-3). Like small children they need to be given light food; they cannot yet take solid food. Although these words contain a reproach, because they are addressed to

101

though by this time you ought to be teachers, you need some one to teach you again the first principles of God's word. You need milk, not solid food; ¹³for every one who lives on milk is unskilled in the word of righteousness, for he is a child. ¹⁴But solid food is for the mature, for those who have their facilities trained by practice to distinguish good from evil.

Eph 4:13f

Phil 1:10
Gen 2:17
Rom 16:19

---

aliquis elementa exordii sermonum Dei, et facti estis, quibus lacte opus sit, non solido cibo. ¹³Omnis enim, qui lactis est particeps, expers est sermonis iustitiae, parvulus enim est; ¹⁴perfectorum autem est solidus cibus, eorum, qui pro consuetudine exercitatos habent sensus ad discretionem boni ac mali.

---

grown-up people, they are said in a tone of tenderness and affection. The rabbis in fact used to affectionately call their disciples "children of the breast", and described themselves as "teachers of children" (cf. Rom 2:20). St Paul often used the image of a child at the breast to describe the situation of those who did not yet know the truth and were therefore blamelessly ignorant (cf. 1 Cor 13:11; Gal 4:1, 3; Eph 4:14). Sometimes he compared his preaching with the loving vigilance of a mother nursing her child (cf. 1 Thess 2:7; Gal 4:20). St Peter also calls recently baptized people "newborn babes" (1 Pet 2:2). So, in spite of being reproachful, the author of the letter sees himself as a teacher and spiritual father. Like little children, his readers need to go back and study the basics of the faith; they are not yet ready to understand the "word of righteousness", that is, the mystery of justification (Rom 6:16; 9:30), nor can they yet distinguish good from evil (cf. Rom 2:18; Phil 1:10; Gen 3:5). He is extending an implicit invitation to become spiritually mature, for a Christian should attain the wisdom and maturity of the perfect man, according to the measure of Christ's perfection (cf. Eph 4:10; 1 Cor 14:20; Col 1:28).

In this connexion St Thomas reminds us that Christian perfection calls for a continuous effort to purify the intentions behind one's actions, to have one's mind and other faculties properly trained, to keep repeating acts of virtue so as to develop good habits, and to distinguish between good and better, bad and worse (cf. *Commentary on Heb, ad loc.*). This is what is involved in having one's "faculties trained by practice".

¹Therefore let us leave the elementary doctrines of Christ and go on to maturity, not laying again a foundation of repentance from dead works and of faith toward God, ²with

Heb 9:14
Acts 20:21

Acts 6:6
1 Tim 4:14

---

¹Quapropter praetermittentes inchoationis Christi sermonem ad perfectionem feramur, non rursum iacientes fundamentum paenitentiae ab operibus mortuis et fidei ad Deum, ²baptismatum doctrinae, impositionis quoque manuum, ac

1-3. The sacred writer wishes to strengthen Christians' faith and confidence, and therefore he reminds his readers that it is not a matter of going over elementary teaching, which is based on repentance for sin and a desire to begin a new life, but of developing this teaching so as to understand it better and draw practical conclusions: "Let us go on to maturity." Basic catechesis or instruction of the faithful was usually imparted before and after Baptism and consisted of various elements, as we can see from the text. It explained who Jesus Christ is and what his mission is (cf. Acts 8:35, 37), and, in particular, that he is the Son of God; it went into the need for penance and for seeking forgiveness of sin (cf. Mk 4:17; Mk 1:15); it dealt with faith in God, the sacraments and the last things—resurrection of the body and the Judgment.

Here we have an admirably clear and simple summary of the basic elements of Christian catechesis. Given its antiquity and the fact that it is inspired, this text bears important witness to the fact that even in the apostolic era there existed a summary of those truths which had to be expounded and accepted before a person could be baptized—a summary which was an early outline of what later became the Creed or Symbol of Faith. The very order in which these articles of faith are given reflects the pedagogical wisdom of the Church, guided by the Holy Spirit—first, faith, then the sacraments, then the last things.

The purpose of catechesis, as St Thomas tells us, is to acquire that teaching "whereby Christ begins to dwell in us through our knowledge of the faith". It involves establishing a vital, active solidarity with our Lord and Redeemer. The Christian can then go on to deepen in this knowledge. "The primary and essential object of catechesis is [. . .] 'the mystery of Christ'. Catechizing is in a way to lead a person to study this Mystery in all its dimensions [. . .]. It is therefore to reveal in the Person of Christ the whole of God's eternal design reaching fulfilment in that Person. It is to seek to understand the meaning of Christ's actions and words and of the signs worked by him, for they simultaneously hide and reveal his mystery. Accordingly, the definitive aim of catechesis is to put people not only in touch but in communion, in intimacy, with Jesus Christ: only he can lead us to the love of the Father in the Spirit and make us share in the life of the Holy Trinity" (John Paul II, *Catechesi tradendae*, 5).

2. Christian salvation goes hand in hand with using certain material things

instruction[k] about ablutions, the laying on of hands, the resurrection of the dead, and eternal judgment. [3]And this we will do if God permits.[l]

The danger of apostasy and the need for perseverance

Heb 10:26f;
12:17
Mt 12:31
1 Jn 5:10
1 Pet 2:3

[4]For it is impossible to restore again to repentance those who have once been enlightened, who have tasted the heavenly gift, and have become partakers of the Holy Spirit, [5]and have tasted the goodness of the word of God and the

---

resurrectionis mortuorum et iudicii aeterni. [3]Et hoc faciemus siquidem permiserit Deus. [4]Impossibile est enim eos, qui semel sunt illuminati, gustaverunt etiam donum caeleste et participes sunt facti Spiritus Sancti [5]et bonum

which confer grace: these are the sacraments. The text alludes to this in very few words. Firstly, there is instruction about "ablutions" or, as the original text suggests, "baptisms". The use of the plural has puzzled scholars because clearly there is only one Baptism—"one hope, one faith, one baptism" (cf. Eph 4:5). But it can be explained fairly easily if one bears in mind that Baptism used to be administered by triple immersion; that there are different forms of baptism (of water, of blood or of desire); and that people used to be baptized in groups. However, it is more likely that the verse refers to the difference between the sacrament of Baptism and the "baptisms" or ritual washings the Jews frequently practised (cf. Mk 7:3-4); the phrase would, in that case, mean "instruction about the difference between Judaic ablutions and Christian Baptism".

The laying on of hands may refer to the rite of Confirmation, which included anointing with chrism (cf. Acts 8:17; 19:6), or to the rite of other sacraments, for example, that of Order (cf. 1 Tim 4:14; 5:22; 2 Tim 1:6; Acts 6:6; 13:3; etc.), Penance or Anointing of the Sick (cf. Jas 5:14). It may perhaps be a reference to the sacraments in general.

It should be remembered that in the New Testament, as St Thomas points out, the laying on of hands refers to a number of different things. For example, when Christ used to lay his hands on sick people to heal them (cf. Lk 4:40), that action did not have a sacramental character: it conferred a gift externally and visibly. In other cases, the laying on of hands was sacramental and referred mainly to the sacraments of Order and Confirmation, which produced an interior change and renewal (cf. *Commentary on Heb, ad loc.*).

4-6. In the context of an exhortation to fidelity and growth in maturity, the letter gives a severe warning about the danger of apostasy. It is true that it is very difficult for an apostate to return to the true faith, very difficult for him to

---

[k]Other ancient manuscripts read *of instruction*
[l]Other ancient manuscripts read *let us do this if God permits*

change his attitudes, difficult also for someone to find the right words to get him to change, for he previously had knowledge of the truth and then voluntarily rejected it. However, it is not impossible for him to return, for God is infinitely merciful, as is shown in the episode of Simon Peter's denials and repentance. "In the case of physical illnesses", St Thomas comments, "there is no more dangerous situation than that of those who suffer a relapse; so too in the spiritual sphere if someone falls into sin after receiving grace it is more difficult for him to recover and do good" (*Commentary on Heb, ad loc.*).

To appreciate these strong words, it should be remembered that the early Christians had a high sense of the dignity of their calling. It is not possible to be really a Christian and at the same time be in league with sin—particularly if it is a sin of apostasy, which involves denial of the faith and therefore of the very source of salvation. On the other hand, the first recipients of the letter seem to have been living in a hostile environment: rejected by the society in which they had been brought up, they had to shed certain Jewish religious practices; they felt isolated and rejected, and therefore the temptation to revert to Judaism was strong. That is why the writer reminds them, firstly, of the gifts their calling to Christianity has brought them: they have been "enlightened", that is, they have received Baptism, "which is the principle of spiritual rebirth whereby the mind is enlightened by faith" (*Commentary on Heb, ad loc.*); God has also given them the light of the Gospel; they have been filled with the "heavenly gift", that is, the Holy Spirit who fills the soul with sweetness (cf. 1 Pet 2:3; Ps 34:9); they have been nourished with the Eucharist, and they have experienced the reassurance of the Good News and the power of the Kingdom of God and all the gifts in its train—divine filiation, joy, gratitude, faith, hope and charity, all of which are the beginnings of eternal life.

The situation referred to in v. 6 suggests a calamitous fall, rather like that of Adam (cf. Rom 5:15-20). It may be similar to that sin against the Holy Spirit which our Lord himself said would not be forgiven either in this world or in the next (cf. Mt 12:31-32; Mk 3:28-29; Lk 12:10). It echoes what St Peter says about an apostate being like a dog going back to its vomit or a sow that is washed but then wallows in the mire: they are worse off than when they started (cf. 2 Pet 2:30-22). Like a skilled preacher the sacred writer wants to show his readers the full horror which rejection of faith involves.

Many heretics have used this text to argue that there are sins which the Church cannot forgive—specifically, the sins of murder, adultery and apostasy. However, if one denies the Church that power it is equivalent to denying the sacrament of Penance. That is why all the Fathers have met this rigourism head on, because it almost always leads to outright laxism. Here is how St John Chrysostom put the case: "'There is no such thing as penance', they say. But penance does exist; what does not exist is second Baptism. Penance exists; it is very powerful and it can free from the burden of sins even a person who is deeply submerged in sins, provided he wants to be freed; it can make someone who is in danger completely safe, even though he may have plumbed the depths of evil [. . .]. If we so desire, Christ can be formed in us anew. Listen to what

Gen 1:11f
Deut 11:11
Heb 10:29
powers of the age to come, ⁶if they then commit apostasy, since they crucify the Son of God on their own account and

---

gustaverunt Dei verbum virtutesque saeculi venturi ⁶et prolapsi sunt, renovari rursus ad paenitentiam, rursum crucifigentes sibimetipsis Filium Dei et ostentui

---

Paul says: 'My little children, with whom I am again in travail until Christ be formed in you!' (Gal 4:9). All that we need do is lay hold of Penance. See how kind God is to us! [. . .] 'We have fallen once again!' Yet not even then did he punish us: instead, he gave us the medicine of Penance, which is powerful enough to destroy and eliminate all our sins, provided we know what type of medicine it is and how to use it" (*Hom. on Heb*, 6). God in his mercy always receives the repentant sinner who has recourse to the sacrament of Penance, no matter how much he has sinned, no matter what sins he has committed. "What depths of mercy there are in God's justice! For, in the judgments of men, he who confesses his fault is punished; and in the judgment of God, he is pardoned. Blessed be the holy Sacrament of Penance!" (Blessed J. Escrivá, *The Way*, 309).

"To restore again to repentance": this points to the fact that the purpose and outcome of interior renewal is repentance and changed behaviour. It is describing the situation of a person who, having been influenced by interior grace and external preaching, takes his first steps on the road of repentance.

It is even more difficult to grasp all the implications of the second part of this verse: "since they crucify the Son of God on their own account and hold him up to contempt". Many Fathers and theologians see here a reference to the impossibility of being baptized a second time, because in baptism we share in the effects of the passion and death of Christ (cf. Rom 6:3-6; 1 Cor 1:13). If apostates were to try to be baptized again to obtain forgiveness, it would be like asking, in a way, for Christ to be crucified again. But Christ is no longer mortal and therefore it is not possible for Baptism to be repeated. Thus, for example, St Thomas comments: "When he says, 'they crucify again (the Son of God)', he is giving the reason why Baptism is not repeated, that is, because Baptism is a kind of conforming to the death of Christ, as we see in Romans 6:3—'all of us who have been baptized into Christ'—and this does not happen more than once because 'Christ being raised from the dead will never die again' (Rom 6:9). So those who would want to be baptized again would want to crucify Christ again" (*Commentary on Heb*, ad loc.).

Without excluding this meaning, a more obvious explanation, proposed by other Fathers, is that sinners are despising Penance even more than they are Baptism, for Penance also cleanses us by virtue of the merits of the passion and death of Christ, and, as long as they remain obstinate in their sins, they crucify him on their own account and hold him up to contempt in the sense that they fail to appreciate the fruits of our Lord's passion: that is the reason they cannot repent or obtain forgiveness. St Thomas comments: "Those who sin after Baptism crucify Christ again, insofar as they can, for Christ died for our sins once and for all. You, who are baptized and commit sin, are crucifying Christ

hold him up to contempt. [7]For land which has drunk the 2 Pet 2:21
rain that often falls upon it, and brings forth vegetation
useful to those for whose sake it is cultivated, receives a
blessing from God. [8]But if it bears thorns and thistles, it is Gen 3:17f
worthless and near to being cursed; its end is to be burned. Mt 7:16

---

habentes. [7]Terra enim saepe venientem super se bibens imbrem et generans herbam opportunam illis propter, quos et colitur, accipit benedictionem a Deo; [8]*proferens* autem *spinas ac tribulos* reproba est et *maledicto* proxima, cuius finis in combustionem. [9]Confidimus autem de vobis, dilectissimi, meliora et viciniora saluti, tametsi ita loquitur; [10]non enim iniustus Deus, ut obliviscatur

---

again insofar as you can; you are thus holding him up to contempt, for you are soiling yourself again after being cleansed by his blood" (*Commentary on Heb*, *ad loc.*).

7-8. To support its exhortations to fidelity the sacred text uses a parable which has a very evangelical ring to it: good ground receives the blessings of God; barren ground is only good for burning. This is a clear evocation of Christ's teaching: the ground is man's heart, his disposition towards God; God, for his part, sows seed generously through those whom he has sent, as in the parable of the sower (cf. Lk 8:5-15 and par.); and he also sends rain as needs be—preaching or instruction or grace itself which works in the interior of the soul (cf. Mt 5:45). The passage is also reminiscent of things that God often said to the chosen people through his prophets. The land is also the vineyard tended by the Almighty with loving care (cf. Is 5:1-6).

This parable dwells further on the sad consequences of unfaithfulness. The heart of the irreligious person or of the apostate is like barren land, which produces only thorns and thistles, as happened after the fall of Adam (cf. Gen 3:18). All it produces is sins, which merit condemnation to eternal fire (cf. Mt 25:41).

God's desire is to encourage everyone to be faithful. "We should tremble, dearly beloved," St John Chrysostom says, "for this warning does not come from Paul; these are not man's words: they are spoken by the Holy Spirit, it is Christ who is speaking through Paul [. . .]. Let us be filled with fear, therefore, let us be filled with fear. 'The wrath of God is revealed from heaven' (Rom 1:18). For it is manifested not only in regard to irreligion but in regard to every sin, great or small. But the mercy of God is also highlighted here too for it says, 'it is worthless and near to being cursed'. What consolation this word brings! For it says, 'near to being cursed'—not 'cursed'. And one is comforted not only by this phrase but also by the one that follows: for it does not say 'it will be burned' but 'its end is to be burned'. What does this mean? That if it remains in this state until the end, it will be subjected to fire. Therefore, if we cut and burn the thistles, we will be able to enjoy innumerable benefits, we will be appreciated and will receive the blessing" (*Hom. on Heb*, *ad loc.*).

Heb 10:32-34;
3:14
Rom 15:25, 31
2 Cor 8:4

1 Cor 11:1
Phil 3:17; 4:9
Gal 3:14, 19

⁹Though we speak thus, yet in your case, beloved, we feel sure of better things that belong to salvation. ¹⁰For God is not so unjust as to overlook your work and the love which you showed for his sake in serving the saints, as you still do. ¹¹And we desire each one of you to show the same earnestness in realizing the full assurance of hope until the end, ¹²so that you may not be sluggish, but imitators of those who through faith and patience inherit the promises.

operis vestri et dilectionis, quam ostendistis nomini ipsius, qui ministrastis sanctis et ministratis. ¹¹Cupimus autem unumquemque vestrum eandem ostentare sollicitudinem ad expletionem spei usque in finem, ¹²ut non segnes efficiamini, verum imitatores eorum, qui fide et patientia hereditant

9-12. The letter now changes to a tone of encouragement. "After speaking harshly about the position of the faithful, to prevent their falling into despair he now reveals why he has written what he has: he wants to lead them well away from danger. And so, in the first place, he tells them what confidence he has in them, and then gives the reason why they should feel confident themselves—because God is not unjust" (St Thomas Aquinas, *Commentary on Heb*, 4, 3).

The readers are called "beloved"; this was how St Paul normally addressed those who embraced the faith through his preaching (cf. 1 Thess 2:8; 1 Cor 10:14; 15:58; 2 Cor 7:1; 12:19; Rom 1:7; Phil 2:12; 4:1; etc.). The writer wants to see the situation improve, perhaps to see the trials pass or become easier; certainly he wants his readers to use their tribulation to help them to achieve salvation. He is moved when he recalls the charity they have shown one another: theirs has been an active fraternity, shown in deeds of service to the "saints", which was the way St Paul often referred to the brethren (cf. Rom 1:7; 1 Cor 1:2; 2 Cor 1:1; Eph 1:1; Phil 1:1; Col 1:2; etc.); their charity is practised "for his sake", for God. In their present circumstances, in the persecution they are experiencing, God will not abandon them (cf. Heb 10:33-34), for they have been generous in the almsgiving and hospitality that is so proper to Christians (cf. Rom 15:25, 31; 1 Cor 16:15; Eph 1:15; 2 Cor 8:4; 9:1, 12). "Now that we hear this—I beg you—let us serve the saints!, for every member of the faithful is a saint by the mere fact of belonging to the faithful [. . .]. Let us not be charitable only towards monks who live in the mountains. It is true that their faith and their lives make them saints, but many of those who live here are also saints: all are saints by virtue of their faith, and many are saints by virtue of their lives too. So, if you see someone suffering, do not doubt it for one moment: his very suffering gives him the right to be helped" (St John Chrysostom, *Hom. on Heb*, 10). It is not enough, however, to have a history of doing good: it is necessary to persevere in doing good, as if to say: By seeing through to the end what you have started you shall obtain everything you hope for. They must do good right "to the end", for he who endures to the end will be saved (cf. Mt

The promises made to Abraham, confirmed by oath, cannot be broken

¹³For when God made a promise to Abraham, since he had no one greater by whom to swear, he swore by himself, ¹⁴saying, "Surely I will bless you and multiply you." ¹⁵And

Rom 4:20
Gen 22:16f

---

promissiones. ¹³Abrahae namque promittens Deus, quoniam neminem habuit, per quem iuraret maiorem, *iuravit per semetipsum* ¹⁴dicens: *"Utique benedicens benedicam te et multiplicans multiplicabo te"*; ¹⁵et sic longanimiter ferens adeptus est repromissionem. ¹⁶Homines enim per maiorem sui iurant, et omnis

---

10:22; 24:13; *Commentary on Heb*, 4, 3). "Eternal life should be set before those who persevere in good works 'to the end' (cf. Mt 10:22) and who hope in God; it should be set before them as being the grace that God, through Jesus Christ, has mercifully promised his sons and 'as the reward' which, according to God's personal undertaking, most assuredly will be given them for their good works and merits (cf. St Augustine, *De natura et gratia*, VIII, 20)" (Council of Trent, *De iustificatione*, chap. 16).

However, there is always the danger of slowing down: lazy people often excuse their inaction by pointing to the suffering and difficulties that doing good involves. The strength of one's resolutions is shown by the way one copes with difficulties: "You will convince me that you sincerely want to achieve your goals when I see you go forward unwaveringly. Do good [. . .]; practise the virtue of justice, right where you are, in your normal surroundings, even if you end up exhausted. Foster happiness among those around you by cheerfully serving the people you work with and by striving to carry out your job as perfectly as you can, showing understanding, smiling, having a Christian approach to life. And do everything for God, thinking of his glory, with your sights set high and longing for the definitive homeland, because there is no other goal worthwhile" (Blessed J. Escrivá, *Friends of God*, 211).

13-15. Abraham is an example, for every generation, of faith that is full of hope and patience; he is a man with great strength of character (cf. Rom 5:3-5). Already in the Epistle to the Romans Abraham is cited as an example of faith and hope (cf. Rom 4:18- 22). There St Paul highlights Abraham's faith in the Lord's promise that he would have innumerable descendants in spite of the fact that he was already an old man and unlikely to father children (cf. Gen 15:5; 17:1, 17). The Apostle may also have been alluding to the episode (cf. Gen 22), when God asked the patriarch to sacrifice Isaac, the son he had so yearned for: at that point Abraham did indeed "believe against hope" (cf. Rom 4:18; Gen 22:15-17). Here, on the other hand, of all the various promises made to Abraham of blessings and numerous offspring (cf. Gen 12:2-3, 7; 13:14-17; 15:5-7; 13:16; 17:4-8, 19), what is explicitly mentioned is the promise made after God prevented him from sacrificing his son. That was the first occasion the Lord "swore by himself" to a man. This divine promise, supported by an oath and seen as the most solemn "word of Yahweh", was the foundation of

Ex 22:10
> thus Abraham,[m] having patiently endured, obtained the
> promise. [16]Men indeed swear by a greater than themselves,

---

controversiae eorum finis ad confirmationem est iuramentum; [17]in quo

Israel's hope for thousands of years. Abraham himself recalled it when he was dying (cf. Gen 24:7); it was the support of Moses in all his great endeavours (cf. Ex 13:5, 11; 32:13); David, too, gave thanks to God for it (1 Chron 16:16; Ps 105:9); and at the dawn of the Redemption Zechariah rejoiced over it (Lk 1:73): it was "the oath which God swore to our Father Abraham" and it was fulfilled in Christ and in the Church (cf. Gal 4:21-31).

Abraham "obtained the promise" in the sense that he was enabled to see with his own eyes his promised son, Isaac, who was born to Sarah despite her old age. Not alone that: the New Testament tells us (cf. Jn 8:56; Gal 3:8) that he was given some sort of prophetic vision which allowed him to see the day of Christ and rejoice at it.

16. Secular writers of antiquity used to define an oath as something attached to a statement which cannot be proved, to provide a divine guarantee (cf. Pseudo-Aristotle, *Speech to Alexander*). This meant that they regarded an oath as a proof at law, to be put alongside the text of the law, the evidence of witnesses, agreement between the parties, and a confession of guilt. The Jews regarded an oath as something so awesome, so solemn, that they never dared swear an oath by God directly; instead they would swear by angels or by the life of men, such as the Messiah, Moses, Solomon, or by the gates of the temple, etc. (cf. Mt 5:34-36; 23:16-22). Philo of Alexandria, an heir to Jewish tradition and Greco-Roman thought, says that "by means of oaths, matters subject to doubt before the courts are resolved; what was not clear is made clear; and what was regarded as unreliable is rendered reliable" (*De sacrificio Abel*, 91).

St Thomas Aquinas developed and combined these ideas by saying that "an oath is an act of the virtue of religion which gives reliability to something previously in doubt. For in the sphere of knowledge nothing becomes certain unless it be demonstrated from something which is more certainly known. When oaths are taken, this certainty is obtained because the oath is sworn on God, who is the greatest and surest there is, since for men nothing is truer than God" (*Commentary on Heb, ad loc.*). The Thomist definition has become widely accepted because it also fits in with the commonly held view that swearing an oath is a way of honouring the sacred name of God. When an oath is properly made—meeting the necessary traditional requirements of truth, justice and judgment—that is, when it is made sincerely, for good reasons and not lightly, it is a morally good and meritorious act because it does honour to God's infinite truthfulness.

On Christ's teachings concerning oath-taking see the notes on Mt 5:33-37 and 23:16-22.

[m]Greek *he*

and in all their disputes an oath is final for confirmation.
[17]So when God desired to show more convincingly to the
heirs of the promise the unchangeable character of his
purpose, he interposed with an oath, [18]so that through two
unchangeable things, in which it is impossible that God
should prove false, we who have fled for refuge might have
strong encouragement to seize the hope set before us. [19]We
have this as a sure and steadfast anchor of the soul, a hope

Num 23:19
1 Sam 15:29

Lev 16:2, 12
Heb 9:3; 10:20
Mt 27:51

abundantius volens Deus ostendere pollicitationis heredibus immobilitatem
consilii sui, se interposuit iure iurando, [18]ut per duas res immobiles, in quibus
impossibile est mentiri Deum, fortissimum solacium habeamus, qui con-
fugimus ad tenendam propositam spem, [19]quam sicut anchoram habemus
animae, tutam ac firmam et incedentem usque in interiora velaminis, [20]ubi

17-18. "Through two unchangeable things": in promises made by God his
veracity is doubly committed—as the taker of the oath and as its guarantor.

God's covenant with Abraham and his oath to give him descendants took
place at separate times (cf. Gen 15:7-18; 22:16-18). However, both episodes
stem from a single act of God's will, in that he wanted to reward Abraham's
obedience and at the same time commit himself by the use of external for-
malities proper to Hebrew legal practice. Among the Hebrews, when people
made a pact, they sacrificed animals; the victims were then quartered and the
contracting parties walked between the carcasses to symbolize that they would
die the same death if they failed to keep the pact. God passed between the pieces
of the animals Abraham sacrificed, in the form of a flaming torch, thereby
giving him to understand that he (God) was under a most solemn obligation to
do what he promised. In the second episode this rite was not repeated, but he
"interposed with an oath", renewing as it were the "passing between" rite that
accompanied the covenant.

God chose to express his promise by following this human form of contract
in order to make his words more intelligible and to give us greater confidence.

19-20. God's promise and oath are the gateway to our salvation, an anchor
which makes us feel safe no matter what hazards threaten us. The Christian,
who is, through faith, the true descendant of Abraham (cf. Rom 4:12) and the
heir of the promise (cf. Gal 3:14, 16, 29), is therefore certain that God will keep
his word. That is why the text says that we should "have strong encouragement
to seize the hope set before us" (v.18). Hope is a kind of hold on what is
promised, a kind of anchor that is "sure and steadfast". "For just as the anchor
thrown overboard prevents the ship from moving, even if it is being battered
by countless winds, but instead keeps it in one place, hope has the same effect"
(Chrysostom, *Hom. on Heb*, 11). Greek and Roman authors often used the
simile of an anchor in connexion with being steadfast in virtue and hopeful of
happier times. The anchor has always been a motif in Christian art expressive

that enters into the inner shrine behind the curtain, [20]where Jesus has gone as a forerunner on our behalf, having become a high priest for ever after the order of Melchizedek.

---

praecursor pro nobis introivit Iesus, *secundum ordinem Melchisedech* pontifex factus *in aeternum.*

---

of much more than a human sense of safety: it symbolizes the Christian's faith, his certainty in the resurrection of the Lord and in his own resurrection; it is a symbol of a confidence which stems from his intimate union with Christ. The sacred text brings together all those ideas: in a certain sense the anchor is Christ himself who through his redemptive sacrifice gives us the conviction that we can with him enter "into the inner shrine", that is, the heavenly sanctuary. "I have asked you to keep on lifting your eyes up to heaven as you go about your work, because hope encourages us to grasp the strong hand which God never ceases to reach out to us, to keep us from losing our supernatural point of view. Let us persevere even when our passions rear up and attack us, attempting to imprison us within the narrow confines of our selfishness; or when puerile vanity makes us think we are the centre of the universe. I am convinced that unless I look upward, unless I have Jesus, I will never accomplish anything. And I know that the strength to conquer myself and to win comes from repeating that cry, 'I can do all things in him who strengthens me' (Phil 4:13), words which reflect God's firm promise not to abandon his children if they do not abandon him" (Blessed J. Escrivá, *Friends of God*, 213). "A man should be tied to hope in the same way as the anchor is tied to the ship. But there is a difference between the anchor and hope: the anchor reaches down to get its hold, whereas hope reaches upwards, laying hold of God" (*Commentary on Heb, ad loc.*).

20. The sacrifice, resurrection and glorification of Christ are the grounds of our hope. In the Old Testament, the high priest entered the Holy of Holies once a year, on the Day of Atonement; this he did after offering one sacrifice in expiation of his own sins and another for the sins of the entire people. By his sacrifice on the cross, Christ entered into the true sanctuary of heaven and gave all men access to it. The reason for our firm hope is the fact that Christ has entered heaven. "It was not into the Holy of Holies (where Moses entered) but behind the curtain, into heaven, that he, Christ Jesus, went as our forerunner and was made a priest forever. He went not like Aaron, to offer the sacrificial victims, but to offer prayer for all the nations, like Melchizedek" (St Ephraem, *Com. in Epist. ad Haebreos*, 6).

The description here of Christ as a "forerunner" has great depth and beauty. This is the only time this word is used in the New Testament, although Christian tradition soon came to use it, on the basis of the prophecy of Malachi (Mal 3:1), to describe St John the Baptist, the envoy sent in advance of Jesus to prepare his way (cf. Mk 1:2; Lk 1:76). Here the perspective is slightly different: it has to do not with preparing for the proclamation of the Gospel but with attaining final beatitude. Christ has gone before us into heaven to prepare a place for us (cf. Jn 14:2): he is our hope (cf. Col 1:27; 1 Tim 1:1), our life (cf. Col 3:4), our way (cf. Jn 14:6), whereby we have access to the Father (cf. Eph 2:18; 2:7). Christ is a "forerunner" in the literal sense of the word—one who "runs ahead", who went on ahead of the party to announce its arrival; or it can be understood in the sense of the first one to reach the finish, the first to finish the race. For our Lord is the first-born among the dead, the first in everything (cf. Col 1:18), the first fruits of those who will arise (cf. 1 Cor 15:20). By his merits he has already obtained the prize that we hope to win. Christian hope cannot falter, for it is based on the perennial value of the sacrifice and priesthood of Christ. Thus, the last words of this chapter remind us of the main theme of the epistle.

Chap. 7. In keeping with biblical interpretation as practised by Jews of the time, the sacred writer now puts forward certain arguments in support of the superiority of Christ's priesthood over the Levitical priesthood. He wants to show the reader that the priesthood of Aaron and his descendants, that is, the Levitical priesthood, which was responsible for divine service in the temple of Jerusalem, was something good and very fitting. However, it was destined to disappear, and part of its mission was to prepare the way for Christ's priesthood, which is eternal and immutable. Earlier, in chapters 5 and 6, the relationships between Judaism and Christianity were examined from the point of view of the Covenant. In this chapter, they are looked at from the point of view of priesthood.

To do this, the writer brings in an Old Testament figure shrouded in mystery and much revered by the Jews—the priest Melchizedek. He appears first in Genesis 14:18-20 as king of Salem, when he comes out to meet Abraham to bless him after his victory over the invading kings. The passage also says that he was a priest of "God Most High" and that he offered Abraham bread and wine and received from the latter a tenth of his booty. In Psalm 110, which deals with the priesthood of the Messiah, Melchizedek is referred to again as being a "priest for ever", invested with an eternal priesthood which the Messiah King will also enjoy.

The Epistle to the Hebrews uses and comments on these two Old Testament texts, taking them as well-known; it does not stop to explore their mysterious aspects. Chapter 7 consists of two parts. The first (7:1-10) may be summarized as saying that Melchizedek's priesthood is superior to the Levitical priesthood; and, because Christ's priesthood belongs to the order of Melchizedek, it also is superior to the Levitical.

The second part (7:11-25) hinges on direct comparison of Christ's priesthood with that of the Old Law. The superiority of Christ's priesthood is clear to see, for it is perfect, permanent and sealed by God with an oath. In fact, because it is a permanent, eternal priesthood, it is unique: Christ is the only true high priest, whereas prior to his coming "the former priests were many in number, because they were prevented by death from continuing in office."

Christ's priesthood (which was heralded by that of Melchizedek), is prolonged in the Christian ministerial priesthood. However, Christ continues to be

7

Jesus Christ is a priest after the order of Melchizedek

Gen 14:17-20 ¹For this Melchizedek, king of Salem, priest of the Most High God, met Abraham returning from the slaughter of the kings and blessed him; ²and to him Abraham apportioned a tenth part of everything. He is first, by translation

---

¹Hic enim *Mechisedech, rex Salem, sacerdos Dei summi,* qui *obviavit Abrahae regresso a caede regum et benedixit ei,* ²cui et *decimam omnium* divisit

---

the only true priest, interceding for us with the Father: Christian priests are only vicars or ministers of Christ, not his successors.

At the end of the chapter (vv. 26-28) Christ's priesthood is extolled as being holy, blameless, unstained, perfect, and exalted above the heavens.

1-3. Melchizedek has special characteristics which make him a "figure" or "type" of Christ. The connexions between Christ and Melchizedek are expounded in accordance with the rules of rabbinical bible commentary; this is particularly obvious in the use of the phrase "without father or mother or genealogy" to refer to the eternity of Melchizedek. It is not surprising that the writer brings in the figure of Melchizedek, for the mysterious mention of this personage in Genesis 14:18-20 and in Psalm 110:4 had for some time intrigued Jewish commentators. For example, Philo of Alexandria sees Melchizedek as a symbol for human reason enlightened by divine wisdom (cf. *De legum allegoria,* 3, 79-82). Also, apocryphal literature identified Melchizedek with other biblical figures—for example, with Shem, Noah's first-born son, or with the son of Nir, Noah's brother. Certainly the epistle is in line with Jewish tradition on one important point: Melchizedek belongs to a priesthood established by God in pre-Mosaic times.

The Jewish historian Flavius Josephus (A.D. 37-100) refers to Melchizedek as a "prince of Canaan", who founded and was high priest of Jerusalem. The name Melchizedek, meaning "my king is righteous" or "King of Righteousness", was a Canaanite name (cf. Josh 10:13). "Salem" is probably an abbreviation of Jerusalem (cf. Ps 76:2); and *Elioh,* that is, God Most High, may also have been the name of one of the divinities worshipped by the inhabitants of Palestine before the Jewish conquest. Genesis tells us that, in spite of living in a Canaanite and polytheistic environment, Melchizedek was a priest of the true God. Despite not being a member of the chosen people, he had knowledge of the Supreme God. Psalm 110 adds a further revelation to that contained in Genesis: the promised Messiah, a descendant of David, will not only be a king (which they already knew) but also a priest; and he will not be a priest of Aaron: by a new disposition of God he will be a priest according to the order, or as the Hebrew text says, "after the manner of Melchizedek".

The Epistle to the Hebrews views the Genesis episode through the prism of

of his name, king of righteousness, and then he is also king of Salem, that is, king of peace. ³He is without father or

Jn 7:27
Ps 110:4

Abraham, primum quidem, qui interpretatur rex iustitiae, deinde autem et *rex Salem*, quod est rex Pacis, ³sine patre, sine matre, sine genealogia, neque initium

---

Psalm 110: Melchizedek is above all a representative of a new priesthood instituted by God independently of the Mosaic Law. That is why it gives so much importance to the words of Genesis: Melchizedek is "king of righteousness", according to one popular etymology, and he is also "king of Salem", that is, "king of peace" according to another which changes the second vowel of the Hebrew word *shalom*, which means "peace". Thus, in Melchizedek the two foremost characteristics of the messianic kingdom meet—righteousness and peace (cf. Ps 85:10; 89:14; 97:2; Is 9:5-7; 2:4; 45:8; Lk 2:14). Moreover, since Genesis says nothing about Melchizedek's background (he did not belong to the chosen people), the sacred writer, following a common rabbinical rule of interpretation (what is not in Scripture—in the Torah—has no existence in the real world"), sees Scripture's silence on this point as symbolic: Melchizedek, since his genealogy is unknown, is a figure or "type" of Christ, who is eternal.

"Resembling the Son of God": it is not Christ who resembles Melchizedek but Melchizedek who is like Christ—indeed, who has been made to resemble Christ. Christ is the perfection of priesthood. Melchizedek was created and made like Christ so that we by reflecting on him might learn something about the Son of God.

Theoderet of Cyrus develops on this idea: "Christ the Lord possesses all these qualifications really and by nature. He is 'without mother', for God as Father alone begot him. He is 'without father', for he was conceived by mother alone, that is, the Virgin. He is 'without genealogy', as God, for he who was begotten by the unbegotten Father has no need of genealogy. 'He has not beginning of days', for his is an eternal generation. 'He has no end of life', for he possesses an immortal nature. For all those reasons Christ himself is not compared to Melchizedek but Melchizedek to Christ" (*Interpretatio Ep. ad Haebreos, ad loc.*). St Ephraem put this very nicely: "Thus, Melchizedek's priesthood continues for ever—not in Melchizedek himself but in the Lord of Melchizedek" (*Com. in Epist. ad Haebreos, ad loc.*).

3. A priest of the true God, of the Most High God, yet not a member of the chosen people, Melchizedek is an example of how God sows the seeds of saving truth beyond limitations of geography, epoch or nation. "The priesthood of Christ, of which priests have been really made sharers, is necessarily directed to all people and all times, and is not confined by any bounds of blood, race, or age, as was already typified in a mysterious way by the figure of Melchizedek. Priests, therefore, should recall that the solicitude of all the churches ought to be their intimate concern" (Vatican II, *Presbyterorum ordinis*, 10).

mother or genealogy, and has neither beginning of days nor end of life, but resembling the Son of God he continues a priest for ever.

Melchizedek's priesthood is higher than that of Abraham's line

Gen 14:20   ⁴See how great he is! Abraham the patriarch gave him a

---

dierum neque finem vitae habens, assimilatus autem Filio Dei, manet sacerdos in perpetuum. ⁴Intuemini autem quantus sit hic, cui et decimam dedit de

At the same time the sacred text, by saying that Melchizedek was "without father or mother", gives grounds for thinking that also in the case of the consecration of Christ's priests they, in order to fulfil their mission, should be ready to leave their family behind—which is what often in fact happens. "The character and life of the man called to be a minister in the worship of the one true God bear the marks of a halo and a destiny to be 'set apart'. This puts him in some way outside and above the common history of other men—*sine patre, sine matre, sine genealogia*, as St Paul says of the mysterious prophetic Melchizedek" (A. del Portillo, *On Priesthood*, p. 44).

Addressing Christians, particularly those consecrated to the service of God, St John of Avila writes: "*Forget your people* (Ps 45:10) and be like another Melchizedek, whom we are told had no father or mother or genealogy. In this way [. . .] example is given to the servants of God who must be so forgetful of their family and relations that they are like Melchizedek in this world, as far as their heart is concerned—having nothing that ties their heart and slows them up on their way to God" (*Audi, filia*, 98).

4-10. The superiority of Melchizedek's priesthood over the Levitical priesthood is argued on two points—tithing and blessing. The same principle applies in each case, as is explicitly stated in v. 7 in regard to blessing: the inferior pays tithes to the superior, and it is the superior who blesses the inferior. Therefore, all the evidence indicates that Melchizedek was superior to Abraham because he was the one who received the tithe and gave the blessing. But Levi, the founder of the priestly line, was "in the loins" of his father Abraham when Abraham made his act of submission to Melchizedek; therefore, Levi is inferior to Melchizedek. Moreover, whereas the Levites or priests of the Mosaic Law are mortal men, Melchizedek is said to "live", because he has "no end of life".

Be that as it may, the passage does underline the exalted nature of priesthood. This applies to the Levitical priesthood , which has a prominent place among the Jewish people, for only priests of the family of Aaron were entitled to receive tithes and not have to pay them (cf. Num 18:26-32). Other Levites, not priests, received tithes of agricultural produce (cf. Deut 12:17-19; 14:22-27; 26:12-13) and livestock (cf. Lev 27:30-32), but they, in their turn, had to pay the tithe of the tithe—the "offering of Yahweh"—to their brothers who were priests. Tithing was a sign of God's absolute power over all things, and, in this

tithe of the spoils. [5]And those descendants of Levi who receive the priestly office have a commandment in the law to take tithes from the people, that is from their brethren, though these also are descended from Abrabam. [6]But this man who has not the genealogy received tithes from

Num 18:21, 25
Deut 14:22

---

praecipuis Abraham patriarcha. [5]Et illi quidem, qui de filiis Levi sacerdotium accipiunt, mandatum habent decimas sumere a populo secundum legem, id est a fratribus suis, quamquam et ipsi exierunt de lumbis Abrahae; [6]hic autem, cuius generatio non annumeratur in eis, decimam sumpsit ab Abraham et eum, qui habebat repromissiones, benedixit. [7]Sine ulla autem contradictione, quod minus

---

sense, by their dedication to the service of God, the Levites also evidenced God's dominion: they were dedicated to Yahweh, standing in for all the first-born of Israel (cf. Num 3:12-13), because every first-born belonged to the Lord. The Levites, therefore, did not have territory assigned to them to cultivate and support themselves on: their "portion" and "lot" was God himself (cf. Ps 16:5-6). That was why they had a right to live on the tithes which every Israelite had a duty to pay to God.

However, despite the dignity of the Levitical priesthood, that of Melchizedek was worthier still. To him no less a personage than Abraham, the first father (the "Patriarch") of all Israel pays the tithe—despite the fact that the king of Salem was not of his tribe. And he pays him tithe of the best part of his booty (according to the Greek text), almost anticipating the Mosaic precept which prescribed that God be given the best portion of the Levitical tithe (cf. Num 18:30). In other words, although the priesthood of the sons of Aaron is on a very high level, Melchizedek's priesthood is more elevated still.

5. In the Law of Moses, that is, the Pentateuch or Torah, the regulations about tithing changed somewhat over the course of the history of Israel (cf. Deut 12:6-17; 14:22-27; 26:12-15; Lev 27:30-33; 2 Chron 31:6); they developed gradually and, after the Exile (around the end of the sixth century), they became quite complex (cf. Neh 13:5, 10-12; Mal 3:8; Sir 35:8-10). A whole series of oral precepts grew up, which were later codified in rabbinical writings and, in some cases, led Jesus to reproach the Pharisees for their hypocrisy and over-emphasis on detail (cf. Mt 23:23; Lk 11:42; 18:12 and notes on same). It is quite likely that this verse, in speaking of "a commandment in the law", is referring to precepts of the oral as well as the written law.

Although it belongs to the Law of Moses and has therefore been replaced by the Law of Christ, the precept about paying tithes is a precept of natural justice and therefore "it was in the Law and is also in the New Testament, where it says, 'the labourer deserves his food' (Mt 10:10) or 'the labourer deserves his wages' (Lk 10:7). But now it is up to the Church to specify these tithes, just as previously, in the Old Testament, the Law specified them" (St Thomas Aquinas, *Commentary on Heb, ad loc.*).

Abraham and blessed him who had the promises. [7]It is beyond dispute that the inferior is blessed by the superior. [8]Here tithes are received by mortal men; there, by one of whom it is testified that he lives. [9]One might even say that Levi himself, who receives tithes, paid tithes through Abraham, [10]for he was still in the loins of his ancestor when Melchizedek met him.

[11]Now if perfection had been attainable through the

Ps 110:4

---

est, a meliore benedicitur. [8]Et hic quidem decimas morientes homines sumunt, ibi autem testimonium accipiens quia vivit. [9]Et ut ita dictum sit, per Abraham et Levi, qui decimas accipit, decimatus est, [10]adhuc enim in lumbis patris erat, quando *obviavit ei Melchisedech.* [11]Si ergo consummatio per sacerdotium

---

7. A priest's blessing always does the recipient good because it draws down on him the holiness of the Church. Some people, for example, members of heretical groups, wrongly treated blessings with contempt. It should be remembered that the beneficial effect of rites and sacred signs established by the Church (sacramentals) derives not from the virtue of the minister but from the prayer of the Church and the dispositions of the recipient.

11-14. On the basis of the superiority of Melchizedek's priesthood over that of Levi, the writer now begins his "demonstration" of the superiority of Christ's priesthood over that of Aaron. If the Levitical priesthood had been able to achieve "perfection", that is, to fulfil God's design perfectly and bring about the salvation of mankind, why should there have been any need to replace it? If it has been replaced it is because that priesthood was unable to do what God designed it for—to bring the Mosaic Law to perfection; the priesthood of Aaron could only proclaim or promise.

It is clear that Christ is not only called (Ps 110:4) a priest "after the order", that is, in line with the role of and in succession to Melchizedek and not after the order of Aaron; but also, as the prophecies repeatedly say (cf. e.g., Num 24:17; Gen 48:10; 2 Sam 7:1; etc.), he belongs to the tribe of Judah—which had no priestly assignment under the Mosaic Law. No Israelite outside the tribe of Levi might perform priestly duties—under pain of death (cf. Num 1:51; 3:10, 38).

11. Broadly, the "perfection" referred to here has to do with true union with God, and therefore must include sanctifying grace and forgiveness of sin.

The Levitical priesthood was at the service of the Law, and the Law was salvific only through faith in the coming of Christ. Thus the Levitical priesthood was intrinsically orientated to Christ: "for, as it would be written (Heb 7:19), 'the law made nothing perfect' [. . .]; it did not provide the ultimate fulness of the heavenly fatherland because it did not enable people to enter Life" (St Thomas, *Commentary on Heb*, 7, 2).

Levitical priesthood (for under it the people received the law), what further need would there have been for another priest to arise after the order of Melchizedek, rather than one named after the order of Aaron? [12]For when there is a

---

leviticum erat, populus enim sub ipso legem accepit, quid adhuc necessarium *secundum ordinem Melchisedech* alium surgere *sacerdotem* et non *secundum ordinem* Aaron dici? [12]Translato enim sacerdotio, necesse est, ut et legis

---

In Romans 3:20 and Galatians 2:16-19 the same idea, so typical of St Paul, is to be found. It is summed up by the Council of Trent in these words: "As the Apostle St Paul testifies, there was no perfection under the former Testament because of the insufficiency of the Levitical priesthood. It was therefore necessary (according to the merciful ordination of God the Father) that another priest arise according to the order of Melchizedek, our Lord Jesus Christ, who could perfect all who were to be sanctified (cf. Heb 10:14)" (*De SS. Missae sacrificio*, chap. 1).

12. On the neccesary connexion between priesthood and covenant, St Thomas writes: "The Law was subject to the ministry of its priests; so, when the priesthood changed, the Law too had to change. This is why that change had to take place: when the end is changed, the means for attaining the end must also change [. . .]. Just as human law regulates how men should live together and how society be arranged, so spiritual and divine law has to do with the order established by God. This divine disposition of things is essentially bound up with priesthood" (*Commentary on Heb, ad loc.*). This teaching, supported by Hebrews, was used by the Council of Trent to explain the connexion between the sacrifice of the New Testament and Christian priesthood: "By divine decree sacrifice and priesthood are so closely connected that both are present in every law. Since the catholic Church received by divine institution the holy and visible sacrifice of the Eucharist, there must be located in her also an external, visible priesthood, which derives from the transfer of the old priesthood [to the New Law]" (*De Sacram. ordinis*, chap. 1). The connexion between priesthood, sacrifice and law is also explained in the *St Pius V Catechism* (II, 7, 8): "The period previous to the written law must have had its priesthood and its spiritual power since it is certain that it had its law; for these two, as the Apostle testifies, are so closely connected that if the priesthood is transferred, the law must necessarily be transferred also. Guided, therefore, by a natural instinct, men recognized that God is to be worshipped; and hence it follows that in every nation some, whose power might in a certain sense be called spiritual, were given the care of sacred things and of divine worship. This power was also possessed by the Jews; but though it was superior in dignity to that with which priests were invested under the law of nature, yet it must be regarded as far inferior to the spiritual power that is found in the New Law. For the latter is heavenly, and surpasses all the power of angels; it is derived not from the

119

change in the priesthood, there is necessarily a change in the law as well. [13]For the one of whom these things are spoken belonged to another tribe, from which no one has ever served at the altar. [14]For it is evident that our Lord was des- cended from Judah, and in connection with that tribe Moses said nothing about priests.

Gen 49:10
Is 11:1
Lk 1:78
Rom 1:3
Rev 5:5

[15]This becomes even more evident when another priest arises in the likeness of Melchizedek, [16]who has become a priest, not according to a legal requirement concerning bodily descent but by the power of an indestructible life. [17]For it is witnessed of him,

Ps 110:4
Heb 5:6

"Thou art a priest for ever,
after the order of Melchizedek."

[18]On the one hand, a former commandment is set aside because of its weakness and uselessness [19](for the law made

Heb 9:9
Rom 7:7; 8:3

---

translatio fiat. [13]De quo enim haec dicuntur, ex alia tribu est, ex qua nullus altari praesto fuit; [14]manifestum enim quod ex Iuda ortus sit Dominus noster, in quam tribum nihil de sacerdotibus Moyses locutus est. [15]Et amplius adhuc manifestum est, si *secundum* similitudinem *Melchisedech* exsurgit alius *sacerdos*, [16]qui non secundum legem mandati carnalis factus est sed secundum virtutem vitae insolubilis, [17]testimonium enim accipit: *"Tu es sacerdos in aeternum secundum ordinem Melchisedech."* [18]Reprobatio quidem fit praecedentis mandati propter infirmitatem eius et inutilitatem, [19]nihil enim ad

---

Mosaic priesthood, but from Christ our Lord who was a priest, not according to the order of Aaron, but according to the order of Melchizedek. For he it is who, himself endowed with the supreme power of granting grace and remitting sins, left to his Church this power, although he limited it in extent and attached it to the sacraments."

13. "The one of whom these things are spoken": the true priest, then, is not Melchizedek, who had only a symbolic role, but Christ, who is truly eternal, higher, perfect, unchangeable, and who brings Redemption.

15-19. The superiority of Christ's priesthood is now demonstrated by reference to the inferiority of the Old Law, in line with the inferiority of its priesthood. The Law is defined as "a legal requirement concerning bodily descent" as opposed to something spiritual (cf. 1 Cor 2:13-15; Gal 6:1; Eph 1:3; Col 1:8; 2 Cor 3:6-8); it is "weak" as opposed to effective; "useless" as opposed to being able to do what it is designed for. From this two things follow: the Law made nothing perfect (cf. note on 7:11); and its function was that of "introducing" us to a better law—that of Christ, a law that is full of hope, and hope enables us to draw near to God (cf. Rom 3:21; Gal 3:24; 1 Tim 1:8).

nothing perfect); on the other hand, a better hope is introduced, through which we draw near to God.

Christ is perfect high priest and his priesthood endures forever

²⁰And it was not without an oath. ²¹Those who formerly

Ps 110:4

perfectum adduxit lex, introductio vero melioris spei, per quam proximamus
ad Deum. ²⁰Et quantum non est sine iure iurando, illi quidem sine iure iurando
sacerdotes facti sunt, ²¹hic autem cum iure iurando per eum, qui dicit ad illum:

The epistle's verdict on the Law of Moses may seem somewhat harsh, but
it fits in exactly with the gratuitous nature of glorification: "The Law",
Theodoret comments, "has come to an end, as the Apostle says, and its place
is taken by hope of better things. The Law has ended, however, not because it
was bad, as some heretics foolishly say, but because it was weak and was not
perfectly useful. But we must understand that it is the [now] superfluous parts
of the Law that are described as weak or useless—circumcision, the sabbath
precept, and similar things. For, the New Testament insistently commands
observance of the 'Thou shalt not kill, Thou shalt not commit adultery' and the
other commandments. In place of the old precepts we have now received hope
of future good things, a hope that makes us God's own household"
(*Interpretatio Ep. ad Haebreos, ad loc.*). St Thomas Aquinas points out that
the commandments were and are useful. The Old Testament was not in itself
bad, but it is unsuited to the new times; there is no reason why the new
priesthood should continue the ways of the old (cf. Ps 40:6f). That was why the
Old Law was abrogated—because it was weak and served no purpose: "We say
something is weak when it fails to produce its [designed] effect; and the effect
proper to the Law and the priesthood is justification [. . .]. This the Law was
unable to do, because it did not bring man to beatitude, which is his end.
However, in its time it was useful, in that it prepared men for faith"
(*Commentary on Heb*, 7, 3).

20-22. The third reason why Christ's priesthood is superior is that it has
been sealed with an oath (cf. Heb 9:15-18). There is an implicit repetition here
of what was said apropos of the promise made to Abraham (6:13-18): God's
oath provides absolute certainty because the oath is made by Truth itself and
supreme Truth bears witness to it. Psalm 110:4 is again quoted but with attention
focused on the oath itself: "The Lord has sworn and will not change his mind."
In developing his argument the author of Hebrews is using different aspects of
the Psalm. First he bases his argument on "Thou art a priest [. . .] after the order
of Melchizedek" to show that Christ's priesthood is different from and superior
to the Levitical priesthood. Then he comments on the words "Thou art a priest
forever" to contrast the eternal nature of Christ's priesthood with the contingent
and temporary nature of the Levitical priesthood. And finally he focuses on the
words "The Lord has sworn and will not change his mind", to show the force
and permanence of the divine decision.

became priests took their office without an oath, but this one was addressed with an oath,

"The Lord has sworn
and will not change his mind,
'Thou art a priest for ever.'"

Heb 8:6-10 [22]This makes Jesus the surety of a better covenant.

[23]The former priests were many in number, because they were prevented by death from continuing in office; [24]but he holds his priesthood permanently, because he continues for

Rom 8:34
Rev 1:18
1 Jn 2:1
Heb 9:24 ever. [25]Consequently he is able for all time to save those who draw near to God through him, since he always lives to make intercession for them.

"Iuravit Dominus et non paenitebit eum: Tu es sacerdos in aeternum", [22]in tantum et melioris testamenti sponsor factus est Iesus. [23]Et illi quidem plures facti sunt sacerdotes, idcirco quod morte prohibebantur permanere; [24]hic autem eo quod manet in aeternum, intransgressibile habet sacerdotium, [25]unde et salvare in perpetuum potest accedentes per semetipsum ad Deum, semper

22. "The surety [mediator] of a better covenant": Christ is mediator (cf. 8:6; 9:15; 12:24) because he is priest, for every priest is established as a mediator between God and men (cf. 1 Tim 2:5; Heb 5:1). Christ's priesthood is superior to the Levitical priesthood because it has been established with an oath, whereas the Levitical has not. Given that covenant or law is bound up with priesthood, the New Covenant is therefore "better" than the old. "The function of a mediator is to get two extremes to agree. Christ brought us the divine gifts, for through him we have become partakers of the divine nature (cf 2 Pet 1:4) [. . .]. In the Old Covenant certain temporal benefits were promised; whereas now it is eternal ones" (*Commentary on Heb*, 7, 2).

23-25. Christ's priesthood is everlasting. Just as Melchizedek had no "end of life", so too the Son of God holds his priesthood permanently. The Levites are mere mortal men; Christ, however, has not been instituted as priest by "bodily descent but by the power of an indestructible life" (v. 16); that is why he can truly be said to be a priest "for ever". This makes sense, for death is a consequence of sin, and Christ has conquered sin and death. Moreover, death makes it necessary for there to be a succession of human priests in order to provide continuity; whereas the everlasting character of Christ's priesthood renders any further priesthood unnecessary.

St Thomas comments that this shows Christ to be the true and perfect Priest in the strict sense of the word, for it was impossible for the Jewish priests to be permanent mediators because death naturally deprived them of their priesthood. The case of Christian priests is quite different, because they are not mediators strictly speaking. There is only one Mediator, Jesus Christ; they are simply representatives of his, who act in his name. Christ is to the Levites as the perfect (which is necessarily one) is to the imperfect (which is always multiple): "Incorruptible things have no need to reproduce themselves [. . .]. Christ is immortal. As the eternal Word of the Father, he abides forever: his divine eternity is passed on to his body, for 'being raised from the dead (he) will never die again' (Rom 6:9). And so 'because he continues for ever, he holds his priesthood permanently.' Christ alone is the true Priest; the others (priests) are his ministers" (*Commentary on Heb, ad loc.*).

The eternal character of Christ's priesthood, St John Chrysostom points out, gives us reason for great confidence: "It is as if the Apostle were saying, 'Do not be afraid or think that (although) he loves us and has the Father's full confidence he cannot live forever: on the contrary, he does live forever!'" (*Hom. on Heb*, 13). We can put our trust in Christ the Priest because his priesthood is an enduring expression of his heartfelt love for all mankind: "The living Christ continues to love us still; he loves us today, now, and he offers us his heart as the fountain of our redemption: 'he always lives to make intercession for (us)' (Heb 7:25). We are always—ourselves and the entire world— embraced by the love of this heart 'which has loved men so much and receives such poor response from them'" (John Paul II, *Hom. in Sacré Coeur, Montmartre, Paris*, 1 June 1980).

Christ's priesthood is an expression of his Love, from which it cannot be separated; since his Love is everlasting, so too is his priesthood. In the first place, his priesthood is everlasting because it is linked to the Incarnation, which is something permanent; secondly, because Christ's mission is that of saving all men in all periods of history and not simply one of helping them by his teaching and his example; thirdly, because Christ continues to be present— St Ephraem says—not in the victims of the sacrifices of Mosaic worship, but in the prayer of the Church (cf. *Com. in Epist. ad Haebreos, ad loc.*), particularly in the permanent efficacy of the sacrifice of the Cross constantly renewed in the Mass, and in the praying of the Divine Office. Finally, it is everlasting because Christ's sacrifice is perpetuated until the end of time in the Christian ministerial priesthood, for bishops and priests "in virtue of the sacrament of Order, are consecrated as true priests of the New Testament to preach the Gospel and shepherd the faithful and celebrate divine worship" (Vatican II, *Lumen gentium*, 28).

Christ not only interceded for us when he was on earth: he continues to make intercession for us from heaven: "This 'always' points to a great mystery," St John Chrysostom observes; "he lives not only here but also there, in heaven; not only here and for a while, but also there, in life eternal" (*Hom. on Heb*, 13). In saying that Christ "makes intercession" for us, the inspired text is saying that Christ "takes the initiative, addresses the Father, presents him with a request or a demand", as if Christ were an advocate before the Father, a help, a defender (a "paraclete": cf. 1 Jn 2:1). But in what sense does he continue to make intercession for us, given that he cannot merit any more than he did when he was on this earth? He intercedes, St Thomas replies, first by again presenting his human nature to the Father, marked with the glorious signs of his passion,

Heb 4:14f

Lev 16:6, 11, 15

Heb 5:9

²⁶For it was fitting that we should have such a high priest, holy, blameless, unstained, separated from sinners, exalted above the heavens. ²⁷He has no need, like those high priests, to offer sacrifices daily, first for his own sins and then for those of the people; he did this once for all when he offered up himself. ²⁸Indeed, the law appoints men in their weak-

---

vivens ad interpellandum pro eis. ²⁶Talis enim et decebat, ut nobis esset pontifex, sanctus, innocens, impollutus, segregatus a peccatoribus et excelsior caelis factus, ²⁷qui non habet necessitatem cotidie, quemadmodum pontifices, prius pro suis delictis hostias offerre, deinde pro populi; hoc enim fecit semel semetipsum offerendo. ²⁸Lex enim homines constituit pontifices infirmitatem

---

and then by expressing the great love and desire of his soul to bring about our salvation (cf. *Commentary on Heb*, 7, 4). Christ, so to speak, continues to offer the Father the sacrifice of his longsuffering, humility, obedience and love. That is why we can always approach him to find salvation. "Through Christ and in the Holy Spirit, a Christian has access to the intimacy of God the Father, and he spends his life looking for the Kingdom which is not of this world, but which is initiated and prepared in this world. We must seek Christ in the Word and in the Bread, in the Eucharist and in prayer. And we must treat him as a friend, as the real, living person he is—for he is risen. Christ, we read in the Epistle to the Hebrews [Heb 7:24-25 follows]" (Blessed J. Escrivá, *Christ is passing by*, 116).

26-28. These last verses form a paean in praise of Christ, summing up and rounding off what has gone before. Christ is proclaimed to be "holy, blameless, unstained," that is, sinless, totally devoted to God the Father, just and faithful. Sacred Scripture uses similar language to describe people of outstanding holiness, such as Zechariah and Elizabeth (cf. Lk 1:6), Simeon, who was "righteous and devout", Joseph of Arimathea (cf. Lk 23:50), the centurion Cornelius (cf. Acts 10:22), etc. The praise given Christ here, however, hints at a perfection which is more than human. Christ is, at the same time, "separated from sinners", not in the sense that he refuses to have any dealings with them or despises them, for, on the contrary, we know that the Pharisees abused him, saying, "Behold, a glutton and a drunkard, a friend of tax collectors and sinners" (Mt 11:19) and "This man receives sinners and eats with them" (Lk 15:2; cf. Mt 9-11:13 and par.; Lk 7:34); he is "separated from sinners" because he can have no sin in him, since the presence of sin in his human nature is absolutely incompatible with the holiness of the unique person that Christ is—the divine Word. He is the perfect embodiment of all the ancient prerequisites for a priest of the true God (cf. Lev 21:4, 6, 8, 15). Christ, finally, from the point of view of his human nature also, has been "exalted above the heavens" not only ethically speaking, by virtue of his sublime holiness, but also in his very body,

ness as high priests, but the word of the oath, which came later than the law, appoints a Son who has been made perfect for ever.

---

habentes, sermo autem iuris iurandi, quod post legem est, Filium in aeternum consummatum.

---

through his glorious ascension (cf. Acts 2:33-26; 10:42); he is therefore the "Son who has been made perfect forever".

"Who was Jesus Christ?" St Alphonsus asks himself. "He was, St Paul replies, holy, blameless, unstained or, even better, he was holiness itself, innocence itself, purity itself" (*Christmas Novena*, 4). And St Fulgentius of Ruspe extols Christ in these beautiful terms: "He is the one who possessed in himself all that was needed to bring about our redemption, that is, he himself was the priest and the victim; he himself was God and the temple— the priest by whose actions we are reconciled; the sacrifice which brings about our reconciliation; the temple wherein we are reconciled; the God with whom we have been reconciled. Therefore, be absolutely certain of this and do not doubt it for a moment: the only-begotten God himself, the Word made flesh, offered himself to God on our behalf in an odour of sweetness as sacrifice and victim—the very one in whose honour as well as that of the Father and the Holy Spirit, the patriarchs, prophets and priests used to offer sacrifices of animals in Old Testament times; and to whom now, that is, in the time of the New Testament, in the unity of the Father and the Holy Spirit, with whom he shares the same unique divinity, the holy catholic Church never ceases to offer on behalf of the entire universe the sacrifice of the bread and wine, with faith and charity" (*De fide ad Petrum*, 22).

The sublimity of Christ's priesthood is a source of encouragement, hope and holy pride for the priests of the New Testament, given that "every priest in his own way puts on the person of Christ and is endowed with a special grace. By this grace, the priest, through his service of the people committed to his care and all the people of God, is able the better to pursue the perfection of Christ, whose place he takes. The human weakness of his flesh is remedied by the holiness of him who became for us a high priest, 'holy, blameless, unstained, separated from sinners' (Heb 7:26)" (Vatican II, *Presbyterorum ordinis*, 12). For all these reasons St Pius X, addressing priests, wrote: "We ought, therefore, to represent the person of Christ and fulfil the mission he has entrusted to us; and thereby attain the end which he has set out to reach [. . .]. We are under an obligation, as his friends, to have the same sentiments as Jesus Christ, who is 'holy, blameless, unstained' (Heb 7:26). As his ambassadors we have a duty to win over men's minds to accept his law and his teaching, beginning by observing them ourselves; insofar as we have a share in his power, we are obliged to set souls free from the bonds of sin, and we must ourselves be very careful to avoid falling into sin" (St Pius X, *Haerent animo*, 5).

125

CHRIST'S SACRIFICE IS MORE EXCELLENT THAN ALL THE SACRIFICES OF THE OLD LAW

8

Christ is high priest of a New Covenant, which replaces the Old

Ps 110:1
Heb 4:14
Acts 2:36
Num 24:6, LXX

[1]Now the point in what we are saying is this: we have such a high priest, one who is seated at the right hand of the throne of the Majesty in heaven, [2]a minister in the sanctuary

---

[1]Caput autem super ea, quae dicuntur: talem habemus pontificem, qui consedit in dextera throni Maiestatis in caelis, [2]sanctorum minister et tabernaculi veri,

---

1-2. The key point of the epistle is now proclaimed with great formality—the superiority of Christ's priesthood. This links up what was already said in 1:3 (about Christ being enthroned at the right hand of the Majesty) with what will be developed in chapters 9 and 10 (about the new temple and new form of worship). In Christ the Old Covenant, which offered worship by means of sacrifice and offerings, finds its total perfection; from Christ onwards the New Covenant begins, with a new sacrifice and a new temple. Little by little, consideration of the priesthood of the Mosaic form of worship gives way to examination of Christ's new form of divine service.

It is not just a matter of one temple or stone being replaced by another or by many such temples. The old temple has given way to a heavenly sanctuary, heaven itself. This is why Christ's ascension and enthronement at the right hand of the Father is so important: it marks the definitive entry of Jesus Christ's sacred humanity into his true temple, one not made by human hands. This makes it easier to understand the sense in which the temple of Jerusalem and the worship connected with it were a foreshadowing of future events.

Christ, then, possesses the true, definitive priesthood, for he exercises his ministry in the sanctuary of heaven, where he is seated at the right hand of the Father. This heavenly ministry of Christ is a further confirmation of the superiority of his priesthood. Firstly, because he is seated at the right hand of the Majesty in heaven (cf. Ps 110:1)—"Majesty" meaning the Godhead itself, for it is a way of referring to God (cf. the "throne of grace" in 4:16). Moreover, the "throne of the Majesty" is the equivalent of supreme authority to rule and judge. This can be seen from descriptions of the Last Judgment: "When the Son of man comes in his glory, and all the angels with him, then he will sit on his glorious throne" (Mt 25:31; cf. Rev 3:21; 20:11; Mt 19:28; etc.). Secondly, Christ carries out his ministry in a new sanctuary and a new tabernacle ("tent"), which are "true" in the sense that the sanctuary and tabernacle of Moses were

126

and the true tent[n] which is set up not by man but by the Lord. [3]For every high priest is appointed to offer gifts and sacrifices; hence it is necessary for this priest also to have something to offer. [4]Now if he were on earth, he would not be a priest at all, since there are priests who offer gifts according to the law. [5]They serve a copy and shadow of the heavenly sanctuary; for when Moses was about to erect the tent,[n] he was instructed by God, saying, "See that you make everything according to the pattern which was shown you on the mountain." [6]But as it is, Christ[o] has obtained a

Heb 5:1

Ex 25:40
Col 2:17
Acts 7:44

Heb 7:22; 9:15;
12:24
1 Tim 2:5

quod fixit Dominus, non homo. [3]Omnis enim pontifex ad offerenda munera et hostias constituitur; unde necesse erat et hunc habere aliquid, quod offerret. [4]Si ergo esset super terram, nec esset sacerdos, cum sint qui offerant secundum legem munera; [5]qui figurae et umbrae deserviunt caelestium, sicut responsum est Moysi, cum consummaturus esset tabernaculum: "Vide enim, inquit, *omnia facies secundum exemplar, quod tibi ostensum est in monte.*" [6]Nunc autem differentius sortitus est ministerium, quanto et melioris testamenti mediator est,

only an "image" of them. The earthly liturgy is a reflection of the true, heavenly liturgy, which is the eternal continuation of Christ's priesthood in the presence of the Father, for "in the earthly liturgy we take part in a foretaste of that heavenly liturgy which is celebrated in the Holy City of Jerusalem toward which we journey as pilgrims, where Christ is sitting at the right hand of God, Minister of the holies and of the true tabernacle" (Vatican II, *Sacrosanctum Concilium*, 8).

Some Fathers see the true sanctuary and tabernacle as representing the Church, in its total sense of Church militant plus Church triumphant. And St Cyril of Alexandria, for example, points out in one of his works that "the old tabernacle was set up in the desert by Moses and it was highly suitable for performing all the sacred ceremonies of the Law. But the mansion which is appropriate to Christ is the city on high, that is, heaven, the divine tent which is not the product of human handiwork but rather something holy and begotten by God. Christ, established therein, offers to God the Father those who believe in him, those sanctified by the Spirit" (St Cyril, *Explanation of Heb*).

3-6. To compare the earthly and heavenly tabernacles, the author resorts to analogy and metaphor, which is all that he can do. Bearing this in mind, one should not interpret the words of this passage as meaning that Jesus Christ consummated his sacrifice only in heaven, for the sacrifice of Calvary happened only once and was complete in itself. What this passage is saying is that, in heaven, Christ, the eternal Priest, continuously presents to the Father the fruits

[n]Or *tabernacle*
[o]Greek *he*

ministry which is as much more excellent than the old as the covenant he mediates is better, since it is enacted on better promises. 7For if that first covenant had been fault-less, there would have been no occasion for a second.

Jer 31:31-34

8For he finds fault with them when he says:
"The days will come, says the Lord,
when I will establish a new covenant with the
house of Israel and with the house of Judah;

Ex 19:5f

9not like the covenant that I made with their fathers
on the day when I took them by the hand
to lead them out of the land of Egypt;
for they did not continue in my covenant,
and so I paid no heed to them, says the Lord.

---

quod in melioribus repromissionibus sancitum est. 7Nam si illud prius culpa vacasset, non secundi locus inquireretur; 8vituperans enim eos dicit: *Ecce dies veniunt, dicit Dominus, et consummabo super domum Israel et super domum Iudae testamentum novum;* 9non secundum testamentum, quod feci patribus eorum in die qua apprehendi manum illorum, ut educerem illos de terra Aegypti, quoniam ipsi non permanserunt in testamento meo, et ego neglexi eos, dicit Dominus. 10Quia hoc est testamentum, quod testabor domui Israel post*

---

of the Cross. In the New Covenant there is only one sacrifice—that of Jesus Christ on Calvary; this single sacrifice is renewed in an unbloody manner every day in the sacrifice of the Mass; there Jesus Christ—the only Priest of the New Law—immolates and offers, by means of priests who are his ministers, the same victim (body and blood) which was immolated in a bloody manner once and for all on the Cross.

7-12. The comparison between the two covenants, the Old made with Moses and written on stone, and the New, engraved on the minds and hearts of the faithful (cf. 2 Cor 3:3; Heb 10:16, 17) is developed with the help of a quotation from Jeremiah (Jer 31:31-34), where the prophet announces the spiritual alliance of Yahweh with his people. Jeremiah's words, quoted from the Greek translation (very close to the original Hebrew), refer directly to the restoration of the Jews after the Exile. Now that the chosen people have been purified by suffering they are fit to be truly the people of God: "I will be their God, and they shall be my people"; this promise of intimate friendship is the core of the prophecy. That is what it means when it says the Law will be written on the minds and hearts of all, and all—even the least—shall know God. It may be that Jeremiah sensed the messianic restoration that lay beyond the restoration of the chosen people on its return from exile; certainly we can see that this oracle finds its complete fulfilment only with the New Covenant: the return from Babylon was merely an additional signal/symbol of the perfect Covenant

¹⁰This is the covenant that I will make with the house of
Israel after those days, says the Lord:
I will put my laws into their minds,
and write them on their hearts,
and I will be their God,
and they shall be my people.
¹¹And they shall not teach every one his fellow
or every one his brother, saying, 'Know the Lord,'
for all shall know me,
from the least of them to the greatest.
¹²For I will be merciful toward their iniquities,
and I will remember their sins no more."
¹³In speaking of a new covenant he treats the first as
obsolete. And what is becoming obsolete and growing old
is ready to vanish away.

Heb 10:16f
2 Cor 3:3;
6:16-18

Rom 10.4
2 Cor 5:17
Rev 21:4f
Heb 9:18

---

*dies illos, dicit Dominus, dando leges meas in mentem eorum, et in corde eorum
superscribam eas; et ero eis in Deum, et ipsi erunt mihi in populum. ¹¹Et non
docebit unusquisque civem suum, et unusquisque fratrem suum dicens:
'Cognosce Dominum'; quoniam omnes scient me, a minore usque ad maiorem
eorum, ¹²quia propitius ero iniquitatibus eorum et peccatorum illorum iam non
memorabor." ¹³Dicendo* "novum" veteravit prius; quod autem antiquatur et
senescit, prope interitum est.

---

which Christ would establish. For it is in that New Covenant that God truly
forgives sins and remembers them no more.

The Old Covenant is said not to have been faultless, or sinless. This does
not mean it was bad; rather; as St Thomas explains, it was powerless to atone
for sins, it did not provide people with the grace to avoid committing sins, it
simply showed people how to recognize sins; those who lived under the Old
Law continued to be subject to sin (cf. *Commentary on Heb*, 7, 2).

9

The rites of the Old Covenant prefigure those of the New

Ex 25:23, 30f
2 Chron 13:11,
LXX [1]Now even the first covenant had regulations for worship and an earthly sanctuary. [2]For a tent^p was prepared, the outer one, in which were the lampstand and the table and Ex 26:31-33 the bread of the Presence;^q it is called the Holy Place. [3]Behind the second curtain stood a tent^p called the Holy of Ex 16:33; Holies, [4]having the golden altar of incense and the ark of

[1]Habuit ergo et prius praecepta cultus et Sanctum huius saeculi. [2]Tabernaculum enim praeparatum est primum, in quo inerat candelabrum et mensa et propositio panum, quod dicitur Sancta; [3]post secundum autem velamentum, tabernaculum, quod dicitur Sancta Sanctorum, [4]aureum habens turibulum et arcam

1-10. In the preceding chapters the superiority of Christ's priesthood is discussed. Now the epistle examines the excellence of his sacrifice. To do so, it describes the sanctuary of the Old Covenant, the tent or tabernacle, where Yahweh dwelt during the period when the people of Israel were making their way through the wilderness and in the early years in the promised land. It also refers to the sacrifice on the great Day of Atonement or *Yom Kippur* (cf. Lev 16:1-34; 23:26-32; Num 29:7-11), whereby Israel was reconciled with its God by purification and the forgiveness of all those sins committed during the year for which no atonement had been made. Both the sanctuary and the rites celebrated in it on this solemn day are a prefiguration of the new sanctuary and new form of worship inaugurated by Christ. This leads on to a discussion of the most essential and specific function of priesthood—sacrifice.

It should be noted that in describing the sanctuary of the Old Covenant the epistle does so in terms not of the temple of Jerusalem but of the tent in the desert. In addition to having certain more traditional connotations and allowing the ark of the Covenant to be included in the description (the ark was destroyed in 587 B.C. when Nebuchadnezzar sacked the temple), reference to the tabernacle is closely connected with an idea which underlies the entire epistle: the Christian is making his way in a new exodus towards his homeland in heaven, entry into which has been opened by Christ's sacrifice (cf. 3:7-11).

3. "The second curtain": separating the Holy Place from the Holy of Holies. It is called the "second curtain" to distinguish it from the curtain at the entrance to the Holy Place, which would have been the first curtain. It was not, then, that there were two tents: there was only one, which was divided into two sections by this "second curtain".

For information about the tabernacle complex cf. pp. 26ff above.

^pOr *tabernacle*
^qGreek *the presentation of the loaves*

the covenant covered on all sides with gold, which contained a golden urn holding the manna, and Aaron's rod
that budded, and the tables of the covenant; [5]above it were
the cherubim of glory overshadowing the mercy seat. Of
these things we cannot now speak in detail.

Ex 25:120;
16:21
Num 17:25
Ex 25:18, 22

[6]These preparations having thus been made, the priests
go continually into the outer tent,[p] performing their ritual
duties; [7]but into the second only the high priest goes and he
but once a year, and not without taking blood which he
offers for himself and for the errors of the people. [8]By this

Num 18:3f

Ex 30:10
Lev 16:2, 14f,
18f

Heb 7:27

Heb 10:19f

---

testamenti circumtectam ex omni parte auro, in quae urna aurea habens manna
et virga Aaron, quae fronduerat, et tabulae testamenti, [5]superque eam cherubim
gloriae obumbrantia propitiatorium; de quibus non est modo dicendum per
singula. [6]His vero ita praeparatis, in prius quidem tabernaculum semper intrant
sacerdotes sacrorum officia consummantes, [7]in secundum autem semel in anno
solus pontifex, non sine sanguine, quem offert pro suis et populi ignorantiis,
[8]hoc significante Spiritu Sancto, nondum propalatam esse sanctorum viam,

---

6-7. This is a reference to the most solemn sacrifice of the Old Testament
Day of Atonement — a penitential service on the tenth day of the month of Tishri
(September-October), five days before the feast of Tabernacles. The Day of
Atonement was the only day in the year when the high priest was permitted to
enter the Holy of Holies, whereas priests entered the Holy Place every day to
do things connected with divine service (renew the incense, change the loaves
of proposition, etc.). The ceremonies of the Day of Atonement are described in
more detail in the Introduction to this volume.

This celebration purified the people of Israel, priests and leaders included,
from their sins and atoned for the faults and uncleanness which the ordinary
sacrifices could not erase; the sanctuary itself was also rendered clean of any
contamination.

Yom Kippur is one of the most important feasts in the Jewish calendar, the
others being the Passover, Pentecost, Tabernacles, and the celebration of the
New Year.

"The errors of the people" probably refers to every kind of sin, both sins
which Leviticus terms "sin" and what it calls "guilt" (cf. Lev 7:37). However,
by referring to them as "errors", sins of ignorance, the point is being made that
voluntary sins cannot be pardoned by the ceremony of *Yom Kippur*. There were
certain rabbis in fact who taught that animal sacrifices were insufficient to erase
the graver types of sin. For that it was necessary for God himself to replace the
sacrifices offered by men with a divine sacrifice of infinite atoning value.

8-10. Old Testament liturgy was a symbol of the new liturgy, whose centre
is the sacrifice of Christ, which alone is capable of sanctifying man, of
"perfecting the conscience of the worshipper". The existence of an outer tent

Lev 11:2; 15:18
Num 19:13
Col 2:16f

the Holy Spirit indicates that the way into the sanctuary is not yet opened as long as the outer tent[p] is still standing [9](which is symbolic for the present age). According to this arrangement, gifts and sacrifice are offered which cannot perfect the conscience of the worshipper, [10]but deal only with food and drink and various ablutions, regulations for the body imposed until the time of reformation.

Christ sealed the New Covenant with his blood once and for all

Heb 4:14;
10:1, 20
2 Cor 5:1

[11]But when Christ appeared as a high priest of the good things that have come,[r] then through the greater and more

---

adhuc priore tabernaculo habente statum; [9]quae parabola est temporis instantis, iuxta quam munera et hostiae offeruntur, quae non possunt iuxta conscientiam perfectum facere servientem, [10]solummodo in cibis et in potibus et variis baptismis, quae sunt praecepta carnis usque ad tempus correctionis imposita. [11]Christus autem cum advenit pontifex futurorum bonorum, per amplius et

---

blocking the way to the inner tent symbolizes this inability of the liturgy to effect justification. Once the curtain is removed the way is open to man to attain union with God—holiness symbolized by entry into the Holy of Holies. By his death Christ tore the curtain (cf. Mt 27:51). He is our Way (cf. Jn 14:6), the Door (cf. Jn 10:7), allowing entry into the heavenly sanctuary. Therefore, as long as there exists the first tabernacle, that is, the Holy Place, separated from the Holy of Holies by the curtain, sacrifices and gifts offered cannot bring about man's interior perfection, because Christ's sacrifice has not yet taken place, the sacrifice which will make satisfaction for the sins of all mankind.

Also, the existence of the tabernacle is a symbol of the ineffectiveness of Jewish rites in the present era, when the redemptive sacrifice has already been offered. It should be remembered that when the Epistle to the Hebrews was being written, the old liturgy was still being enacted in the temple. But the rites of the Old Law were valid only up to the Redemption wrought by Christ, that is, up to his death and resurrection.

11-14. The sacrifices of the Old Law could only promise ephemeral benefits, whereas Christ's redemptive sacrifice obtained for man, once and for all, "the good things to come", that is, the heavenly and eternal benefits proper to the messianic age—sanctifying grace and entry to heaven. Like the high priest on the Day of Atonement, Christ entered once for all into the Holy of Holies, through the curtain. This sanctuary which he entered is the heavenly one; that is why it is "greater and more perfect" and not made by men (cf. 8:2). Christ passed through the heavens into the very presence of the Father (cf. 7:26) and is seated in heaven at his right hand (cf. 8:1).

[r]Other manuscripts read *good things to come*

perfect tent[p] (not made with hands, that is, not of this creation) [12]he entered once for all into the Holy Place,

perfectius tabernaculum, non manufactum, id est non huius creationis, [12]neque per sanguinem hircorum et vitulorum sed per proprium sanguinem introivit

Many Fathers, Doctors of the Church and modern scholars see the expression "through the greater and more perfect tent" as referring to the sacred humanity of our Lord, virginally conceived in the womb of Mary, that is, "not made with hands". The tent or tabernacle would be our Lord's body, in which the Godhead dwells. The text then says that it is "not of this creation", because Jesus as man was conceived without the action of a man and without original sin: he did not follow "the law of nature which holds sway in the created world" (Theodoret, *Interpretatio Ep. ad Hebraeos, ad loc.*). In this case the inspired text would be saying that Christ redeemed us by means of his human nature (cf. v. 12). However, the words "through the greater and more perfect tent" can also be understood as referring to heaven, in the sense of a greater and more perfect sanctuary. In any event, whether by passing through the heavens or through his most sacred body, Christ achieved Redemption by offering his own blood. This does not have a temporary value—like the blood of animals shed each year when the priest entered the Holy of Holies: Jesus secured eternal Redemption. In the Old Law the Jews were cleansed by the blood of sacrificed animals from legal impurities which prevented them from taking part in the liturgy; but Christ's blood does so much more, for it cleanses man of his sins. "Do you want to know how effective the blood of Christ is? Let us go back to the symbols which foretold it and remind ourselves of the ancient accounts of (the Jews in) Egypt. Moses told them to kill a year-old lamb and put its blood on the two doorposts and the lintel of each house [. . .]. Would you like an additional way to appreciate the power of Christ's blood? See where it flowed from, what its source is. It began to flow from the very Cross and its source was the Lord's side. For, as the Gospel says, when our Lord was already dead, one of the soldiers went up to him with a lance and pierced his side and at once there came out water and blood—water, the symbol of Baptism; blood, the symbol of the Eucharist. The soldier pierced his side, he opened a breach in the wall of the holy temple, and there I discover the hidden treasure and I rejoice at the treasure I have found" (Chrysostom, *Baptismal catechesis*, III, 13-19).

And so the Church includes in the prayers it recommends to be said after Mass, one which reads: "I beseech thee, most sweet Lord Jesus, may your passion be the virtue which strengthens, protects and defends me; your wounds, food and drink to nourish, inebriate and delight me; your death, everlasting life for me; your cross, my eternal glory" (*Roman Missal of St Pius V*, recommended prayer of thanksgiving after Mass).

12. "Thus securing an eternal redemption": the Greek text uses "having found", here translated as "securing". St John Chrysostom points out that the

[p]Or *tabernacle*

takings not the blood of goats and calves but his own blood,
Num 19:9, 17-20 thus securing an eternal redemption. [13]For if the sprinkling
of defiled persons with the blood of goats and bulls and with
the ashes of a heifer sanctifies for the purification of the
1 Pet 1:18f
1 Jn 1:7 flesh, [14]how much more shall the blood of Christ, who

---

semel in Sancta, aeterna redemptione inventa. [13]Si enim sanguis hircorum et taurorum et cinis vitulae aspersus inquinatos sanctificat ad emundationem carnis, [14]quanto magis sanguis Christi, qui per Spiritum aeternum semetipsum

---

verb "to find" in this context has a shade of meaning that implies finding something unexpected: the reference is to finding, "as it were, something very unknown and very unexpected" (*Hom. on Heb, ad loc.*). However, taking into account the whole context and the possible Hebraic background of the expression, the verb "to find" is synonymous with "to search keenly, to reach, to attain": in other words, Christ eagerly sought to redeem man and he did so by his sacrifice. The verse refers to an "eternal" redemption, in contrast to the provisional nature of Mosaic sacrifices.

13. These words refer to a ceremony of purification described in the Old Testament (cf. Num 19). To cleanse a person from certain transgressions of the Law, the Israelites could avail of certain expiatory ablutions. These were done with water mixed with the ashes of a heifer, which the high priest had sacrificed in front of the tabernacle and then burned in its entirety. Into the fire cedar-wood, hyssop and scarlet wool (9:19) had also to be thrown. Thus lustral water was only useful for legal purification or "purification of the flesh", as distinct from purification of the spirit.

14. The Messiah acts "through the eternal Spirit", which may be taken as a reference to the Holy Spirit, as St Thomas, for example, interprets it: "Christ shed his blood, because the Holy Spirit did so; that is to say, it was by the Spirit's influence and prompting, that is, out of love of God and love of neighbour, that he did what he did. For it is the Spirit who purifies" (*Commentary on Heb, ad loc.*).

Pope John Paul II has referred to this text to show the presence of the Holy Spirit in the redemptive sacrifice of the Incarnate Word: "In the sacrifice of the Son of Man the Holy Spirit is present and active just as he acted in Jesus's conception, in his coming into the world, in his hidden life and in his public ministry. According to the Letter to the Hebrews, on the way to his 'departure' through Gethsemani and Golgotha, the same *Jesus Christ* in his own humanity *opened himself totally* to this *action of the Spirit-Paraclete*, who from suffering enables eternal salvific love to spring forth" (*Dominum et Vivificantem*, 40).

The Son of God desired that the Holy Spirit should turn his death into a perfect sacrifice. Only Christ "in his humanity was worthy to become this

sGreek *through*

through the eternal Spirit offered himself without blemish
to God, purify your[t] conscience from dead works to serve
the living God.

15Therefore he is the mediator of a new covenant, so that

1 Cor 15:45
2 Cor 13:13

1 Tim 2:5
Heb 8:6; 12:24
Gal 3:19; 4:1-7

---

obtulit immaculatum Deo, emundabit conscientiam nostram ab operibus mortuis ad serviendum Deo viventi. 15Et ideo novi testamenti mediator est, ut, morte

---

sacrifice, for *he alone* was 'without blemish' (Heb 9:14). But he offered it 'through the eternal Spirit', which means that the Holy Spirit acted in a special way in this absolute self-giving of the Son of Man, in order to transform this suffering into redemptive love" (*ibid.*).

It is also possible that "the eternal Spirit" is a more general reference to the Godhead present in Christ; in which case it would be the same as saying that Christ, being God and man, offered himself as an unblemished victim and therefore this offering was infinitely efficacious. Thus, as Pius XII says, Christ "laboured unceasingly by prayer and self-sacrifice for the salvation of souls until, hanging on the Cross, he offered himself as a victim unblemished in God's sight, that he might purify our consciences and set them free from lifeless observances to serve the living God. All men were thus rescued from the path of ruin and perdition and set once more on the way to God, to whom they were now to give due glory by co-operating personally in their sanctification, making their own the holiness that springs from the blood of the unspotted Lamb" (*Mediator Dei*, 1).

Christ's sacrifice purifies us completely, thereby rendering us fit to worship the living God. As St Alphonsus puts it, "Jesus Christ offered himself to God pure and without the trace of a fault; otherwise he would not have been a worthy mediator, would not have been capable of reconciling God and sinful man, nor would his blood have had the power to purify and cleanse our conscience from 'dead works', that is, from sins which are given that name because (our) works are in no way meritorious or else are worthy of eternal punishment. 'So that you might serve the living God'" (*Reflections on the Passion*, 9, 2).

15-22. The covenant is shown to be new because it has been ratified by the death and by the shedding of the blood of the testator or mediator. "Man, having fallen into sin, was in debt to divine justice and was the enemy of God. The Son of God came into the world and clothed himself in human flesh; being both God and man he became the mediator between man and God, the representative of both sides, so as to restore peace between them and obtain divine grace for man, giving himself as an offering to pay man's debt with his blood and his death. This reconciliation was prefigured in the Old Testament in all the sacrifices that were offered in that period and in all the symbols which God ordained—the tabernacle, the altar, the veil, the lampstand, the thurible and the

---

[t]Other manuscripts read *our*

those who are called may receive the promised eternal inheritance, since a death has occurred which redeems them from the transgressions under the first covenant.[u] [16]For where a will[u] is involved, the death of the one who made it

---

intercedente in redemptionem earum praevaricationum, quae erant sub priore testamento, repromissionem accipiant, qui vocati sunt aeternae hereditatis. [16]Ubi enim testamentum, mors necesse est afferatur testatoris; [17]testamentum

---

ark where the rod of Aaron and the tables of the Law were kept. All these were a sign and type of the promised redemption; and it was because that redemption would come about through the blood of Christ that God specified the blood of animals—a symbol of the blood of the divine Lamb—and laid it down that all the symbolic objects mentioned above should be sprinkled with blood: 'Hence even the first Covenant was not ratified without blood'" (*ibid.*, 9, 2).

For a third time Christ is stated to be the mediator of a New Covenant. Hebrews 7:22 and 8:6 say that he is the mediator of a better covenant because it can give eternal life. Here, as in 12:24, it is explained that Christ is the mediator of a New Covenant, ratified by blood which gives an eternal inheritance. The emphasis is on the sacrificial aspect: Christ is the mediator insofar as he is the atoning victim and at the same time the offerer of the sacrifice: in his sacrifice he is both priest and victim. "Christ is priest indeed; but he is priest for us, not for himself. It is in the name of the whole human race that he offers prayer and acts of human religious homage to his Eternal Father. He is likewise victim; but victim for us, since he substitutes himself for guilty mankind. Now the Apostle's exhortation, 'Yours is to be the same mind as Christ Jesus showed' (Phil 2:5), requires all Christians, so far as human power allows, to reproduce in themselves the sentiments that Christ had when he was offering himself in sacrifice—sentiments of humility, of adoration, praise, and thanksgiving to the divine Majesty. It requires them also to become victims, as it were; cultivating a spirit of self-denial according to the precepts of the Gospel, willingly doing works of penance, detesting and expiating their sins" (*Mediator Dei*, 22).

Christ's sacrifice is not only effective to forgive our sins; it is a manifestation of our Redeemer's love for us and it sets an example which we should follow. "And if God forgives us our sins it is so that we might use the time that remains to us in his service and love. And the Apostle concludes, saying, 'Therefore he is the mediator of a new covenant.' Our Redeemer, captivated by his boundless love for us, chose to rescue us, at the cost of his blood, from eternal death; and he succeeded in doing so, for if we serve him faithfully until we die we shall obtain from the Lord forgiveness and eternal life. Such were the terms of the testament, mediation or compact between Jesus Christ and God" (*Reflections on the Passion*, 9, 2).

15-17. As the RSV note points out the Greek word can be translated as either "covenant" or "will". The context and the parallel with the covenant of Sinai

[u]The Greek word here used means both *covenant* and *will*

136

must be established. [17]For a will[u] takes effect only at death, since it is not in force as long as the one who made it is alive. [18]Hence even the first covenant was not ratified without blood. [19]For when every commandment of the law had been declared by Moses to all the people, he took the blood of calves and goats, with water and scarlet wool and hyssop, and sprinkled both the book itself and all the people, [20]saying, "This is the blood of the covenant which God commanded you." [21]And in the same way he sprinkled with the blood both the tent[p] and all the vessels used in worship. [22]Indeed, under the law almost everything is

Ex 24:3-8
Lev 14:4
Num 19:6

Ex 24:8
Mt 26:28
Heb 7:22

Lev 8:15, 19
Ex 40:9
Lev 17:11
Eph 1:7

autem in mortuis est confirmatum, nondum enim valet, dum vivit, qui testatus est. [18]Unde ne prius quidem sine sanguine dedicatum est; [19]enuntiato enim omni mandato secundum legem a Moyse universo populo, accipiens sanguinem vitulorum et hircorum cum aqua et lana coccinea et hyssopo, ipsum librum et omnem populum aspersit [20]dicens: *"Hic sanguis testamenti quod mandavit ad vos Deus"*; [21]etiam tabernaculum et omnia vasa ministerii sanguine similiter

suggest the idea of covenant or pact, since the covenant with the chosen people was an unilateral pact, that is, a concession granted by God; however, it too can also be taken in a broad sense as a "will". Both the word "mediator" and the word "testator" (the one who makes the will) applied here to Christ serve to emphasize that his death needed to involve the shedding of blood. His is a death whereby we are called to "receive the promised eternal inheritance": "The work of our Redemption has been accomplished. We are now children of God, because Jesus has died for us and his death has ransomed us. *Empti enim estis pretio magno!* (1 Cor 6:20), you and I have been bought at a great price.

"We must bring into our life, to make them our own, the life and death of Christ. We must die through mortification and penance, so that Christ may live in us through Love. And then follow in the footsteps of Christ, with a zeal to co-redeem all mankind" (Blessed J. Escrivá, *The Way of the Cross*, XIV).

18-22. The shedding of Christ's blood was necessary for the ratification of the New Covenant, just as the shedding of blood was needed for that of the Sinai covenant. Moses' action following on his solemn dialogue with God is described here in more detail than in the Exodus 24 account, probably following a Jewish oral tradition. Verse 22 gives the reason why Moses sprinkled the book of the Law, the people, the tabernacle and the ritual vessels: he did so to purify them; it is formulating a very important principle, which rounds off the whole point being made in this chapter—that the shedding of blood is needed for purification and for forgiveness of sins.

Although the Old Testament had "purifications" carried out with water, fire or cereal offerings—for example, cleansing from leprosy and from legal

[p]Or *tabernacle*

uncleanness (cf. Lev 22:6; 14:1ff), or the purification of booty captured from idolators (cf. Num 31:22-23)—in keeping with the Law (cf. Lev 17:11) almost everything was purified with blood in the sense that the sprinkling or anointing which the high priest carried out implied involvement in the essential act of sacrifice—the shedding of blood.

The Jews thought that the principle of life resided in blood, because no one could live without blood. Life and blood were taken as almost identical, and therefore God, the Lord of Life, was also the only owner of the blood. Hence the prohibition, in the Law of Moses, on eating food with blood in it: when a sacrifice was offered, the blood of the victim was reserved to Yahweh. Since many types of purification were done by blood offerings, the text says that "almost everything is purified by blood".

In the case of the simpler types of purification, sprinkling with blood was the most perfect but not the only method; but when it was a matter of obtaining "forgiveness" of sins and not just legal purification, the only recourse was a blood offering. That is why the rabbis used to say, "There is no atonement without blood". It is true that the Old Testament does speak of sins being forgiven through almsgiving (cf. Tob 4:8-11; 12:9; Dan 4:27), fasting, prayers and other penitential practices, but it is referring to attitudes which express repentance. These attitudes or dispositions would have been ineffective were they not accompanied by worship of the true God by means of sacrifice. In fact both blood sacrifices and interior sacrifices (fasting and penance) were all orientated towards the ultimate sacrifice—the shedding of Christ's blood. Therefore, the principle enunciated by the rabbis, which is the background to v. 22, finds its perfect fulfilment only in Christ's sacrifice: without the shedding of his blood, there is no forgiveness of sin.

"In our case it was Christ, not Moses, who sprinkled us with blood, through the words he spoke: 'This is the blood of the new covenant for the forgiveness of sins.' By these words, not by hyssop smeared by blood, did he sprinkle all. Previously, people's bodies were cleansed externally, because it was a matter of physical purification; whereas now, since the cleansing is spiritual, it penetrates the soul and purifies it, not by mere sprinkling but, as it were, by a fount which wells up in our souls" (St John Chrysostom, *Hom. on Heb*, 16).

The shedding of Christ's blood is in some way renewed when any sacrament is being administered, particularly so at the eucharistic consecration when the priest repeats the words of consecration, "this is the cup of my blood, the blood of the new and everlasting covenant. It will be shed for you and for all so that sins may be forgiven". Therefore, the Church, in awe at the efficacy of Christ's sacrifice, commemorates his passion in these words: "But when thirty years were over, / time had made that fame mature; / now, his long-predestined passion / Christ will willingly endure: / on the cross the Lamb is lifted— / Lo! the Victim they secure. / Of the gall he drinks, out-wearied, / thorns and nails and spear have vied, / till the blood and water issue / from his gentle riven side: / earth, sea, stars, yea all creation / lave them in that cleansing tide" (*Liturgy of the Hours*, Hymn at lauds in Passiontide, trs. Fitzpatrick).

purified with blood, and without the shedding of blood
there is no forgiveness of sins.

[23]Thus it was necessary for the copies of the heavenly   Heb 8:5
things to be purified with these rites, but the heavenly things

---

aspersit. [22]Et omnia paene in sanguine mundantur secundum legem, et sine
sanguinis effusione non fit remissio. [23]Necesse erat ergo figuras quidem

---

23-28. In these verses the sacred writer adds some additional considerations
to the main line of his argument. His thought centres on linking the sanctuary,
the sacrifices which were offered in the Old Testament sanctuary, and the
sacrifice of the New Covenant. It was "necessary" for Christ to shed his blood
so that men might "receive the promised eternal inheritance" (9:15), that is,
forgiveness of their sins (cf. 9:14). This shedding of blood is also necessary for
the "purification" of the heavenly things (9:23). The sacrifices of the Mosaic
liturgy purified the things of the old sanctuary and, in some way, pointed to
forgiveness of sins (9:9, 10). The sacrifice of Christ, on the other hand, really
does blot out sin and opens for us the way to heaven itself, giving us entry into
that new sanctuary (7:25; 9:12). But the parallel is not a perfect one, for the old
sacrifices were multiple and were constantly repeated in petition of forgiveness
(9:25). The sacrifice of Christ, on the contrary, is a unique sacrifice, because it
is eternally effective (7:27; 9:12). Moreover, whereas the high priest offered a
sacrifice not with his own blood but with the blood of animals, Christ offered
his own blood in sacrifice. Therefore, Christ has offered himself "once" (7:28;
9:12, 26, 28) in the same sort of way as every man has to die only once and
then undergoes judgment. Furthermore, through his sacrifice Christ has passed
through the heavens once and for all and will not return to earth to renew his
sacrifice. He will not return until the end of time, when he will come in glory.

Two truths interweave here a number of times. The first is that Christ entered
forever not into a temple made by man but into heaven itself (9:24; 7:26; 8:1).
The second is that Christ also enables us to enter into glory; that is, his sacrifice
and his entry into heaven enable man to attain his last end.

23. The text might seem to be saying that the heavenly sanctuary, like the
Mosaic sanctuary, also needs purification. However, it is impossible for
heavenly things to need purification from any stain or imperfection. This has
led to many different interpretations being offered to explain what the purification mentioned here means. Some have seen the "heavenly things" as
referring to the Church on earth, an as yet imperfect image of the Church in
heaven and still in need of purification. Others see them as referring to the
Church in heaven, the Church triumphant, in the sense that it has to purify
sinners so as to be able to receive them into its bosom and destroy the roots of
evil. St Thomas interprets the text as referring to the abolition of impediments
to entry to the sanctuary. Men need to be purified of sin in order to enter heaven.

The words "heavenly things" seem to refer to the dedication or inauguration

themselves with better sacrifices than these. [24]For Christ has entered, not into a sanctuary made with hands, a copy of the true one, but into heaven itself, now to appear in the presence of God on our behalf. [25]Nor was it to offer himself

caelestium his mundari, ipsa autem caelestia melioribus hostiis quam istis. [24]Non enim in manufacta Sancta Christus introivit, quae sunt similitudo verorum, sed in ipsum caelum, ut appareat nunc vultui Dei pro nobis; [25]neque ut saepe offerat semetipsum, quemadmodum pontifex intrat in Sancta per

of heaven—conceived as a sanctuary, where God has his dwelling-place—with the blood of Christ. The old sanctuary was inaugurated and dedicated by a large number of blood sacrifices (cf. 1 Kings 8:62-64; 1 Mac 4:52-56). The new worship in the heavenly sanctuary cannot begin without the shedding of Christ's blood. Although the Christian has access to the sanctuary which Christ has inaugurated, he needs to remember that because it is so great and so perfect he cannot enter it if he has any stain or imperfection. Therefore, God has established that the souls of those who die in his friendship but who are not completely free from venial sin, are to be cleansed in purgatory. "To that [the beatific] vision no rational creature can be elevated unless it be thoroughly and entirely purified [. . .]. But it does at times happen that such purification is not entirely perfected in this life; one remains a debtor for the punishment [. . .]. Nevertheless, he is not entirely cut off from the reward, because such things can happen without mortal sin, which alone takes away the charity to which the reward of eternal life is due [. . .]. They must, then, be purged after this life before they achieve the final reward" (St Thomas Aquinas, *Summa contra Gentiles*, IV, 91, 6).

24. By his glorious ascension into heaven Jesus Christ crowns his re-demptive sacrifice and thenceforth intercedes for us as our advocate in the presence of God the Father (cf. Heb 4:14; 7:25; 8:1; 9:11-12). "What is this the Apostle is saying here about its being fitting that Christ, after suffering on our behalf, should go up into heaven and sit at the right hand of the Father, appearing before the face of God? What is this, Lord? He had to do this for us so that he could stand before the Father's house and show him his wounds and his sufferings, and say to him, 'Eternal Father, if you truly love me, so also truly love those whom I gave birth to and for whom I have laboured" (St John of Avila, *Sermon 31 on Whit Monday*).

25-26. Between the sacrifices of the Old Covenant and the sacrifice of Christ there are numerous points of contact and a degree of continuity, for the former are a foreshadowing of the latter. However, there are also substantial differences: the sacrifices of the Mosaic Law were multiple, Christ's sacrifice was unique; the Mosaic sacrifices did not really have the power to forgive sins, Christ's sacrifice does; the Mosaic ones were done with the blood of animals, Christ shed his own blood; the Mosaic ones belong to the time of waiting and

repeatedly, as the high priest enters the Holy Place yearly with blood not his own; [26]for then he would have had to suffer repeatedly since the foundation of the world. But as it is, he has appeared once for all at the end of the age to

1 Cor 10:6, 11
Gal 4:4
1 Pet 1:20
Heb 12
1 Jn 3:5

---

singulos annos in sanguine alieno. [26]Alioquin oportebat eum frequenter pati ab origine mundi; nunc autem semel in consummatione saeculorum ad destitutionem peccati per sacrificium sui manifestatus est. [27]Et quemadmodum

---

preparation, Christ's sacrifice marks the beginning of "the fulness of time" (cf. Mt 13:40-49; 24:3; 28:20; 1 Cor 10:11; Gal 4:4; Eph 1:10).

On the excellence of Christ's sacrifice over those of the Old Law, a further short proof is added, similar to that used in 8:3-5: if Christ's sacrifice consists essentially in his passion, and if the passion did not have the power to forgive all past, present and future sins, it would have had to be repeated, but that would be absurd, for Christ could die only once; therefore, Christ's sacrifice, offered once for all, is infinitely efficacious.

The celebration of the Sacrifice of the Mass is not at odds therefore with the efficacy and unicity of the sacrifice of Christ, because the Mass is not a new sacrifice involving the shedding of blood, a numerical repetition of the sacrifice of the Cross: it is an unbloody renewal of that sacrifice, to apply its infinite efficacy. "It is one and the same victim—he who now makes the offering through the ministry of priests and he who then offered himself on the Cross; the only difference is in the manner of the offering" (Council of Trent, *De SS. Missae sacrificio*, chap. 2), since the sacrifice of Calvary was a blood sacrifice whereas the Mass is an unbloody sacrifice; "a commemorative showing forth of the death which took place in reality on Calvary is repeated in each Mass, because by distinct representations Christ Jesus is signified and shown forth in the state of victim" (Pius XII, *Mediator Dei*, 20).

The Mass, then, receives all its efficacy from Christ's death on the cross, and applies that sacrifice in time and space.

"Among the instruments for distributing to believers the merits that flow from the cross of the divine Redeemer, the august sacrifice of the altar is pre-eminent: 'As often as the commemoration of this victim is celebrated, the work of our Redemption is performed' (*Roman Missal*, Ninth Sunday after Pentecost). This in no way derogates from the dignity of the sacrifice of the Cross; on the contrary, it is a clear proof—as the Council of Trent asserts—of its greatness and necessity. The daily immolation is a reminder to us that there is no salvation but in the cross of our Lord Jesus Christ (cf. Gal 6:14) and that the reason why God wills the continuation of this sacrifice 'from the rising of the sun to its setting' (Mal 1:11) is in order that there may be no pause in that hymn of praise and thanksgiving. This is a debt which men owe and to their Creator precisely because they stand in constant need of his help, and in constant need of the divine Redeemer's blood to destroy the sins that call for just retribution" (*Mediator Dei*, 21).

Gen 3:19
Is 53:12
Heb 10:12, 14
1 Tim 6:14
Phil 3:20
1 Pet 2:24

put away sin by the sacrifice of himself. [27]And just as it is appointed for men to die once, and after that comes judgment, [28]so Christ, having been offered once to bear the sins of many, will appear a second time, not to deal with sin but to save those who are eagerly waiting for him.

---

statutum est hominibus semel mori, post hoc autem iudicium, [28]sic et Christus, semel oblatus ad multorum auferenda peccata, secundo sine peccato apparebit exspectantibus se in salutem.

27-28. These verses look at three basic truths of Christian belief about the last things—1) the immutable decree of death; 2) the fact that there is a judgment immediately after death; 3) the second coming of Christ, in glory.

"Not to deal with sin": this phrase means that the second coming of Christ, or Parousia, will not be for the purpose of redeeming men from sin but rather to bring salvation, that is, glory, to those who placed their hope in him. Christ will come into the world for a second time, but not as Redeemer, for his sacrifice has already eliminated sin once for all; rather, he will come as Judge of all. His coming "is appointed": it is as necessary as death and judgment. These three truths are closely interconnected.

Although man is mortal, "a spiritual element survives and subsists after death, an element endowed with consciousness and will, so that the 'human self' subsists. To designate this element, the Church uses the word 'soul', the accepted term in the usage of Scripture and Tradition" (SCDF, *Letter on Certain Questions concerning Eschatology*, 17 May 1979).

Man, then, is made up of a spiritual and immortal soul and a corruptible body. However, when God originally endowed man with supernatural grace, he gave him additional gifts, the so-called "preternatural" gifts, which included bodily immortality. Adam's disobedience resulted in the loss of his friendship with God and the loss of this preternatural gift. From that point onwards death is "the wages of sin" (Rom 6:23), and it is to this divine decision that the text refers when it says that it "is appointed for men to die" (cf. Gen 3:19, 23; Rom 5:12). The Church has repeatedly stressed that death is a punishment; cf., for example, Pius VI, *Auctorem fidei*, prop. 1, 7: "in our present state (death) is inflicted as a just punishment for sin"; immortality was an "unmerited gift and not a natural condition". Verses 27-28 are an implicit exhortation to watchfulness (cf. also 1 Cor 7:29; Sir 14:12; and *Lumen gentium*, 48).

Immediately after death everyone will be judged on the conduct of his life. All "are to give an account of their lives; those who have done good deeds will go into eternal life; those who have done evil will go into everlasting fire" (*Athanasian Creed*). This is something which reason with the help of God's Word can discover, because people with a correct moral sense realize that good deserves to be rewarded and evil punished, and that it is impossible for this to occur completely in this life. It is difficult to say whether Hebrews 9:27 is referring to the "particular judgment", which happens immediately after death,

10

The sacrifices of the Old Covenant could not take away sins

¹For since the law has but a shadow of the good things to come instead of the true form of these realities, it can never, by the same sacrifices which are continually offered year

Col 2:17
Heb 7:19; 8:5

---

¹Umbram enim habens lex bonorum futurorum, non ipsam imaginem rerum, per singulos annos iisdem ipsis hostiis, quas offerunt indesinenter, numquam

---

or to the general judgment, which will take place on the last day. Both interpretations can be supported, for the judgment the verse refers to is connected, on the one hand, with death, and on the other with the second coming of Christ. In any event, it is clear that what is meant is a "personal" judgment, a trial at which each individual will be judged by Christ (cf. 2 Cor 5:10; Rom 14:10). The existence of a general judgment does not conflict with the certainty that there is a particular judgment, for the Church, in line with Sacred Scripture, although it awaits the glorious revealing of our Lord Jesus Christ on the last day, sees that event as distinct from and separate in time from the judgment which every individual will undergo immediately after death (cf. *Letter on Eschatology, op. cit.*).

The idea of death and judgment, however, should not only inspire fear; it should also lead us to hope in Christ, for our Lord will come a second time to show himself a merciful judge to "those who are eagerly waiting for him".

Christians, therefore, combine their joyful hope in the establishment of the Kingdom of God, which they wholeheartedly desire, with a desire to make the best possible use of the time allotted to them in this life. "This urgent solicitude of the Church, the Spouse of Christ, for the needs of men—for their joys and hopes, their griefs and labours—is nothing other than her intense desire to share them in full, in order to illuminate men with the light of Christ and to gather together and unite all in him who alone is the Saviour of each one of them. This solicitude must never be taken to mean that the Church conforms herself to the things of this world, or that her longing for the coming of her Lord and his eternal reign grows cold" (Paul VI, *Creed of the People of God*).

1. The sacred writer once more compares the Old Testament sacrifices with the sacrifice of Christ (cf. 7:27; 9:9-10, 12-13), examining them now from the point of view of their efficacy.

The Law is "a shadow", that is, something without substance. The term used to be employed by artists to describe the first sketch on a canvas, a bare outline before the application of colour. Thus, the Old Law in relation to the New Testament is like a first sketch as compared with the finished painting. However, because it speaks of the New Testament as "the true form of these realities", it allows us to see the New Covenant as not yet giving possession of

after year, make perfect those who draw near. ²Otherwise, would they not have ceased to be offered? If the worshippers had once been cleansed, they would no longer have any consciousness of sin. ³But in these sacrifices there is a reminder of sin year after year. ⁴For it is impossible that the blood of bulls and goats should take away sins.

Num 5:15, LXX

Is 1:11

---

potest accedentes perfectos facere. ²Alioquin nonne cessassent offerri, ideo quod nullam haberent ultra conscientiam peccatorum cultores semel mundati? ³Sed in ipsis commemoratio peccatorum per singulos annos fit, ⁴impossibile

---

these "good things to come", but as being a kind of anticipation of them, a reflection of them. Yet it is a true, a faithful, reflection, insofar as the New Law already has the power to forgive sins and to link men with God through charity. "The New Law", St Thomas says, "represents the good things to come more clearly than does the Old. Firstly, because in the words of the New Testament express mention is made of the good things to come and the promise, whereas in the Old reference is made only to material good things. Secondly, because the New Testament draws its strength from charity, which is the fulness of the Law. And this charity, even if it be imperfect, is similar to Christ's charity by virtue of the faith to which it is joined. That is why the new law is called the 'law of love'. And that is also why it is called the 'true form', because it has imprinted on it the image of the good things to come" (*Commentary on Heb, ad loc.*).

Moreover, an image, to some degree at least, coincides with the reality it reflects: Christ himself, for example, is the image of God. Therefore, "in Christ one already possesses, in a permanent way, these good things of heaven—both the present ones and the future ones" (Chrysostom, *Hom. on Heb, ad loc.*).

2-4. These verses repeat and complete what is said in v. 1 and in 9:12-13. "Tell me, then, what is the point of having more victims and more sacrifices when a single victim would suffice for atonement for sins [. . .]. Multiple sacrifices in effect show that the Jews needed to atone for their sins because they had failed to find forgiveness: it points to the inefficacy of the victims offered, rather than to their power" (Chrysostom, *Hom. on Heb*, 17). The ultimate reason for this inefficacy is explained by a striking statement: "It is impossible that the blood of bulls and goats should take away sins" (v. 4). There is here an echo of those proclamations of the prophets which reminded the people that true purification comes not from external actions but from conversion of heart (cf. Jer 2:22; 4:14; 11:15; Mic 6:7-8; Ps 51:18-19; etc.).

And yet, is it not the case that the priests of the New Testament renew Jesus' sacrifice in the Mass everyday? St John Chrysostom answers: "Yes, that is true, but not because we regard the original sacrifice, Christ's sacrifice, as ineffective or impotent. We priests repeat it to commemorate his death. We have but one victim, Christ—not many victims [. . .]. There is but one and the same sacrifice

Christ's offering of himself has infinite value

⁵Consequently, when Christ[v] came into the world, he said,   Ps 40:7-9

"Sacrifices and offerings thou hast not desired,
but a body hast thou prepared for me;
⁶in burnt offerings and sin offerings thou hast taken no
pleasure.
⁷Then I said, 'Lo, I have come to do thy will, O God,'
as it is written of me in the roll of the book."

---

enim est sanquinem taurorum et hircorum auferre peccata. ⁵Ideo ingrediens mundum dicit: *"Hostiam et oblationem noluisti, corpus autem aptasti mihi; ⁶holocautomata et sacrificia pro peccato non tibi placuerunt. ⁷Tunc dixi: Ecce*

[. . .], one Christ whole and entire, here as elsewhere, the same everywhere—the same Christ on all the altars. Just as Jesus Christ, although offered in different places, has only one body, so everywhere there is but one sacrifice [. . .]. What we do is a commemoration of Christ's offering, for at the Supper he said, 'Do this in memory of me.' Therefore, we do not offer, as the high priest of the Law did, a new, additional, victim: it is not one sacrifice more, but always the same one" (*Hom. on Heb*, 17).

The Mass "is the sacrifice of Christ, offered to the Father with the co-operation of the Holy Spirit—an offering of infinite value, which perpetuates the work of the Redemption in us and surpasses the sacrifices of the Old Law. The holy Mass brings us face to face with one of the central mysteries of our faith, because it is the gift of the Blessed Trinity to the Church. It is because of this that we can consider the Mass as the centre and the source of a Christian's spiritual life. It is the final end of all the sacraments" (Blessed J. Escrivá, *Christ is passing by*, 86-87).

5-10. This passage carries a quotation from Psalm 40:7-8, but one taken from the Greek translation, the Septuagint, not from the Hebrew. Where the Hebrew says, "thou hast opened my ears", the Greek reads, "a body thou hast prepared for me". The difference is not substantial, because the Hebrew expression points to the docility and obedience of the speaker, who is the Messiah himself. The Greek translation gives the sentence a more general meaning: God has not only opened the ears of the Messiah; he has given him life as a man (cf. Phil 2:7). The words of this psalm "allow us as it were to sound the unfathomable depths of this self-abasement of the Word, his humiliation of himself for love of men even to death on the Cross [. . .]. Why this obedience, this self-abasement, this suffering? The Creed gives us the answer: 'for us men and for our salvation' Jesus came down from heaven so as to give man full entitlement to ascend (to heaven) and by becoming a son in the Son to regain

[v]Greek *he*

145

⁸When he said above, "Thou has neither desired nor taken
pleasure in sacrifices and offerings and burnt offerings and

1 Sam 15:22
Jn 6:38

sin offerings" (these are offered according to the law), ⁹then
he added, "Lo, I have come to do thy will." He abolishes

Heb 9:14, 28
Eph 5:2

the first in order to establish the second. ¹⁰And by that will
we have been sanctified through the offering of the body of
Jesus Christ once for all.

---

venio, in capitulo libri scriptum est de me, ut faciam, Deus, voluntatem tuam."
⁸Superius dicens: *"Hostias et oblationes et holocautomata et sacrificia pro
peccato noluisti, nec placuerunt* tibi", quae secundum legem offeruntur, ⁹*tunc*
dixit: *"Ecce venio, ut faciam voluntatem tuam."* Aufert primum, ut secundum
statuat; ¹⁰in qua voluntate sanctificati sumus per oblationem corporis Christi
Iesu in semel. ¹¹Et omnis quidem sacerdos stat cotidie ministrans et easdem

the dignity he lost through sin [. . .]. Let us welcome Him. Let us say to him,
'Here I am; I have come to do your will'" (John Paul II, *General Audience*, 25
March 1981).

The author of the letter, elaborating on the text of the psalm, asserts that the
Messiah's sacrifice is greater than the sacrifices of the Old Law, unbloody as
well as bloody, sin-offerings as well as burnt offerings as they were called in
the liturgy (cf. Lev 5:6; 7:27). The sacrifice of Christ, who has "come into the
world", has replaced both kinds of ancient sacrifice. It consisted in perfectly
doing the will of his Father (cf. Jn 4:34; 6:38; 8:29; 14:31), even though he was
required to give his life to the point of dying on Calvary (Mt 26:42; Jn 10:18;
Heb 5:7-9). Christ "came into the world" to offer himself up to suffering and
death for the redemption of the world. "He knew that all the sacrifices of goats
and bulls offered to God in ancient times were incapable of making satisfaction
for the sins of men; he knew that a divine person was needed to do that [. . .].
My Father (Jesus Christ said), all the victims offered you up to this are not
enough and never will be enough to satisfy your justice; you gave me a body
capable of experiencing suffering, so that you might be placated by the shedding
of my blood, and men thereby saved; *'ecce venio*, here I am, ready'; I accept
everything and in all things do I submit to your will. The lower part of his human
nature naturally felt repugnance and reacted against living and dying in so much
pain and opprobium, but its rational part, which was fully subject to the Father's
will, had the upper hand; it accepted everything, and therefore Jesus Christ
began to suffer, from that point onwards, all the anguish and pain which he
would undergo in the course of his life. That is how our divine Redeemer acted
from the very first moments of his coming into the world. So, how should we
behave towards Jesus when, come to the use of reason, we begin to know the
sacred mysteries of Redemption through the light of faith?" (St Alphonsus,
Advent Meditations, II, 5).

The psalm speaks of "the roll of the book": this may refer to a specific book
or else to the Old Testament in general (cf. Lk 24:27; Jn 5:39, 46, 47).

Heb 10:1-4
Deut 10:8

Ps 110:1
Acts 2:33
Mt 22:44

Jn 17:19

¹¹And every priest stands daily at his service, offering repeatedly the same sacrifices, which can never take away sins. ¹²But when Christ[w] had offered for all time a single sacrifice for sins, he sat down at the right hand of God, ¹³then to wait until his enemies should be made a stool for his feet. ¹⁴For by a single offering he has perfected for all time those who are sanctified. ¹⁵And the Holy Spirit also bears witness to us; for after saying,

---

saepe offerens hostias, quae numquam possunt auferre peccata. ¹²Hic autem, una pro peccatis oblata hostia, in sempiternum *consedit in dextera Dei*, ¹³de cetero expectans, *donec ponantur inimici eius scabellum pedum eius*; ¹⁴una enim oblatione consummavit in sempiternum eos, qui sanctificantur. ¹⁵Testificatur autem nobis et Spiritus Sanctus; postquam enim dixit: ¹⁶*"Hoc est*

11-14. Teaching given elsewhere in the letter (8:5; 9:9-10, 12-13, 25; 10:1-4) is now reiterated in order to show the universal efficacy of Christ's sacrifice. However, here it is expounded by comparing the posture of the Old Testament priests with that of Christ. They did in fact have to *stand* in the presence of Yahweh, offering victims repeatedly. Standing was the correct posture for servants and employees. The reference is to Old Testament priests who repeatedly, every day, went through the same motions and offered the same sacrifices. By contrast, Christ, as is stated in Psalm 110:1, after his Ascension is *seated* at the right hand of God the Father (see notes on Mt 16:19 and Heb 1:3). In addition to conveying the idea of repose and rest, being seated would be equivalent to receiving royal investiture or to exercising authority (cf. Heb 7:26; 8:1); also, a king's chief minister or heir used to sit on the right of the king, as in a place of special honour (cf. Mt 26:24; Mk 14:62; Lk 26:69); and it might be pointed out that David pitched his tent to the right of the tabernacle: cf. 2 Sam 7:18). What has happened is that by virtue of the efficacy of his single sacrifice, Christ has taken possession of heaven for ever more and has merited royal dignity; all that remains to happen, and it shall happen, is for all his enemies to submit to him (cf. 1 Cor 15:25-28). So fruitful is his sacrifice that those who take part in it, "those who have been sanctified", are thereby perfected: they obtain forgiveness of sins, purity of conscience, access to and union with God. In other words, the source of holiness in men is the sacrifice of Calvary.

15-18. The last proof of the superiority of Christ's sacrifice for the forgiveness of sins is based on this passage of Jeremiah 31:33-34, already quoted in 8:10-12. The letter is insisting on the spiritual character of the New Covenant —ratified with the blood of Christ—which is impressed on the hearts and minds of men. And it is also emphasizing the effects of this Covenant—forgiveness of sins by God.

ʷGreek *this one*

147

Heb 8:10
Jer 31:33
^{16}"This is the covenant that I will make with them
after those days, says the Lord:
I will put my laws on their hearts,
and write them on their minds,"
Heb 8:12
Jer 31:34
^{17}then he adds,
"I will remember their sins and their misdeeds no more."
^{18}Where there is forgiveness of these, there is no longer any
offering for sin.

MORAL SECTION
FAITH AND PERSEVERANCE IN FAITH

AN EXHORTATION TO PERSEVERANCE

Motives for perseverance

Jn 14:6
Heb 6:19f;
9:8, 11f

Zech 6:11ff
^{19}Therefore, brethren, since we have confidence to enter
the sanctuary by the blood of Jesus, ^{20}by the new and living
way which he opened for us through the curtain, that is,
through his flesh, ^{21}and since we have a great priest over

---

testamentum, quod testabor ad illos *post dies illos, dicit Dominus, dando leges meas in cordibus eorum et in mente eorum superscribam eas;* ^{17}*et peccatorum eorum et iniquitatem eorum iam non recordabor amplius.*" ^{18}Ubi autem horum remissio, iam non oblatio pro peccato. ^{19}Habentes itaque, fratres, fiduciam in introitum Sanctorum in sanguine Iesu, ^{20}quam initiavit nobis viam novam et viventem per velamen, id est carnem suam, ^{21}et sacerdotem magnum super

---

19-21. Throughout the epistle there is a constant interweaving of dogmatic and moral considerations, with the former points often giving rise to exhortations to the faithful to be unwavering in faith and hope. The epistle now moves on from its theological reflections on Christ's priesthood to its practical application in the Christian life: the Christian should put his trust in the efficacy of Christ's sacrifice, and through faith, hope and charity associate himself with Christ's priesthood. He should do this for three reasons—the redemptive value of the blood of Jesus, the access to glory signified by his entry into the sanctuary of heaven, and Christ's enthronement at the right hand of the Father. The sprinkling of the blood of Christ gives the believer full assurance that he too will enter heaven, because the paschal mystery of Christ—his passion, death and resurrection—has made this possible.

"The new and living way": a translation of the original Greek expression, which literally reads "the recently sacrificed and living way"; this is a metaphorical expression indicating that Christ is a way, and that this way has been recently opened up, has been sacrificed and is alive. There is, then, a personi-

the house of God, [22]let us draw near with a true heart in full assurance of faith, with our hearts sprinkled clean from an evil conscience and our bodies washed with pure water. [23]Let us hold fast the confession of our hope without wavering, for he who promised is faithful; [24]and let us consider how to stir up one another to love and good works, [25]not neglecting to meet together, as is the habit of some, but encouraging one another, and all the more as you see the Day drawing near.

Eph 5:26
Ezek 36:25
Heb 3:6; 4:16
Rom 6:4

Heb 4:14

Heb 3:13
2 Thess 2:1
Jas 2:2

---

domum Dei, [22]accedamus cum vero corde in plenitudine fidei, aspersi corda a conscientia mala et abluti corpus aqua munda; [23]teneamus spei confessionem indeclinabilem, fidelis enim est, qui repromisit; [24]et consideremus invicem in provocationem caritatis et bonorum operum, [25]non deserentes congregationem nostram, sicut est consuetudinis quibusdam, sed exhortantes, et tanto magis

---

fication of "way" which recalls what Jesus said about his being "the way, and the truth, and the life" (Jn 14:6); and there is also a reference to Christ's sacrifice, to the fact that his body did not experience corruption and that he lives for ever (cf. Heb 7:25).

The *Pius V Catechism*, referring to the benefits brought us by Christ's passion, specifies how he opened to us the gates of heaven, closed due to mankind's sin: "Nor are we without a type and figure of this mystery in the Old Law. For those who were prohibited to return into their native country before the death of the high priest (cf. Num 35:25) typified that no one, however just and holy may have been his life, could gain admission into the celestial country until the eternal High Priest, Jesus Christ, had died, and by his death immediately opened heaven to those who, purified by the sacraments and gifted with faith, hope and charity, become partakers of his passion" (I, 5, 14).

The reference to Christ's flesh as a "curtain" not only recalls the curtain in the temple separating the Holy of Holies from the rest of the sanctuary, but also points to the fact that the deepest dimension of Christ is his Godhead, in which the Christian must believe, but without separating it from his humanity. Christ's human nature is at the same time a "way" because it reveals his divinity, and a "curtain" because it masks it. "Just as the priest (of the Old Law) entered the Holy of Holies, so too if we want to enter holy glory, we must enter by way of Christ's flesh, the curtain (concealing) his divinity [. . .]. For, faith in the one God is insufficient if one does not have faith in the Incarnation" (St Thomas Aquinas, *Commentary on Heb, ad loc.*).

22-25. The epistle now exhorts its readers to purity of heart, steadfastness in faith and mutual charity.

It speaks of a clean heart, recalling the purity which the water of Baptism brings. The Christian should stay true to the faith he received and professed at

²⁶For if we sin deliberately after receiving the knowledge of the truth, there no longer remains a sacrifice for sins,

---

quanto videtis appropinquantem diem. ²⁶Voluntarie enim peccantibus nobis, post acceptam notitiam veritatis, iam non relinquitur pro peccatis hostia,

---

Baptism, and maintain the purity which it brings. To live in this way the baptized should count on the help provided by the Church and on the grace God continually gives. As Vatican I teaches, referring to those who have received the light of faith, "God does not abandon them, unless he is abandoned [. . .]. Therefore, the position of those who have embraced Catholic truth by the heavenly gift of faith, and of those who have been misled by human opinions and follow a false religion is by no means the same, for the former, who have accepted the faith under the teaching authority of the Church, can never have just reason for changing that faith or calling it into question" (*Dei Filius*, chap. 3).

Along with its exhortation to practise the three theological virtues, the passage includes a call not to neglect to attend Christian assemblies. We know that the first Christians were expected to come together daily or weekly (cf. Acts 2:46; 20:7) and, as we can see here, some gave up going to those meetings through carelessness, or because they preferred private to public prayer, or because they did not want others to know they were Christians. In Judaism much emphasis was placed on the duty to attend synagogue meetings. The meetings referred to in this passage, whether for the celebration of the Christian liturgy or for instruction in apostolic teaching, had a clearly eschatological focus in the sense that they built up people's hope in the coming of our Lord (cf. 1 Thess 5:4; 1 Cor 3:13; Rom 13:12; Phil 4:5; Jas 5:8; 1 Pet 4:7). The author's insistence on the need to meet together recalls another exhortation which goes back to the early Church: "Now that you are members of Christ, do not choose to cut yourselves off from the Church by failing to attend the assembly; having Christ your head present and in touch with you, as he promised, do not underestimate yourselves or choose to separate the Saviour from his members, or divide or scatter his body, or give your everyday needs more importance than the Word of God; rather, on the Lord's Day leave everything aside and come to the Church" (*The Teaching of the Twelve Apostles*). On the basis of the apostolic tradition, the Church has established a grave obligation to attend Mass on Sundays (cf. *Code of Canon Law*, can. 1247). "On this day Christ's faithful are bound to come together into one place. They should listen to the word of God and take part in the Eucharist, thus calling to mind the passion, resurrection and glory of the Lord Jesus and giving thanks to God, 'who has begotten them anew to a living hope through the resurrection of Jesus Christ from the dead' (1 Pet 1:3)" (Vatican II, *Sacrosanctum Concilium*, 106).

In the same way—by listening to and meditating on the Word of God— Christians fulfil their equally serious obligation to improve their understanding of Christian doctrine.

²⁷but a fearful prospect of judgment, and a fury of fire which will consume the adversaries. ²⁸A man who has violated the law of Moses dies without mercy at the testimony of two or three witnesses. ²⁹How much worse punishment do you think will be deserved by the man who has spurned the Son of God, and profaned the blood of the covenant by which he was sanctified, and outraged the Spirit of grace? ³⁰For we know him who said, "Vengeance is mine, I will repay."

Is 26:11, LXX

Num 35:30
Deut 17:6

Heb 2:3; 6:6;
9:20
Ex 24:8

Deut 32:35f
Ps 135:14
Rom 12:19

---

²⁷terribilis autem quaedam exspectatio iudicii et ignis aemulatio, quae consumptura est adversarios. ²⁸Irritam quis faciens legem Moysis sine ulla miseratione *duobus vel tribus testibus moritur*: ²⁹quanto deteriora putatis merebitur supplicia, qui Filium Dei conculcaverit, et sanguinem testamenti communem duxerit, in quo sanctificatus est, et Spiritui gratiae contumeliam fecerit? ³⁰Scimus enim eum, qui dixit: *"Mihi vindicta, ego retribuam"* et iterum:

26-31. This passage is not saying that there are some sins that are unforgivable (cf. Heb 6:4-6), as early rigorists taught. The Church has received from her divine Redeemer the power to forgive all sins, no matter how grave (cf. Mt 18:18; Jn 20:18-20). Pope St Gelasius I explained this as follows: "So, there is no sin for whose forgiveness the Church does not pray; no sin which, by virtue of the God-given power it has, that cannot be forgiven; for it was (the Church) that was told, 'If you forgive the sins of any . . .' (cf. Jn 20:23); 'whatever you loose on earth shall be loosed in heaven' (Mt 18:18). The word 'whatever' covers everything, no matter how grave the sins be, or what kind they be. That view is correct which argues that there is to be no forgiveness for him who persists in committing sins; but that does not apply to one who later repents of them" (*Ne forte*, 4). The letter speaks of "deliberate" sins, sins a person commits knowing that they are sins and consenting in them *and* acting maliciously; that is, fully deliberate sins—what the Old Testament calls "acting presumptuously" (cf. Deut 17:12; 18:22). Because the sinner is pertinacious, in practice there is no hope of his repenting. It is similar to what is called in the Gospel "speaking against [or blaspheming] the Holy Spirit" (cf. Mt 12:32 and note): "'blasphemy' does not properly consist in offending against the Holy Spirit in words; it consists rather *in the refusal to accept the salvation which God offers to man through the Holy Spirit*, working through the power of the Cross. If man rejects the 'convincing concerning sin' which comes from the Holy Spirit and which has the power to save, he also rejects the 'coming' of the Counsellor—that 'coming' which was accomplished in the Paschal Mystery, in union with the redemptive power of Christ's blood—the blood which 'purifies the conscience from dead works'" (John Paul II, *Dominum et Vivificantem*, 46).

Specifically, the writer seems to be referring to Christian apostates who had already received "the knowledge of the truth", which may mean instruction prior to Baptism and reception of the Eucharist; no part of Christ's redeeming

And again, "The Lord will judge his people." [31]It is a fearful thing to fall into the hands of the living God.

"Iudicabit Dominus populum suum." [31]Horrendum est incidere in manus Dei viventis. [32]Rememoramini autem pristinos dies, in quibus illuminati magnum

---

sacrifice can help people in that position, because they have deliberately and explicitly rejected Redemption. All they can look forward to is condemnation when God comes to judge them, and punishment by fire (cf. the fate of Korah, Dathan and Abiram: Num 16:16-35). Punishment by fire is also something often proclaimed by the prophets as a part of divine justice on the day of Yahweh (cf. Is 66:24). The fire referred to here has to do not only with God's fury but with eternal torment (cf. Mk 9:47-49; Rev 11:5).

To emphasize the gravity of the sin of apostasy, which outrages the Holy Spirit, profanes the redeeming sacrifice of Christ and shows contempt for the very Son of God, the epistle recalls that under the Law of Moses, there were certain sins which on the evidence of two or three witnesses (cf. Deut 19:15-21), merited capital punishment. This was the case, for example, with fully conscious deliberate and scandalous sins (cf. Num 15:30-31), blasphemy (Lev 24:13-16), adultery, incest, sodomy, bestiality, murder, idolatry and prophecy in the name of other gods. If sinners who committed such sins did not deserve "remission", obstinate apostates deserve it less.

Some commentators see this passage as also saying that there cannot be second baptism, contrary to the position taken by certain heretics.

31. This verse rounds off an entire passage designed to inspire horror of deliberate grave sin and to encourage Christians to have a holy fear of God. This fear includes, firstly, fear of eternal punishment and a sense of shame at the moral ugliness of sin, which are characteristics of attrition. But it can also include other dispositions which are proper to contrition, to the extent that one's fear is motivated by a sense of the outrage done to Christ, who suffered out of love for us; in which case love and fear are linked; in fact, the right kind of fear is filial fear, that of someone who is afraid of offending his father. Sorrow for having offended our heavenly Father is one of the key features of the Law of Christ.

"There are two motives which lead a person to do good and avoid evil. The first is fear. The motive that first leads a person to avoid sin is the thought of the pains of hell and the Last Judgment [. . .]. It is true that a person who refrains from sinning simply out of fear is not just; but that is where his justification begins. That is how the Law of Moses works to draw people away from sin and lead them to do good [. . .]. But this method, the method of fear, is inadequate; the Law promulgated by Moses was inadequate: it relied on that kind of fear to frustrate sin; although it did discourage a person from actually committing sin, it failed to purify his intentions. There is, however, another way to draw people away from sin and encourage them to act rightly—the way of love. That

³²But recall the former days when, after you were enlightened, you endured a hard struggle with sufferings, ³³sometimes being publicly exposed to abuse and affliction, and sometimes being partners with those so treated. ³⁴For you had compassion on the prisoners, and you joyfully

Heb 6:4
Eph 5:14

1 Cor 4:9
Phil 4:14

Heb 13:3
Mt 5:40; 6:20

certamen sustinuistis passionum, ³³in altero quidem opprobriis et tribulationibus spectaculum facti, in altero autem socii taliter conversantium effecti; ³⁴nam et vinctis compassi estis et rapinam bonorum vestrorum cum gaudio suscepistis, cognoscentes vos habere meliorem substantiam et manentem.

is the way followed by the Law of Christ, that is, the law of the Gospel, which is the law of love" (St Thomas Aquinas, *On the two commandments*, I).

"'*Timor Domini sanctus*. The fear of God is holy.' Fear which is the veneration of a son for his Father; never a servile fear, for your Father-God is not a tyrant" (Blessed J. Escrivá, *The Way*, 435).

32-34. A Christian is called to share the persecution which Christ suffered. "A disciple is not above his teacher", our Lord said (cf. Mt 10:22-25; Lk 12:11-12; Jn 15:18); anyone who wanted to follow him would have to carry his cross (cf. Mt 10:38; 16:24; Mk 8:34; Lk 9:23; 14:27). These words of our Lord have always been borne out in practice. In the Acts of the Apostles we are told of how the Sanhedrin persecuted the Apostles, and of how certain Jews acted against Stephen, and Herod against James and Peter, etc. The early Christians bore these afflictions bravely and even availed of them to spread the faith—first to Samaria, then to Antioch, and later throughout the whole Roman empire. The text here speaks of their courage. It may be thinking of the severe persecution instituted by Nero after the burning of Rome. Given these circumstances, the addressees, and Christians in general, need to keep their baptismal faith, their "enlightenment", intact: they should be mindful of "the former days" and copy those who compete and fight in public not minding that they are making a "public exhibition" of themselves (cf. 1 Cor 4:9).

Undoubtedly the persecution suffered by Christians who were converted from Judaism was severe. They were subject to "abuse" and "affliction", words which point to affronts, insults, ridicule, and treatment typical of religious persecution—confiscation of property, imprisonment and even flogging and other forms of punishment. Our early brethren in the faith not only bore these afflictions but also showed their solidarity and charity by generously sharing the suffering of those who were thrown in gaol.

And yet even these persecutions had very good effects (cf. 1 Pet 1:6-9; Jas 1:3-4), in that they helped the people concerned to be detached from material things and place their hope in divine rewards. In the same type of way, every Christian needs to face up to the difficulties and contradictions he experiences in life.

"Are things going against you? Are you going through a rough time? Say very slowly, as if relishing it, this powerful and manly prayer: 'May the most

accepted the plundering of your property, since you knew that you yourselves had a better possession and an abiding one. ³⁵Therefore do not throw away your confidence, which has a great reward. ³⁶For you have need of endurance, so that you may do the will of God and receive what is promised.

Heb 11:6
Is 26:20, LXX

Jn 14:19
Hab 2:3
Jas 5:8
Hab 2:4
Rom 1:17

1 Pet 1:9
1 Tim 6:9
1 Thess 5:9

³⁷"For yet a little while, and the coming one shall come and shall not tarry;
³⁸but my righteous one shall live by faith,
and if he shrinks back,
my soul has no pleasure in him."
³⁹But we are not of those who shrink back and are destroyed, but of those who have faith and keep their souls.

³⁵Nolite itaque abicere confidentiam vestram, quae magnam habet remunerationem; ³⁶patientia enim vobis necessaria est, ut voluntatem Dei facientes reportetis promissionem. ³⁷Adhuc enim *modicum quantulum, qui venturus est, veniet et non tardabit.* ³⁸*Iustus autem meus ex fide vivet;* quod *si subtraxerit se, non sibi complacet in eo anima mea.* ³⁹Nos autem non sumus subtractionis in perditionem, sed fidei in acquisitionem animae.

just and lovable will of God be done, be fulfilled, be praised and eternally exalted above all things. Amen. Amen.' I assure you that you will find peace" (*The Way*, 691).

35-39. The "confidence" mentioned in v. 35 is a translation of a Greek word which refers to the ease and trusting frankness with which a person addresses a good friend or God.

The sacred writer renews his call to endurance in the face of persecution. St John Chrysostom compares the situation of the Christians addressed in this letter with that of an athlete who has won a competition and is now simply waiting for the president of the games to award him the laurels. "From now on there is no further combat; all you must do is hold on to the merit you have won, and you will not lose your reward [. . .]. No further combat is called for: all that is necessary is perseverance. Just hold out and you will gain your laurels; you have already suffered all you need to obtain them—contentions, chains, pain, loss of property. What more could you have done? All that remains for you to do is wait patiently for the prize to be given you. If there is a delay, it will only be for a short while" (*Hom. on Heb, ad loc.*).

Here, as St Thomas comments, endurance refers to two things—the strength that enables one to stay loyal despite persecution, and the assurance of one who is confident of obtaining certain things he does not yet possess. The letter's exhortation to endurance is supported by two quotations from Sacred Scripture. The first, from Isaiah 26:20, is a reminder that God will soon judge the impious; the second from Habakkuk 2:3-4 (also quoted by St Paul in Rom 1:17; Gal

11

The good example of the Patriarchs

Heb 3:14
Rom 1:16; 8:24

¹Now faith is the assurance of things hoped for, the con-

---

¹Est autem fides sperandorum substantia, rerum argumentum non apparentium.

3:11), announces the coming liberation of the people of Israel. The sacred text accurately prophesied that those Jews who remained faithful to God would be released from captivity in Babylon and survive the experience. Moved by the Holy Spirit, the present writer states that the ancient prophecy has been fulfilled in Christ; he is "the coming one", that is, he will come a second time. Therefore, the Christian should await the outcome of persecution loyally and cheerfully. "Stand your ground like an anvil under the hammer. The mark of a true champion is to stand up to punishment and still come out victorious. It is our duty, particularly when the cause is God's, to accept trials of all kinds, if we ourselves are to be accepted by him" (St Ignatius of Antioch, *Letter to Polycarp*, III, 1).

1. Although the text does not aim to provide a precise definition of faith, it does in fact very clearly describe the essence of that virtue, linking it to hope in future things and to certainty concerning supernatural truths. By means of faith, the believer acquires certainty concerning God's promises to man, and a firm conviction that he will obtain access to heaven. The Latin translates as "*substantia*" the word the RSV translates as "assurance"; *substantia*, which literally means "that which underlies", here refers to the solid basis provided by hope.

This verse indicates that faith, which is a type of knowledge, is different from other types of human knowledge. Thus, man can know things by direct evidence, by reasoned proof or by someone else's testimony. As regards knowledge based on information provided by someone else, that is, knowledge based on faith, we can distinguish two types—human faith, when it is another human being whose word one relies on (as in the case of pupil/teacher, child/parent), and supernatural faith (when the testimony comes from God himself, who is Supreme Truth). In this latter case the knowledge provided is most certain.

However, the object of supernatural faith, that is, *what* one believes in (God and the unchanging decrees of his will), is not something that is self-evident to man, nor is it something that can be attained by the use of unaided reason. That is why it is necessary for God himself to bear witness to what he reveals. Faith, then, is certain knowledge, but it is knowledge of things which are not self-evident, things which one does not see but which one can hope for.

The verse also says that faith is "conviction" concerning things not seen. It is therefore different from opinion, suspicion or doubt (none of which implies certainty). By saying that it has to do with things unseen, it is distinguishing faith from knowledge and intuitive cognition (cf. *Summa theologiae*, II-II, q. 4, a. 1).

Summing up, we can say that "when God makes a revelation, we are obliged to render by faith a full submission of intellect and will. The faith, however, which is the beginning of human salvation, the Catholic Church asserts to be a supernatural virtue whereby, with the inspiration and help of God's grace, we believe that what he has revealed is true—not because its intrinsic truth is seen by the natural light of reason, but because of the authority of God who reveals it, of God who can neither deceive nor be deceived" (Vatican I, *Dei Filius*, chap. 3).

It is, therefore, a feature of faith that it makes us *certain* about things which are not self-evident. That is why in order to believe one must want to believe, why the act of believing is always free and meritorious. However, faith can, with God's help, reach a certainty greater than any proof can provide. "This faith", St John of Avila comments, "is not based on reasons [. . .]; for when a person believes on the basis of reasons, he is not believing in such a way that he is totally convinced, without any doubt or scruple whatever. But the faith which God infuses is grounded on divine Truth, and it causes one to believe more firmly than if one saw it with one's own eyes, and touched it with one's hands—and to believe more certainly than he who believes that four is greater than three, the sort of thing that is so obvious that the mind never hesitates a moment, nor can it even if it wants to" (*Audi, Filia*, chap. 43).

The faith which God gives a person—supernatural faith—is necessarily the point of departure for hope and charity: it is what is usually called "living faith".

When one lives with this kind of faith it is easy to see that the three "theological" virtues (faith, hope and charity) are bound up with one another. Faith and hope lead a person to unite himself to God as the source from which all good things flow; charity unites us to God directly, by loving affection, because God is the supreme Good. Faith is as it were the first step: it means accepting what God says as true. We then unite ourselves to him through hope, insofar as we rely on God's help to attain beatitude. The goal of this process is charity, the fulness of which is eternal possession of God, the Supreme Good. "Let us grow in hope, thereby strengthening our faith which is truly 'the assurance of things hoped for, the conviction of things not seen' (Heb 11:1). Let us grow in this virtue, let us beg our Lord to increase his charity in us; after all, one can only really trust what one loves with all one's might. And it is certainly worthwhile to love our Lord" (Bl. J. Escrivá, *Friends of God*, 220).

If hope in general is the conviction of being able to obtain something worthwhile in the future, something difficult to obtain, theological hope is the conviction of being able, with the help of God, to attain heaven. And faith is precisely what provides certain knowledge of those two truths—that heaven is our goal and that God wants to help us to get there (cf. *Summa theologiae*, II-II, q.17, a. 5 and 7). Therefore, nothing should dishearten us on this road to our ultimate goal because we put our trust in "three truths: God is all-powerful, God has a boundless love for me, God is faithful to his promises. And it is he, the

viction of things not seen. [2]For by it the men of old received
divine approval. [3]By faith we understand that the world was
created by the word of God, so that what is seen was made
out of things which do not appear.

    [4]By faith Abel offered to God a more acceptable sacrifice

Gen 1
Rom 1:20

Gen 4:4, 10
Mt 23:35

---

[2]In hac enim testimonium consecuti sunt seniores. [3]Fide intellegimus aptata
esse saecula verbo Dei, ut ex invisibilibus visibilia facta sint. [4]Fide ampliorem

---

God of mercies, who enkindles this trust within me, so that I never feel lonely
or useless or abandoned but, rather, involved in a plan of salvation which will
one day reach its goal in Paradise" (John Paul I, *Address*, 20 September 1978).

3. The creation of the world from nothing is one of the first articles of faith.
The text is reminiscent in a way of v. 1, in that faith gives conviction about
things we cannot see; that is how we know the origin of all created things and
discover God from things we can see.

Essentially the text is emphasizing the importance of belief in God as Creator
and in Creation as coming from nothing. This is a truth found in all the creeds
and it has been often defined by the Church Magisterium (cf., for example,
Lateran IV and Vatican I). "We believe in one God, the Father, the Son and the
Holy Spirit, Creator of what is visible—such as this world where we live out
our lives—and of the invisible—such as the pure spirits which are also called
angels" (Paul VI, *Creed of the People of God*, 8).

4. The Book of Genesis (4:3-5) tells of the offerings made to Yahweh by
Cain and Abel, the sons of Adam and Eve. God was pleased with Abel's
offering but not with Cain's. God said to Cain, "Why are you angry, and why
has your countenance fallen? If you do well, will you not be accepted? And if
you do not do well, sin is couching at the door ready to waylay you" (Gen
4:6-7). Many Jewish commentators saw this as meaning that Cain's sin may
have been one of meanness because he did not offer the best of his crop.
Additionally there would have been a sin of envy towards Abel (Wisdom 10:3
speaks of Cain's evil and his fratricidal hatred). In contrast to Cain, the
prototype of the envious, selfish, violent and fratricidal man, Jewish literature
extolled Abel as an example of generosity, uprightness and piety.

Against this background of Jewish religious thought come the words of Jesus
(Mt 23:25) and St John (1 Jn 3:12) who describe Abel as "righteous", that is
holy and devout. The Hebrews text stresses that what made Abel's offering the
better one was his faith, commitment to God and generosity. That was why God
bore witness to his righteousness by accepting the victims he offered and
perhaps—according to an ancient oral Jewish tradition—sending fire down
upon them to burn them. For God "looked more to the offerer than to what he
offered, because the acceptability of an oblation is determined by the
righteousness of the offerer, in cases other than of a sacrament," as St Thomas

Gen 5:24
Sir 44:16
Wis 4:10

than Cain, through which he received approval as righteous, God bearing witness by accepting his gifts; he died, but through his faith he is still speaking. ⁵By faith Enoch was taken up so that he should not see death; and he was not found, because God had taken him. Now before he was

---

hostiam Abel quam Cain obtulit Deo, per quam testimonium consecutus est esse iustus, testimonium perhibente muneribus eius Deo, et per illam defunctus adhuc loquitur. ⁵Fide Enoch translatus est ne videret mortem, et *non*

Aquinas says (*Commentary on Heb, ad loc.*). The text says literally that "God himself bore witness to his offerings", as if to imply that he "came down" or that he "sent down fire" to consume them (cf. the famous oblation of Elijah in 1 Kings 18:38; that of Moses and Aaron in Leviticus 9:24; and that of Gideon in Judges 6:21).

"He died, but through his faith he is still speaking": this is reminiscent of the passage in Genesis where God tells Cain that "the voice of your brother's blood is crying to me from the ground" (Gen 4:10). Abel is God's witness, his "martyr", because he confesses God's greatness by his faith, sacrifice and generosity. "By leading others towards virtue, Abel proves to be an eloquent speaker. Any words must be less effective than (the example of) this martyr dom. So, just as heaven speaks to us by simply revealing itself to us, this great saint exhorts us simply by impinging on our memory" (*Hom. on Heb*, 22).

It is comforting to know that the first example of faith in God was given by the son of Adam and Eve, and that it took the form of a sacrifice. It is understandable therefore that Fathers have, in fact, seen Abel as a figure of Christ: he was a shepherd, he offered an oblation pleasing to God, he shed his blood, and was therefore a "martyr for the faith".

When renewing Christ's sacrifice, the Liturgy asks God to look with favour on the offerings and accept them as once he accepted the gifts of his "servant Abel" (cf. *Roman Missal*, Eucharistic Prayer I).

5. There was also quite an amount of Jewish tradition about Enoch, one of the Patriarchs from the pre- Flood period; this stemmed from the fact that the Book of Genesis, instead of rounding off mention of him with the usual words "and he died" (as is the case with the other patriarchs), says that he "walked with Elohim, and he was not, for God took him" (cf. Gen 5:21-24). This led people to think that Enoch did not die and that therefore he was in the presence of God preparing the way for the Messiah who would set man free: that is, he must be one of the Messiah's precursors, like Elijah, of whose death also there is no mention. The Greek translation of the Old Testament (the Septuagint) elaborates a little on the Hebrew text of Genesis 5:23: it says, "Enoch walked with God; and he was not, for the Lord took him", and the RSV Genesis passage reflects this. It might also be pointed out that the Book of Sirach mentions Enoch with great respect, proposing him as an example to all generations; it says that

taken he was attested as having pleased God. ⁶And without faith it is impossible to please him. For whoever would draw near to God must believe that he exists and that he

Heb 7:25; 10:35
Ex 3:14

inveniebatur, quia transtulit illum Deus; ante translationem enim testimonium accepit *placuisse Deo*. ⁶Sine fide autem impossibile placere; credere enim

"Enoch pleased the Lord, and was taken up" (Sir 44:16), and elsewhere it adds that "no one like Enoch has been created on earth" (Sir 49:14). In apocryphal Jewish writing Enoch came to assume great importance: he was attributed great power as an astrologer and described as engaging in a series of fantastic exploits to prepare the way for the Messiah. It therefore became widely believed that Enoch would return to the world prior to the coming of the Anointed.

The Epistle to the Hebrews uses the Sirach texts and the Greek version of Genesis as its ground for stating that Enoch "was attested as having pleased God", and therefore it proposes Enoch as an example of faith.

The sentence "Enoch was taken up so that he should not see death" is not just referring to his being an upright man: it connects him with the coming of the Messiah and with the end of the world. The text is not saying or denying that Enoch died, but simply that he was "taken up". In view of the fact that it is decreed that all men should die (cf. Heb 9:27), for death is a consequence of original sin (cf. Rom 5:12), most probably the words "was taken up" should be seen as a reference to death, and the following words, "so that he should not see death," should be taken either in a moral sense—that is, "not experience the spiritual death of sin "—or else as meaning that he arose immediately after our Lord's death, as happened in the case of some saints (cf. Mt 27:52-53).

6. Faith is a virtue which is necessary for salvation, but faith alone is insufficient; it must be "faith working through love" (Gal 5:6). However, faith is of decisive importance because it is "the beginning of man's salvation" (St Fulgentius, *De fide ad Petrum*, 1) and because it is "the foundation and source of all justification" (Council of Trent, *De iustificatione*, chap. 8); we are referring not only to faith in the sense of a personal act—the act of faith—but also to faith in the sense of a body of truths which one holds as certain. Thus, theology says that two things are necessary—the faith by which one believes (the attitude of the believer) and the truths of faith which have to be believed (articles of faith). The verse speaks of both, but it dwells mainly on the second—the content or "object" of faith—whereas earlier (11:1) it looked more at the importance of the act as such. No one can please God unless he draws near him; but it is not possible to do that without faith; therefore no one can please God unless he has faith. God himself moves us and helps us to approach him, but man needs to respond freely to God's action; it is by the act of faith that he does so: faith is that disposition of soul "by which we yield our unhesitating assent to whatever the authority of our Holy Mother the Church teaches us has been revealed by God; for the faithful cannot doubt those things of which God, who is truth itself, is the author" (*St Pius V Catechism*, I, 1, 1).

That is why, among truths of faith, we distinguish those which are accessible to human reason and those which man could never come to know on his own; the latter are called "mysteries". The former can be reduced to three—the existence of God, the immortality of the soul, and the existence of a moral order established by God.

It is clear that if one does not believe in the existence of God and in the moral order established by him there is no possibility of salvation. What does the passage mean when it says that "whoever would draw near to God must believe that he exists and that he rewards those who seek him"? We might reply, with St Thomas, that, after original sin, no one can be saved unless he have faith in the promised mediator (Gen 3:15). For pagans, who have received no revelation, it was and is sufficient to believe that God rewards good and punishes evil (cf. *Commentary on Heb, ad loc.*).

The words of the sacred writer also pose another problem: how can those be saved who do not know Christ? The first thing to bear in mind is the absolute necessity of true and upright faith. Man has an obligation to seek truth, particularly religious truth, and he must not content himself with just any religion, as if all religions were more or less equal (cf. Pius IX, *Syllabus of Errors*, 15 and 16). That is why adult pagans who request Baptism when they are in danger of death or in a situation of dire need must be given before Baptism a short instruction (adapted to the situation and to their intellectual capacity) on the main mysteries of faith—the Trinity and the Incarnation (cf. *Reply of the Holy Office*, 26 January 1703).

All this, however, does not mean that people who are not Christians cannot be saved. What it means, Vatican II teaches, is that "they could not be saved who, knowing that the Catholic Church was founded as necessary by God through Christ, would refuse either to enter it, or to remain in it" (*Lumen gentium*, 14). "Those who, through no fault of their own, do not know the Gospel of Christ or his Church, but who nevertheless seek God with a sincere heart, and, moved by grace, try in their actions to do his will as they know it through the dictates of their conscience—those too may achieve eternal salvation. Nor shall divine providence deny the assistance necessary for salvation to those who, without any fault of theirs, have not yet arrived at an explicit knowlege of God, and who, not without grace, strive to lead a good life" (*Lumen gentium*, 16).

Therefore, when in its apostolic and missionary work, the catholic Church encounters other religions, it "rejects nothing of what is true and holy in these religions. It has a high regard for the manner of life and conduct, the precepts and doctrines which, although differing in many ways from its own teaching, nevertheless often reflect a ray of that truth which enlightens all men. Yet it proclaims, and is in duty bound to proclaim without fail, Christ who is the way, the truth and the life (Jn 14:6). In him, in whom God reconciled all things to himself (cf. 2 Cor 5:18-19), men find the fulness of their religious life" (Vatican II, *Nostra aetate*, 2). In the last analysis, "although in many ways known to himself God can lead those who, through no fault of their own, are ignorant of

160

rewards those who seek him. ⁷By faith Noah, being warned by God concerning events as yet unseen, took heed and constructed an ark for the saving of his household; by this he condemned the world and became an heir of the right-eousness which comes by faith.

Gen 6:8ff
Heb 7:1
Rom 3:22
2 Pet 2:5
1 Pet 3:20

⁸By faith Abraham obeyed when he was called to go out

Gen 12:1, 4

---

oportet accedentem ad Deum quia est et inquirentibus se remunerator fit. ⁷Fide Noe responso accepto de his, quae adhuc non videbantur, reveritus aptavit arcam in salutem domus suae; per quam damnavit mundum, et iustitiae, quae secundum fidem est, heres est institutus. ⁸Fide vocatus Abraham oboedivit in

---

the Gospel to that faith without which it is impossible to please him (Heb 11:6), the Church, nevertheless, still has the obligation (cf. 1 Cor 9:16) and also the sacred right to evangelize. And so, today as always, missionary activity retains its full force and necessity" (Vatican II, *Ad gentes*, 7).

Similarly every Christian should always desire to seek God and have others seek him also. "If there is someone who is going to reward us, let us do everything possible not to lose the reward that is given to virtue [. . .]. But, how can one find the Lord? Think of how gold is found—by much effort and trouble [. . .]. So, we must seek God in the same way as we look for something we have lost. Is it not true that we rack our brains? Don't we look everywhere? Don't we look in out of the way places? Don't we spend money searching? If, for example, we have lost a child, what will we not do? What regions, what seas, will we not cross? How much more in the case of God, given that those who seek him have such need of him!" (St John Chrysostom, *Hom. on Heb*, 22).

7. When Noah received God's order to build the ark (cf. Gen 6-9; Mt 24:37-39; 1 Pet 3:20; 2 Pet 2:5), there was as yet no sign of a flood; in other words, he had to rely totally on God's word. He took heed, he acted "*reveritus*", with religious fear, that is, with a deeply religious attachment to God, an attitude which led him to obey very exactly what God told him to do.

Noah's faith "condemned the world" because the worldly and unbelieving men of his time jeered at him when he was making the ark. "What do these words mean—'by this he condemned the world'? They mean that he showed up the world as deserving of punishment, because even though they saw him building (the ark) they did not mend their ways or repent" (*Hom. on Heb*, 23, 1). By acting in line with his faith Noah condemns, in spite of himself, the incredulity of his contemporaries. Today also the life of a person of faith can be a reproach to those around him, but that should not lead him to act any differently.

8. Abraham, "our father in faith", is the greatest example, in the Old Testament, of faith in God (cf. Gen 12:1-4; Rom 4:1ff; Gal 3:6-9; Heb 6:13ff).

Gen 23:4; 26:3;
35:12

Rev 21:10-22

to a place which he was to receive as an inheritance and he went out, not knowing where he was to go. ⁹By faith he sojourned in the land of promise, as in a foreign land, living in tents with Isaac and Jacob, heirs with him of the same promise. ¹⁰For he looked forward to the city which has

---

locum exire, quem accepturus erat in hereditatem, et exivit nesciens quo iret. ⁹Fide peregrinatus est in terra promissionis tamquam in aliena in casulis

---

It is not surprising that the author pauses to dwell on the faithful life of the father of the chosen people. Putting all his trust in the divine word, Abraham gave up all the security and comfort of his native land in Ur of the Chaldeans, to set out for a distant and unknown place, the land of Canaan, which God had promised to give his descendants. "Neither the love for his homeland nor the pleasure of his neighbours' company nor the comforts of his father's home were able to weaken his resolve. He set out courageously and ardently to where God willed to lead him. What self-abasement and abandonment! One cannot love God perfectly unless one renounces all attachment to perishable things" (St Francis de Sales, *Treatise on the Love of God*, book 10). Abraham symbolizes the need for detachment if one is to obtain redemption and to be a good servant of God and of others.

"Never forget that Christ cannot be reached without sacrifice. You have to get rid of everything that gets in the way [. . .]. You have to do the same in this battle for the glory of God, in this struggle of love and peace by which we are trying to spread Christ's kingdom. In order to serve the Church, the Pope and all souls, you must be ready to give up everything superfluous" (Blessed J. Escrivá, *Friends of God*, 196).

9-10. Abraham, and his son Isaac and grandson Jacob like him, far from settling down comfortably in a permanent place, lived a nomadic existence, a stranger in a foreign land (cf. Gen 23:4). By faith the patriarch "looked forward to the city which has foundations", the city God would build. Instead of the provisionality of tents and the weak foundations of cities built by men, a heavenly city was being established, eternal and permanent, built by God on solid foundations, which Abraham hoped one day to possess. The promised land was a symbol of the definitive fatherland to which God called the father of Israel. There was even a late Jewish tradition which spoke of Abraham being given a vision of the heavenly Jerusalem after he ratified his covenant with God.

Christians live in the world by the will of God, and they love the world, but at the same time they realize they should not settle down in it as if it were the final goal of their lives. "They are residents at home in their own country but their behaviour is more like that of people who are passing through [. . .]. For them any foreign country is a homeland, and any homeland a foreign country" (*Letter to Diognetus*, V, 5).

162

foundations, whose builder and maker is God. [11]By faith Sarah herself received power to conceive, even when she was past the age, since she considered him faithful who had promised. [12]Therefore from one man, and him as good as dead, were born descendants as many as the stars of heaven and as the innumerable grains of sand by the seashore.

[13]These all died in faith, not having received what was

Gen 17:19; 21:2
Rom 4:19-21
Gen 22:17;
32:13
Dan 3:36, LXX
Ex 32:13

Jn 8:56
Gen 23:4
1 Chron 29:15

---

habitando cum Isaac et Iacob, coheredibus promissionis eiusdem; [10]exspectabat enim fundamenta habentem civitatem, cuius artifex et conditor Deus. [11]Fide— et ipsa Sara sterilis—virtutem in conceptionem seminis accepit etiam praeter tempus aetatis, quoniam fidelem credidit esse, qui promiserat; [12]propter quod et ab uno orti sunt, et hoc emortuo, *tamquam sidera caeli* in multitudine *et sicut arena, quae est ad oram maris innumerabilis*. [13]Iuxta fidem defuncti sunt omnes isti, non acceptis promissionibus, sed a longe eas aspicientes et salu- tantes, et confitentes quia peregrini et hospites sunt supra terram; [14]qui enim

---

11-12. Sarah, like Abraham, was very elderly when God announced that she was going to have a child. At first she was puzzled and even sarcastically sceptical (cf. Gen 18:9f), but soon her attitude changed into a faith which God rewarded by her conceiving Isaac. The faith of Sarah and her husband can be said to exceed that of the earlier patriarchs because what God promised could come true only by means of a miracle, since Abraham, like his wife, was old and incapable of begetting children. That is why it says that from one man "and him as good as dead" innumerable descendants were born. God is generous in rewarding man's faith. "'*Si habueritis fidem, sicut granum sinapis!*—If your faith were the size of a mustard seed! . . .'

"What promises are contained in this exclamation of the Master!" (Blessed J. Escrivá, *The Way*, 585).

The conception of Isaac is also a "type" of that of Christ. "All the miraculous conceptions which occurred in the Old Testament were prefigurements of the greatest of all miracles, the Incarnation of the Word. It was fitting that his birth from a Virgin should be prefigured by other births so as to prepare people's minds for faith. But there is this difference: God miraculously enabled Sarah to conceive by means of human seed, whereas the blessed Virgin conceived without it" (St Thomas Aquinas, *Commentary on Heb*, 11, 3).

13-16. After speaking about the faith of Abel, Noah and Abraham, the sacred writer goes on to give a brief panoramic account of the entire history of the Patriarchs and the Exodus. It does not deal with events in chronological order. By recalling that the Patriarchs left their own country to journey abroad "seeking a homeland", he brings in the exodus from Egypt. Between Abraham, who left Ur to travel to the land of Canaan, and the people of Israel, who left Egypt for the promised land, there is an obvious parallel, which is even more marked if one bears in mind that neither Abraham nor the Israelites led by

163

Ps 39:13
1 Pet 1:1; 2:11 promised, but having seen it and greeted it from afar, and having acknowledged that they were strangers and exiles on the earth. ¹⁴For people who speak thus make it clear that they are seeking a homeland. ¹⁵If they had been thinking of Ex 3:6
Rev 21:2
Mt 23:32 that land from which they had gone out, they would have had opportunity to return. ¹⁶But as it is, they desire a better

---

haec dicunt, significant se patriam inquirere. ¹⁵Et siquidem illius meminissent, de qua exierant, habebant utique tempus revertendi; ¹⁶nunc autem meliorem

---

Moses were destined to take possession of the land: that was reserved to their descendants. The only thing Abraham managed to do was to purchase the cave of Machpelah, near Hebron, and the land immmediately around it, for which he had to pay a very high price in silver. The cave became the burial ground of Sarah, Abraham himself, Isaac, Rebecca, Jacob and Leah. But Abraham publicly admitted he was "a stranger and a sojourner" in Canaan when he bought the cave from the Hittites (Gen 23:4). Nor did the Hebrews of Moses' generation manage to enter Canaan. The nearest they got to it was descriptions brought by their spies; and Moses himself was only able to view it from a distance, from Mount Nebo, just prior to his death (cf. Deut 32:49-52; 33:1-4). Abraham, and later Isaac and Jacob (who led a nomadic existence in Canaan), like the Israelites in the wilderness, prefigure Christians, who are also in search of a land of their own, a better homeland, that is, heaven (cf. Heb 13:14). It certainly is moving to recall the Patriarchs and the Exodus, and very helpful to the faith and hope of Christians amid the difficulties they encounter in this world. Those men of faith are said to have "seen" what was promised: this may be a reference to some special grace God gave them, as was the case with Abraham (cf. Jn 8:56), or else to the intuitive vision of supernatural things which faith provides (cf. *Commentary on Heb, ad loc.*). "They greeted it from afar," happy to do so. "They greeted the promises and rejoiced," St John Chrysostom says, "for they already had such faith in those promises that they could make signs of greeting. This comparison is taken from seafaring: when from afar sailors espy the city they are making for, even before entering the port they cheer in greeting" (*Hom. on Heb*, 23).

The Patriarchs' attitude was a true indication of their faith in a future life, for, as St Thomas points out, by describing themselves as strangers and sojourners (Gen 23:4; 47:9; cf. Deut 26:5) they showed they were heading towards their homeland, the heavenly Jerusalem. They did not set their hearts on an earthly homeland, or on their parental homestead, for if so they could in fact have chosen to return to it (cf. *Commentary on Heb, ad loc.*). Thus the promises made to them found their fulfilment not in something earthly but in the eternity of heaven: "Therefore God is not ashamed" to be called the God of Abraham and Isaac and Jacob: seeing their faith and fidelity, he overlooked their sins and faults. And he is disposed to act in the same way towards Christians.

country, that is, a heavenly one. Therefore God is not ashamed to be called their God, for he has prepared for them a city.

¹⁷By faith Abraham, when he was tested, offered up Isaac, and he who had received the promises was ready to offer up his only son, ¹⁸of whom it was said, "Through Isaac

Gen 22
Jas 2:21
Sir 44:20

Gen 21:12, LXX
Rom 9:7

---

appetunt, id est caelestem. Ideo non confunditur Deus vocari Deus eorum, paravit enim illis civitatem. ¹⁷Fide obtulit Abraham Isaac, cum tentaretur, et unigenitum offerebat ille, qui susceperat promissiones, ¹⁸ad quem dictum erat:

In vv. 14 and 16, in the Greek text and the New Vulgate—and in the RSV—the verbs are in the present tense, as distinct from the past (aorist) used generally in this passage. This is because the whole paragraph is recalling the life of the Patriarchs, but with the intention of stressing that their faith is an example to all generations. What we have here is a mixture of history and sapiential writing, using verbs which indicate that the action—or at least some of its effects—is still going on.

17-19. It is very difficult for us to imagine what Abraham thought when God asked him to sacrifice Isaac, the son of the promise, his only son, in the mountains of Moriah (cf. Gen 22:2). The Old Testament shows how resolute Abraham was, his absolute docility, his serenity even in the midst of suffering, his trust in God (cf. Gen 22:1-18). This is revealed in the touching conversation between the Patriarch and his son, when Isaac asks him where is the lamb for the offering and Abraham replies, "God will provide himself with the lamb for a burnt offering, my son". In St Paul's epistles generally Abraham's faith is proposed as an example (cf. Gal 3:7; Rom 4:3, 11-12; 4:17-22); but that was in the context of his faith in God's promise that he would have a multitude of descendants. Here, however, the Patriarch's faith is to be seen in the way he approaches a commandment which seems to negate that promise: how could God possibly ask him to sacrifice his only son? The answer lies in the fact that God knew that Abraham had faith in his ability to bring the dead back to life.

Abraham's obedience to God in this episode is the most striking proof of his faith. Here most of all the Patriarch "believed against hope [. . .]; he grew strong in his faith as he gave glory to God" (Rom 4:18, 21). "The Patriarch hears words which deny the promise; he hears the very author of the promise contradict himself, but he is not dismayed; he is going to obey as if everything were completely consistent. And in fact the two things were compatible: the two things God said were contradictory as far as human logic was concerned; but faith brought them into agreement [. . .].

"God tested Abraham's faith. Did he not know the strength and integrity of that great man? Undoubtedly he did, very well. Why, then, did he put them to the test? He did not do it to prove to himself the Patriarch's virtue; he did it to show the world how excellent Abraham was. The Apostle, moreover, shows

165

Rom 4:17

Gen 27:27-29, 39f

shall your descendants be named." [19]He considered that God was able to raise men even from the dead; hence he did receive him back, and this was a symbol. [20]By faith

---

"*In Isaac vocabitur tibi semen*", [19]arbitratus quia et a mortuis suscitare potens est Deus; unde eum et in parabola reportavit. [20]Fide et de futuris benedixit Isaac

---

the Hebrews one of the causes of our temptations, so that anyone who is afflicted should not think that God has abandoned him" (*Hom. on Heb*, 25). We know, moreover, that precisely on account of Abraham's generosity and faith, God renewed his promise to him, now ratifying it with an oath (cf. Gen 22:16; Heb 6:13-18).

19. "Hence he did receive him back, and this was a symbol": after offering Isaac, Abraham was given him back, because God stepped in before Isaac was sacrificed (Gen 22:11-12). And he received him as "a symbol" (literally, as "a parable"). Tradition has always seen the sacrifice of Isaac, the only Son, as a symbol of the redemptive sacrifice of Christ; and, particularly, it has seen God's intervention on Mount Moriah as a symbol of the Resurrection. "He saw it as a symbol," Theodoret comments, "that is, as a prefigurement of the Resurrection. (Isaac) was brought to death by his father's will, and then brought back to life by the voice which prevented his death. All this amounts to a prefiguring of the passion of the Saviour, and that is why the Lord told the Jews, 'Your father Abraham rejoiced that he was to see my day; he saw it and was glad' (Jn 8:56)" (*Interpretatio Ep. ad Haebreos, ad loc.*).

Origen, a writer of Christian antiquity, reflects this tradition very beautifully when he says that the sacrifice of Isaac helps us to understand the mystery of Redemption. "Isaac carrying the wood for the burnt offering is a symbol of Christ, who carried his (own) cross. But it is also the function of the priest to carry the wood for the burnt offering [. . .]. Christ is the Word of God, but the Word made flesh. Therefore, there is in Christ an element which comes from above and another which comes from human nature, which he took on in the womb of the Virgin. This is why Christ experiences suffering: he suffers in the flesh, and he dies, but what suffers death is the flesh, and the ram is a figure of this, as St John said, 'Behold the Lamb of God, who takes away the sin of the world' (Jn 1:29) [. . .]. Christ is at one and the same time victim and high priest. Thus, according to the spirit he offers the victim to his father; according to his flesh, he himself is offered on the altar of the cross" (*Homilies on Genesis*, 8, 6 and 9).

For all these reasons, Eucharistic Prayer I links Christ's sacrifice with those of Abel, Isaac and Melchizedek.

20. Prompted by his mother Rebecca, Jacob disguised himself as Esau and managed to obtain from Isaac the blessing that belonged to the latter as first-born; as a result the promises made to Abraham passed to Jacob (cf. Gen

Isaac invoked future blessings on Jacob and Esau. [21]By Gen 47:31, LXX;
faith Jacob, when dying, blessed each of the sons of Joseph, 48:15f
bowing in worship over the head of his staff. [22]By faith Gen 50:24
Joseph, at the end of his life, made mention of the exodus
of the Israelites and gave directions concerning his burial.[x]

Iacob et Esau. [21]Fide Iacob moriens singulis filiorum Ioseph benedixit et
adoravit super fastigium virgae suae. [22]Fide Ioseph moriens de profectione
filiorum Israel memoratus est et de ossibus suis mandavit. [23]Fide Moyses natus
occultatus est mensibus tribus a parentibus suis, eo quod vidissent formosum

---

27:27-29). When Isaac discovered that he had been tricked, he saw in this trick
a design of Providence and he confirmed what he had done (cf. Gen 27:33): "I
ate it before you came, and I have blessed him—yes, and he shall be blessed."
The only blessing that could then be bestowed on Esau was a general blessing
to the effect that he was free to go his own way and would possess a land which
was far from fertile. Isaac is an example of faith, because it was his faith which
allowed him to recognize and accept God's plans.

Isaac bestowed "future blessings"—not material goods but hope in the future
fulfilment of God's promises.

21. "Bowing in worship over the head of his staff": two gestures of Jacob
are combined here. One was when he had finished blessing his sons, the
ancestors of the twelve tribes: "he drew up his feet into the bed, and breathed
his last, and was gathered to his people" (Gen 49:32); the other, slightly earlier,
had to do with the Patriarch's final illness (cf. Gen 47:31). He had Joseph swear
that he would bury him in the promised land; then he took ill and "bowed
himself upon the head of his bed". The Greek translation of the Old Testament
(the Septuagint), by a slight change of vowels in one Hebrew word, said that
"Jacob bowed reverentially over the head of his staff". What the sacred writer
is stressing here is Jacob's reverence towards God: he ended his life with an
act of adoration of God.

22. When Joseph was on the point of dying he remembered the ancient
promise made by God to Abraham (cf. Gen 15:13f), according to which, after
a period of slavery and oppression in a foreign country, the children of Israel
would return to the promised land. Although Joseph enjoyed a privileged
position in Egyptian society, he still firmly believed in God's promise to his
forefathers to give them the land of Canaan, and he wanted his body to lie there:
"I am about to die; but God will visit you, and bring you up out of this land to
the land which he swore to Abraham to Isaac, and to Jacob [. . .]. God will visit
you, and you shall carry up my bones from here" (Gen 50:24-25; cf. Ex 13:19;
Josh 24:32).

[x]Greek *bones*

The faith of Moses, of the Judges and of the Prophets

Ex 2:2f
Acts 7:20

Ex 2:11

Ps 69:10, LXX;
89:51f, LXX
Heb 10:35

Ex 2:15
1 Tim 1:17

²³By faith Moses, when he was born, was hid for three months by his parents, because they saw that the child was beautiful; and they were not afraid of the king's edict. ²⁴By faith Moses, when he was grown up, refused to be called the son of Pharaoh's daughter, ²⁵choosing rather to share ill-treatment with the people of God than to enjoy the fleeting pleasures of sin. ²⁶He considered abuse suffered for the Christ greater wealth than the treasures of Egypt, for he looked to the reward. ²⁷By faith he left Egypt, not being

infantem et non timuerunt regis edictum. ²⁴Fide Moyses grandis factus negavit se dici filium filiae pharaonis, ²⁵magis eligens affligi cum populo Dei quam temporalem peccati habere iucunditatem, ²⁶maiores divitias aestimans

23-29. After the Patriarchs, Moses was the figure most revered by the Jewish people; he was for them the founder and lawgiver of their nation (cf. Heb 3:1-5 and notes). This passage sketches key episodes in his life when he gave great example of faith, and it begins with the faith of his parents, who dared to disobey the Pharaoh's edict (cf. Ex 1:16, 22). The Book of Exodus (cf. Ex 2:2) tells us of his mother's tender care, but Hebrew tradition speaks also of his father's decision to disobey the edict. The reason they disobeyed Pharaoh would initially have been parental love and the fact that the child was so beautiful. However, St Stephen (cf. Acts 7:20) says that Moses was "beautiful before God", that is, pleasing to God: his beauty was a sign of God's favour; so, his parents must have in some way realized that the child was specially favoured by God (cf. *Commentary on Heb, ad loc.*.

Another example of Moses' faith was the fact that he left Pharaoh's court (and the career that was opening up before him, and for which his entire education equipped him: cf. Acts 7:22) over an incident to do with repression of the Israelites; he killed an Egyptian overseer and had to flee for his life (cf. Ex 2:11-15). When Yahweh charged him with the mission of liberating his people, Moses was not afraid to confront Pharaoh. He unleashed the plagues; exposed the magicians of Egypt; and strove relentlessly until he achieved his goal. To do all this he drew his strength from the vision he had seen on Mount Sinai, when the invisible God revealed himself to him in the mysterious burning bush. Finally the text recalls the faith of all those Israelites who followed Moses in the epic journey of the Exodus. God enabled them to cross the Red Sea without wetting their feet, whereas the army of the Egyptians there met its doom (cf. Ex 14:26-31).

The central point of the teaching in this passage is the choice which faith obliges—the pleasures of sin v. ill-treatment shared with the people of God; "the treasures of Egypt" v. "abuse suffered for the Christ". This last expression indicates that the sufferings of the Israelites in Egypt prefigured the sufferings of the Messiah.

afraid of the anger of the king; for he endured as seeing him who is invisible. [28]By faith he kept the Passover and sprinkled the blood, so that the Destroyer of the first-born might not touch them.

Ex 12:11, 21-23

[29]By faith the people crossed the Red Sea as if on dry land; but the Egyptians, when they attempted to do the same, were drowned. [30]By faith the walls of Jericho fell

Ex 14:22, 27
1 Cor 10:10
Wis 18:25

Josh 6:20

---

thesauris Aegypti improperium Christi; aspiciebat enim in remunerationem. [27]Fide reliquit Aegyptum non veritus animositatem regis, invisibilem enim tamquam videns sustinuit. [28]Fide celebravit Pascha et sanguinis effusionem, ne, qui vastabat primogenita, tangeret ea. [29]Fide transierunt mare Rubrum tamquam per aridam terram, quod experti Aegyptii devorati sunt. [30]Fide muri

---

Jewish teachers in the time of St Paul usually saw the future Messiah as being a new and greater Moses: the Anointed would embody, again and definitively, all the functions of Moses—liberator, convoker of the people, lawgiver, mediator of the Covenant, wonder-worker etc. Hence the inevitable Moses-Christ parallel.

"Abuse suffered for the Christ" also refers to suffering and contempt experienced by Christ's followers. There is no earthly prize comparable to attaining the Lord through grace. For the true disciple of Christ no suffering is too great provided he can follow the Messiah and be like him.

"The true servants of Jesus Christ, when they find themselves despised and ill-treated because of their love for him, regard it as a great honour [. . .]. Moses could have escaped Pharaoh's wrath simply by letting himself be taken for the son of the king's daughter, but he rejected such kinship and preferred (to share) the affliction of his Hebrew brethren" (St Alphonsus, *Shorter Sermons*, 40, II, 1).

Our faith should be like that of Moses: we should despise the "fleeting pleasures of sin" in order to suffer with Christ. This commitment to stay with Christ, to stand by his cross, is what gives serenity and joy. "Is it not true that as soon as you cease to be afraid of the Cross, of what people call the cross, when you set your will to accept the Will of God, then you find happiness, and all your worries, all your sufferings, physical or moral, pass away?

"Truly the Cross of Jesus is gentle and lovable. There, sorrows cease to count; there is only the joy of knowing that we are co-redeemers with him" (J. Escrivá, *The Way of the Cross*, II).

30. By putting their faith in the word of God, who had given Joshua detailed instructions about how to take Jericho (cf. Josh 6:2-5), the Israelites obtained victory: the walls protecting the city crumbled before their eyes. "Even if it lasted for ten centuries", St John Chrysostom comments, "the sound of trumpets could not knock walls down, whereas for faith nothing is impossible" (*Hom. on Heb*, 27).

169

Josh 2:11; 6:17, 23
Jas 2:25
Judg 6:11; 4:6; 13:24;
15:20; 12:7
1 Sam 16:10
Acts 3:24
Dan 6:23
Judg 4:15f
1 Sam 17:34f
down after they had been encircled for seven days. ³¹By faith Rahab the harlot did not perish with those who were disobedient, because she had given friendly welcome to the spies.

³²And what more shall I say? For time would fail me to tell of Gideon, Barak, Samson, Jephthah, of David and Samuel and the prophets— ³³who through faith conquered

---

Iericho ruerunt circuiti diebus septem. ³¹Fide Rahab meretrix non periit cum incredulis, quia exceperat exploratores cum pace. ³²Et quid adhuc dicam? Deficiet enim me tempus enarrantem de Gedeon, Barac, Samson, Iephte, David et Samuel atque prophetis, ³³qui per fidem devicerunt regna, operati sunt

31. Before embarking on the conquest of the promised land Joshua sent two spies to bring back detailed information about Jericho. When they reached the city they lodged in the house of Rahab, a prostitute, who hid them and helped them to escape when the king's men came searching. Rahab believed in the true God and she also believed that the Hebrews were his chosen people: that was why she risked her life for them. She asked them to swear to leave herself and her family untouched (cf. Josh 2:1-21). Joshua kept the promise the spies made her, but the rest of the inhabitants of Jericho, who were unbelieving, perished (cf. Josh 6:22-25).

Because of her action and despite the fact that she was a prostitute and a foreigner, Rahab has ever since been the object of praise. The Fathers often saw her as a symbol of "the Church of the Gentiles", that is, of pagans who find their way into the Church.

32-38. Up to this point, the passage has been recalling outstanding examples of faith from the time of the Patriarchs down to that of Joshua (18th to 13th century B.C.). The epistle now goes on to their exploits and sufferings, wherein their faith brought them victory; the sacred writer then mentions the testimony of faith of heroes, judges, kings, prophets and martyrs from the time of the conquest of Palestine to that of the Maccabees (13th to 2nd centuries B.C.). Not in any strict chronological order, he mentions only the most important Judges (Gideon, Barak, Samson and Jephthah), the greatest of the kings (David) and the most famous of the early prophets (Samuel). Finally he refers to exploits and other deeds inspired by faith and fidelity, without giving names.

We know from Sacred Scripture that many of these people had shortcomings and, in some cases, committed grave sins. However, those weaknesses did not prevent their filling key roles in God's plans: they let themselves be used by God to apply his policy and are therefore worthy of being proposed as examples of faith.

33-35a. "Through faith (they) conquered kingdoms": a reference to the men who conquer the promised land: Barak, who overcame the Canaanites (cf. Judg

kingdoms, enforced justice, received promises, stopped the mouths of lions, [34]quenched raging fire, escaped the edge of the sword, won strength out of weakness, became mighty in war, put foreign armies to flight. [35]Women received their

Dan 3:23-25
Ps 46:7, LXX

1 Kings 17:23
2 Kings 4:36

---

iustitiam, adepti sunt repromissiones, obturaverunt ora leonum, [34]extinxerunt impetum ignis, effugerunt aciem gladii, convaluerunt de infirmitate, fortes facti sunt in bello, castra verterunt exterorum; [35]acceperunt mulieres de resurrectione

---

11), Gideon, who conquered the Midianites (cf. Judg 7), Jephthah, who conquered the Amonnites (cf. Judg 11), Samson, who defeated the Philistines (cf. Judg 14), and David, who succeeded in subduing all the enemies of Israel (cf. 2 Sam 5:17-25; 8:1f; 10).

"Enforced justice": a reference to the authority exercised by the Judges on a tribal basis, and by Samuel and the kings over the whole of Israel (cf. 1 Sam 12:3; 2 Sam 8:15); it can also be understood as meaning those who practised righteousness in God's name and made it effective, the prophets being the oustanding examples.

"Received promises": the righteous of the Old Testament received an earnest of the messianic promises in the form of the fulfilment of certain prophecies made by God. Barak defeated Sisera as God had promised (cf. Judg 4:14f); Gideon overcame the Midianites (cf. Judg 6:14; 7:7); David brought peace to the whole land, as Nathan had predicted (cf. 2 Sam 7:11); etc.

"Stopped the mouths of lions": a reference to feats performed by Samson (cf. Jud 14:6), David (cf. 1 Sam 17:34-35), and Benaiah (cf. 2 Sam 23:20); it especially recalls the episode of Daniel in the lion's den: when thrown there by the king on account of his faith, he told him, "My God sent his angel and shut the lions' mouths, and they have not hurt me" (Dan 6:22).

Sacred history also includes people who "quenched raging fire" (like the three young men in the fiery furnace in Babylon: cf. Dan 3:21-94); or who "escaped the edge of the sword" (as Moses did, in his flight from Pharaoh's wrath: cf. Ex 18:4); or like David, who "won strength out of weakness" in his victories over Goliath and Saul (cf. 1 Sam 17:34ff; 18:11; 19:11). Thanks to his faith Elijah found protection from Jezebel's persecution (cf. 1 Kings 19:1f); and the Jewish people were able to escape extermination during King Ahasuerus' reign thanks to the prayer and intercession of Esther and Mordecai (cf. Esther 3:6ff).

Through faith King Hezekiah was miraculously cured of mortal illness (cf. Is 38) and Samson received his strength after becoming weak and blind (cf. Judg 15:19; 16:28-30). Faith enabled the Hebrews, under the Judges, to take on and defeat the pagan peoples of Palestine; it led Judith to behead Holofernes and bring about the destruction of his army; and it enabled the Maccabees to repel the foreign armies of Antiochus (cf. 1 Mac 1:38).

Then there is the example of the widow of Zarephath, who sheltered Elijah and had her son restored when the prophet cured him (cf. 1 Kings 17:17f). And

2 Mac 6:18-7:42   dead by resurrection. Some were tortured, refusing to
accept release, that they might rise again to a better life.
Jer 20:37f   ³⁶Others suffered mocking and scourging, and even chains
2 Chron 24:21
Mt 23:37   and imprisonment. ³⁷They were stoned, they were sawn in

mortuos suos; alii autem distenti sunt, non suscipientes redemptionem, ut
meliorem invenirent resurrectionem; ³⁶alii vero ludibria et verbera experti sunt,
insuper et vincula et carcerem; ³⁷lapidati sunt, secti sunt, in occisione gladii

Elisha brought back to life the son of the Shunammite widow (cf. 2 Kings
4:33f).

All these examples show the effectiveness of faith, when it involves a
person's whole life and lifestyle, influencing both everyday events and great
exploits.

35b-36. Faith not only enables people to perform exploits and miracles: it
also enables them to persevere in doing good and to bear all kinds of moral and
physical pain, even torture and the most cruel forms of death. And so the text
refers to various sorts of suffering inflicted on the prophets and many other just
members of the people of Israel.

The writer may have in mind, for example, the death of Eleazar (cf. 2 Mac
6:19ff) and of the seven brothers (cf. 2 Mac 7), who underwent most cruel
torture during the persecution mounted by Antiochus IV Epiphanes. The king
had promised them their lives if they gave up their faith and laws by eating
forbidden meat; but they stayed true to God and were mercilessly martyred.
However, they had unshakeable faith in the rightness of God's judgment and
in future resurrection (2 Mac 7:19, 14, 23, 29). They desired to "rise again to a
better life": they put their faith in an incomparably more valuable, more real,
life than that of a few more years on earth, which would have been the reward
of apostasy. "They did not escape death," St Thomas writes, "not because God
was not looking after them but so that they might obtain eternal life, which is
a more excellent thing than being set free from any present affliction or being
raised up again to this life" (*Commentary on Heb*, 11, 5).

The example of these men and women whom faith strengthened to endure
suffering, should encourage Christians to face persecution courageously and
defend their faith at all costs. "Let us pray to God that we do not suffer
persecution, but if that does happen, let us bear it bravely. It befits a prudent
man not to fling himself lightly into danger, but it befits a brave man to rise to
the occasion when danger falls on him" (*Hom. on Heb*, 5).

37-38. Some righteous men were stoned for their faith—Zechariah, for
example, who was killed by order of King Joash (cf. 2 Chron 24:20-21);
Naboth, condemned to death through the lies spread by Jezebel (cf. 1 Kings
21:13); and the prophet Jeremiah also, according to an ancient tradition. Others
were sawn in two—Isaiah, for example, whom another Jewish tradition says
was martyred by King Manasseh.

two,[y] they were killed with the sword; they went about in skins of sheep and goats, destitute, afflicted, ill-treated— [38]of whom the world was not worthy—wandering over deserts and mountains, and in dens and caves of the earth.

[39]And all these, though well attested by their faith, did not receive what was promised [40]since God had foreseen something better for us, that apart from us they should not be made perfect.

1 Pet 1:10-12; 3:19

---

mortui sunt, circumierunt in melotis, in pellibus caprinis, egentes, angustiati, afflicti, [38]quibus dignus non erat mundus, in solitudinibus errantes et montibus et speluncis et in cavernis terrae. [39]Et hi omnes testimonium per fidem consecuti non reportaverunt promissionem, [40]Deo pro nobis melius aliquid providente, ut ne sine nobis consummarentur.

Elijah, in flight from persecution, went around dressed in skins (cf. 1 Kings 19:3ff); similarly Mattathias and his sons during the war against the Seleucid kings, were forced to hide in the mountains and had only goatskins to wear (cf. 1 Mac 2:28).

In our own time there are also people who profess their faith in God by undergoing comparable persecution; but usually hatred of Christ and his followers takes more subtle forms.

40. This verse is the conclusion following from all the examples provided. The righteous of the Old Law were outstanding for their faith and endurance, but for all that they did not have the strength that the grace of Christ bestows; Jesus remarked, when John the Baptist was praised to him, "Truly, I say to you, among those born of women there has arisen no one greater than John the Baptist; yet he who is least in the kingdom of heaven is greater than he" (Mt 11:11); and he reminded his disciples of their privileged position: "Blessed are the eyes which see what you see! For I tell you that many prophets and kings desired to see what you see, and did not see it, and to hear what you hear, and did not hear it" (Lk 10:23-24; cf. Mt 13:16-17).

God did not deny their reward to the righteous of the Old Testament, but he postponed it until heaven's gates were opened by the death and resurrection of our Lord. They too now enjoy eternal life and they will attain their final perfecting when their bodies rise in glory on the last day. God is like a good father, St John Chrysostom comments, who says to his beloved children when they finish their work, that he will not give them their supper until their other brothers come back also. "And you, are you annoyed because you have not received your reward? What should Abel do, then? He was the first to gain the victory, but remained uncrowned. And Noah? And all those of those times who

[y]Other manuscripts add *they were tempted*

THE EXAMPLE OF CHRIST AND THE DUTIES OF CHRISTIANS

12

1 Tim 6:12
2 Tim 4:7

The example of Christ

¹Therefore, since we are surrounded by so great a cloud of

---

¹Ideoque et nos tantam habentes circumpositam nobis nubem testium, deponentes omne pondus et circumstans nos peccatum, per patientiam curramus

---

are waiting for you and for those who will come after you? Do you not see how much better off we are? That is why he says: God in his providence had arranged something better for us. And, in order that it should not be thought that those people were superior to us because they received their crown earlier, God disposed that all should be crowned at the very same time; and he who won his many years earlier will be crowned along with you [. . .]. For if we are all the one body, this body will the more rejoice if all are crowned at the same time and not one by one" (*Hom. on Heb*, 28).

1-3. After recalling the exemplary faith and fidelity of the righteous of the Old Testament, a moral lesson is now drawn: Christians should be no less faithful—particularly since they have as a model not only patriarchs, kings and prophets but also Christ Jesus himself, "the pioneer and perfecter of our faith", in other words, he is the perfect example of obedience, of faithfulness to his mission, of union with the Father, and of endurance in suffering.

Christ is depicted as the strong, generous athlete who runs a good race (cf. 1 Cor 9:24; 1 Tim 6:12; 2 Tim 2:6), who starts and finishes well, who does not flag and who wins the race. A Christian should live in the same way (cf. Gal 2:2; Phil 2:16; 5:7). It is as if we were listening again to what St Paul says in Philippians 2:5-9: "Have this mind among yourselves, which was in Christ Jesus." Christ's example helps us to overcome contempt and it reminds us that we should not be surprised to meet up with humiliation and hostility rather than success and rejoicing (cf. Mt 10:24; Lk 6:40). "Cross, toil, anguish: such will be your lot as long as you live. That was the way Christ went, and the disciple is not above his Master" (Blessed J. Escrivá, *The Way*, 699).

1. This verse contains three remarkable expressions which stress the need to be faithful in spite of difficulties. The first is the "cloud of witnesses", a reference to the multitude of holy people in the course of the history of Israel who stayed faithful to God (cf. 11:2, 4, 5, 39); they are a cloud, a huge number filling the sky. In classical literature one often finds an army advancing in battle array being compared with a storm forming in the sky. Also, the image of the

witnesses, let us also lay aside every weight, and sin which
clings so closely, and let us run with perseverance the race
that is set before us, [2]looking to Jesus the pioneer and

Mt 25:21
Ps 110:1
Heb 2:10

---

propositum nobis certamen, [2]aspicientes in auctorem fidei et consummatorem
Iesum, qui pro gaudio sibi proposito sustinuit crucem, confusione contempta,

---

cloud suggests that these witnesses are high up, near the sun, a sign of their
spiritual stature.

They are "witnesses", that is, active spectators of the combat in which
Christians are involved. This evokes the idea of spectators at the Games who
follow the events from the stands, applauding, shouting and gesticulating.

"Sin which clings so closely": one interpretation of the original is "sin which
watches us closely, like an enemy, to see where he can attack us". It is the same
kind of idea as occurs in 1 Pet 5:8, where it says that the devil prowls around
like a roaring lion seeking whom he may devour, and as in Gen 4:7 where God
describes sin as couching at the door (like a hungry wild animal ready to
pounce). The verb used to describe sin indicates it is something which surrounds
one on all sides (cf. RSV) and can easily get a foothold and is persistent. "We
may have here an allusion to occasions of sin, to the fact that sin is present all
around us, that is, in the world, in the flesh, in our neighbour and in the devil"
(St Thomas, *Commentary on Heb, ad loc.*). Sin is also a "weight" which hinders
our movements and reduces our agility; there may also be a reference here to
being overweight. The athlete needs to shed any surplus weight and keep to a
strict training schedule involving many small renunciations (cf. 1 Cor 9:25).
His only hope of success in the Games depends on this.

Finally, Christians are invited to "run with perseverance". Theirs is not a
short race but a long test which calls for endurance and an ability to cope with
pain and fatigue. "Just as in a race and in combat we need to shed everything
that cramps our movements, the same happens in the struggle of tribulation. 'I
have fought the good fight, I have finished the race,' St Paul says (2 Tim 4:7).
So, he who wants to run well towards God in the midst of tribulation should
shed all useless weight. The Apostle describes this encumbrance as 'weight,
and sin which clings so closely'. This weight is the sins we have committed,
which pull the soul downwards and incline it to sin again" (*Commentary on
Heb, ad loc.*).

Essentially, the verse emphasizes the need for detachment if one is to win
in the struggle of life: "Anything that does not lead to God is a hindrance. Root
it out and throw it far from you" (Blessed J. Escrivá, *The Way*, 189).

2. The Christian should fix his gaze on Jesus, in the same way as a runner,
once the race has begun, lets nothing distract him from his determination to
reach his goal.

"If you want to be saved," St Thomas writes, "look at the face of your Christ.
He is the pioneer of our faith, in two senses. He teaches it through his preaching

and he also impresses it on our heart. In two senses also is he the perfecter of our faith: he confirms faith by his miracles and it is he who gives faith its reward" (*Commentary on Heb, ad loc.*).

Christ is the "pioneer" of our faith in the sense that he has marked out the path Christians should take. He is the captain and guide of all the faithful, the champion who takes the lead and opens the way, setting the pace. The reference evokes what Hebrews 6:20 says about Jesus being our "forerunner".

Christ is the "pioneer" of our faith, the cause of our faith; it is he that we first believe in and, as author of grace, it is he who infuses this virtue into our souls. The title of "pioneer", initiator, may also indicate that Christ is for the Christian—and for the universe—beginning and end, alpha and omega (cf. Rev 1:17; 2:8; 22:13). In the same line, Jesus is also the "perfecter" of our faith, for it is he who will lead us to perfection in faith and will transform it into the perfection of glory. He will crown his work in us (cf. St Augustine, *Letter 194*, 5), for if we believe it is because he has moved us to faith, and if we are glorified it will be because he has helped us to stay true to the end.

Everything Christ did in his life is a perfect example for us to follow, particularly the way he underwent his passion. "In the passion of Christ there are three things to consider: in the first place what he gave up, then what he suffered, and thirdly what he merited. As far as the first is concerned, (Hebrews) speaks of his leaving 'the joy that was set before him', that is, joy or happiness here on earth, as when the crowd sought him out to make him king and he fled to the mountain despising that honour [. . .]. Then describing the happiness of eternal life as his reward, he 'endured the cross': that is the second thing, namely, that he suffered the cross. 'He humbled himself and became obedient unto death, even death on a cross' (Phil 2:8). In this the terrible severity of his suffering is manifested, for he was nailed to the cross by his hands and feet, and the opprobrium of this death, for it was an ignominous death [. . .]. The third thing, that is, what he merited, is being seated at the right hand of the Father. Thus, the exaltation of Christ's human nature was the reward for his passion" (*Commentary on Heb, ad loc.*).

Christ is the pioneer of our faith by his death on the Cross, and its perfecter by his glorification. Only those who share in Christ's sufferings will be raised up like him in glory (cf. Rom 6:8). The Christian life begins in Christ and finds its climax in him.

To bring about our redemption any form of suffering would have sufficed; but such was our Lord's love for us that he accepted the ignominy of death on a cross.

"By now they have fastened Jesus to the wooden cross. The executioners have ruthlessly carried out the sentence. Our Lord, with infinite meekness, has let them have their way.

"It was not necessary for him to undergo so much torment. He could have avoided those trials, those humiliations, that ill-usage, that iniquitous judgment, and the shame of the gallows, and the nails and the lance. . . . But he wanted to suffer all this for you and for me. And we, are we not going to respond?

perfecter of our faith, who for the joy that was set before Phil 2:8
him endured the cross, despising the shame, and is seated
at the right hand of the throne of God.

[3]Consider him who endured from sinners such hostility Lk 2:34
Gal 6:9
against himself, so that you may not grow weary or faint-

---

atque in dextera throni Dei sedet. [3]Recogitate enim eum, qui talem sustinuit a
peccatoribus adversum semetipsum contradictionem, ut ne fatigemini animis

---

"Very likely there will be times, when alone in front of a crucifix, you find
tears coming to your eyes. Don't try to hold them back. . . . But try to ensure
that those tears give rise to a resolution" (Blessed J. Escrivá, *The Way of the
Cross*, XI, 1).

3. "What does Christ teach you from the height of the Cross, from which
he chose not to come down, but that you should arm yourself with valour against
those who revile you, and be strong with the strength of God?" (St Augustine,
Enarrationes in Psalmos, 70, 1). The difficulties Jesus had to contend with were
quite exceptional: Jews and Gentiles opposed him; he suffered every kind of
humiliation, to the extreme of his passion and death; but what pained him most
was the hardheartedness, spiritual blindness and impenitence of those whom
had come to save. The "sinners" who proved "hostile" to Jesus are not only
Caiaphas, Herod, Pilate, etc. but also those who continue to sin despite his
redemptive sacrifice. Yet our Lord bore all this patiently and exhibited to a
supreme degree the virtues and qualities he asks of his disciples.

In Christ, and in Christians, weakness becomes strength, humiliation and
glory. "(Jesus) dies nailed to the Cross. But if at the same time in this *weakness*
there is accomplished his *lifting up*, confirmed by the power of the Resurrection,
then this means that the weaknesses of all human sufferings are capable of being
infused with the same power of God manifested in Christ's Cross" (John Paul
II, *Salvifici doloris*, 23).

The sacred text seeks to inspire the faithful with hope and strength by
suggesting that they contemplate Christ's sufferings. That in fact has led many
Christians to turn over a new leaf. St Teresa of Avila describes how it changed
her: "By this time my soul was growing weary, and, though it desired to rest,
the miserable habits which now enslaved it would not allow it to do so. It
happened that, entering the oratory one day, I saw an image which had been
procured for a certain festival that was observed in the house and had been
taken there to be kept for that purpose. It represented Christ sorely wounded;
and so conducive was it to devotion that when I looked at it I was deeply moved
to see him thus, so well did it picture what he suffered for us. So great was my
distress when I thought how ill I had repaid him for those wounds that I felt as
if my heart were breaking, and I threw myself down beside him, shedding floods
of tears and begging him to give me strength once for all so that I might not
offend him" (*Life*, IX, 1).

Heb 10:32-36 hearted. [4]In your struggle against sin you have not yet resisted to the point of shedding your blood.

Perseverance in affliction

Prov 3:11f, LXX [5]And have you forgotten the exhortation which addresses you as sons?—

"My son, do not regard lightly the discipline of the Lord, nor lose courage when you are punished by him.

Rev 3:19 [6]For the Lord disciplines him whom he loves, and chastises every son whom he receives."

---

vestris deficientes. [4]Nondum usque ad sanguinem restitistis adversus peccatum repugnantes [5]et obliti estis exhortationis, quae vobis tamquam filiis loquitur: *"Fili mi, noli neglegere disciplinam Domini neque deficias, dum ab eo argueris:* [6]*quem enim diligit, Dominus castigat, flagellat autem omnem filium, quem recipit."* [7]Ad disciplinam suffertis; tamquam filios vos tractat Deus. Quis

---

4-13. Following Christ's example, Christians should struggle to avoid sin; they should put up with tribulation and persecution because if such adversity arises it means that the Lord permits it for our good. The letter's tone of encouragement seems to change here to one of reproach. It is as if the writer were saying, "Christ gave his life for your sins, contending even to the point of dying for you; how is it that you do not put up with suffering, out of love for him? It is true that you are being persecuted: God is disciplining you as a Father disciplines his children. But you are children of God and therefore your attitude should be one of abandonment to his will even when it seems hard. That is the way a Father brings up his children."

The main point is that the only important thing is fidelity to God, and that the sin of apostasy is the greatest of all misfortunes. "Don't forget, my son, that for you on earth there is but one evil, which you must fear and avoid with the grace of God: sin" (Blessed J. Escrivá, *The Way*, 386).

5-11. Suffering, the sacred writer teaches, is a sign of God's paternal love for us; it proves that we really are his children.

This teaching is supported by the quotation from Proverbs 3:11-12, taken from a long discourse in which a father exhorts his son to acquire true wisdom. In the present passage the father is identified with God and we with the sons whom he is addressing.

By being incorporated into Christ through Baptism a person becomes a child of God: this is the very basis of the Christian life and it should be a source of serenity and peace in every difficulty we meet in the course of life. The term "discipline" which appears so much in this passage does not convey the full richness of the original Greek word, *paideia*, which has to do with the educational upbringing of child by parent, of pupil by teacher, and also the punishment meted out in this context. Here the focus is largely on the second aspect.

⁷It is for discipline that you have to endure. God is treating you as sons; for what son is there whom his father does not discipline? ⁸If you are left without discipline, in which all have participated, then you are illegitimate children and not sons. ⁹Besides this, we have had earthly fathers to discipline us and we respected them. Shall we not much more be subject to the Father of spirits and live? ¹⁰For they disciplined us for a short time at their pleasure, but he disciplines us for our good, that we may share his holiness. ¹¹For the moment all discipline seems painful rather than

Num 16:22

2 Cor 4:17
Jas 3:18

enim filius, quem non corripit pater? ⁸Quod si extra disciplinam estis, cuius participes facti sunt omnes, ergo adulterini et non filii estis! ⁹Deinde patres quidem carnis nostrae habebamus eruditores et reverebamur; non multo magis obtemperabimus Patri spirituum et vivemus? ¹⁰Et illi quidem ad tempus paucorum dierum, secundum quod videbatur illis, castigabant, hic autem ad id, quod utile est ad participandam sanctitatem eius. ¹¹Omnis autem disciplina in

However, it should be remembered that in ancient times education and instruction always involved the idea of punishment. God, therefore, should not be seen as a cruel or pitiless father, but as a good father who brings up his children in an affectionate yet firm way. Adversity and suffering are a sign that this divine teaching method is at work: God uses them to educate us and discipline us. "You suffer in this present life, which is a dream, a short dream. Rejoice, because your Father-God loves you so much, and if you put no obstacles in his way, after this bad dream he will give you a good awakening" (Bl. J. Escrivá, *The Way*, 692). If we were illegitimate children he would not bother to educate us; but because we are true sons he disciplines us, to make us worthy of bearing his name. "Everything that comes to us from God," an ancient ecclesiastical writer reminds us, "and that we initially see as beneficial or disadvantageous, is sent to us by a father who is full of tenderness and by the wisest of physicians, with our good in mind" (Cassian, *Collationes*, VII, 28).

When the soul has this kind of attitude, that is, when the trials the Lord sends are willingly accepted, "with peaceful fruit of righteousness" and it yields fruit of holiness which fills it with peace: "Jesus prays in the garden: *Pater mi* (Mt 26:39), *Abba, Pater!* (Mk 14:36). God is my Father, even though he may send me suffering. He loves me tenderly, even while wounding me. Jesus suffers, to fulfil the Will of the Father. . . . And I, who also wish to fulfil the most holy Will of God, following in the footsteps of the Master, can I complain if I too meet suffering as my travelling companion?

"It will be a sure sign of my sonship, because God is treating me as he treated his own divine Son. Then I, as he did, will be able to groan and weep alone in my Gethsemani; but, as I lie prostrate on the ground, acknowledging my nothingness, there will rise up to the Lord a cry from the depths of my soul: *Pater mi, Abba, Pater, . . . fiat!*" (Bl. J. Escrivá, *The Way of the Cross*, I, 1).

179

pleasant; later it yields the peaceful fruit of righteousness to those who have been trained by it.

Striving for peace; purity; reverent worship

Is 35:3
Prov 4:26, LXX
Ps 34:15
Rom 12:18
Mt 5:8f
1 Jn 3:2
2 Tim 2:22

¹²Therefore lift your drooping hands and strengthen your weak knees, ¹³and make straight paths for your feet, so that what is lame may not be put out of joint but rather be healed. ¹⁴Strive for peace with all men, and for the holiness without

---

praesenti quidem videtur non esse gaudii sed maeroris, postea autem fructum pacificum exercitatis per eam reddit iustitiae. ¹²Propter quod *remissas manus et soluta genua erigite* ¹³et *gressus rectos facite pedibus* vestris, ut, quod

12-13. This exhortation follows logically from the previous one. It seems to evoke the world of athletic competition referred to at the beginning of the chapter. Verse 12 is like a shout of encouragement to a runner who is beginning to flag in the middle of a race.

The author uses a quotation from Isaiah (Is 35:3) in which drooping hands and weak knees indicate moral decline (cf. 2 Sam 2:7; 4:1; Jer 47:3). He then goes on to use words from Proverbs 4:26 to encourage right living: "make straight steps with your feet": if the Christian perseveres in his efforts even if he is somewhat "lame", that is, even if he is someone whose faith is weak and is in danger of apostasy, he will be able to return to fitness in spite of everything.

However, this exhortation can be taken as addressed not only to those who need to mend their ways but also to Christians in general, who should be exemplary and never in any way be a stumbling-block to their weaker brethren.

14. These words echo what our Lord says in the Sermon on the Mount: "Blessed are the peacemakers, for they shall be called sons of God". Jesus promises those who promote peace that they will be sons of God and therefore share in God's inner life, which makes man holy. The Apostles and disciples of the Lord often repeat this teaching (cf. Jas 3:18; Rom 12:18; 1 Pet 3:11). Being at peace with God, which comes from docility to his plans (v. 11), necessarily leads one to foster and maintain peace with others. Peace with God and with one's neighbour is inseparable from the search for holiness. Christ brings about the fulfilment of the ancient promises which foretold a flowering of peace and righteousness in the messianic times (cf. Ps 72:3; 85:11-12; Is 9:7; etc.).

"Holiness": it is not just a matter of avoiding sin. One needs to cultivate virtue and to desire to attain holiness with the help of grace. Holiness or Christian perfection is the common goal of all Christ's disciples. Salvation and holiness are really one and the same thing, for only saints can obtain entry into the presence of God: only those who are holy can see the Holy One.

"You must be perfect, as your heavenly Father is perfect" (Mt 5:48). These words of our Lord are always echoing through the Church; today more than

which no one will see the Lord. [15]See to it that no one fail to obtain the grace of God; that no "root of bitterness" spring up and cause trouble, and by it the many become defiled; [16]that no one be immoral or irreligious like Esau, who sold his birthright for a single meal. [17]For you know

Deut 29:17, LXX
Acts 8:23

Gen 25:33f
Gen 27:30-40
Heb 6:4-6

claudum est, non extorqueatur, magis autem sanetur. [14]Pacem sectamini cum omnibus et sanctificationem, sine qua nemo videbit Dominum, [15]providentes, ne quis desit gratiae Dei, ne qua radix amaritudinis sursum germinans perturbet, et per illam inquinentur multi, [16]ne quis fornicator aut profanus ut Esau, qui

ever. "Today, once again, I set myself this goal and I also remind you and all mankind: this is God's will for us, that we be saints.

"In order to bring peace, genuine peace, to souls; in order to transform the earth and to seek God our Lord in the world and through the things of the world, personal sanctity is indispensable" (Blessed J. Escrivá, *Friends of God*, 294).

15. Theodoret comments on this passage as follows: "Do not be concerned only about yourselves; rather let each of you look after the other; strengthen the waverer and assist him who needs your helping hand" (*Interpretatio Ep. ad Huebreos, ad loc.*). A Christian needs to be concerned not only about his own soul, his own salvation; on his conscience should also lie the salvation of his brothers and sisters in the faith. He should be like a gardener who cares for his plants and makes sure no weeds or diseases spread through his garden. In the Old Testament, the man who denies his faith is described as a root bearing poisonous and bitter fruit (cf. Deut 29:18). Anyone who is indifferent to a brother's infidelity endangers those around him, for bad example can spread like an epidemic. This passage is reminiscent of St Paul's reproach to the Corinthians: "Do you not know that a little leaven leavens the whole lump?" (1 Cor 5:6).

Hence the need to be ever vigilant to ensure that no one through his own fault loses the gifts God has given him; "the true apostle is on the lookout for occasions of announcing Christ by word, either to unbelievers to draw them towards the faith, or to the faithful to instruct them, strengthen them, incite them to a more fervent life; 'for Christ's love urges us on' (2 Cor 5:14), and in the hearts of all should the Apostle's words find echo: 'Woe to me if I do not preach the Gospel' (1 Cor 9:16)" (Vatican II, *Apostolicam actuositatem*, 6).

16-17. Esau is an example of the way excessive interest in temporal things can lead to irresponsible behaviour. In rabbinical literature the first-born son of Isaac gained notoriety as a man inclined to vice through his marriages to Hittite women (cf. Gen 26:34-35; 27:46). The letter describes him as a "fornicator" (translated by RSV as "immoral", the word can be interpreted in a strict sense as meaning "unchaste"); but it can also be taken metaphorically as indicating apostasy, which is often its sense in the Old Testament. Esau is

181

that afterward, when he desired to inherit the blessing, he was rejected, for he found no chance to repent, though he sought it with tears.

Ex 19:12, 16, 18

Deut 4:11

Ex 19:16, 19; 20:18f

Ex 19:12f

Deut 9:19

Rev 14:1

Ps 74:4

[18]For you have not come to what may be touched, a blazing fire, and darkness, and gloom, and a tempest, [19]and the sound of a trumpet, and a voice whose words made the hearers entreat that no further messages be spoken to them. [20]For they could not endure the order that was given, "If even a beast touches the mountain, it shall be stoned." [21]Indeed, so terrifying was the sight that Moses said, "I

---

propter unam escam vendidit primogenita sua. [17]Scitis enim quoniam et postea cupiens hereditare benedictionem reprobatus est, non enim invenit paenitentiae locum, quamquam cum lacrimis inquisisset eam. [18]Non enim accessistis ad tractabilem et ardentem ignem et turbinem et caliginem et procellam [19]et tubae sonum et vocem verborum, quam qui audierunt, recusaverunt, ne ultra eis fieret verbum; [20]non enim portabant mandatum: *"Et si bestia tetigerit montem,*

---

also described as "irreligious", that is, "impious", lacking in the piety due to his parents, because he sold his birthright (cf. Gen 25:29-34). He later tried to obtain from his father, Isaac, the blessing proper to the first-born, which Jacob had inherited through deceit (Gen 27). But he did not succeed in getting his father to change his mind and bless him, even though he pleaded with him with tears in his eyes, according to ancient Jewish tradition.

Esau "did not repent of having sold his birthright; he repented of having lost it; what pained him was not the sin of selling (it) but the disadvantage of losing (it). That is why his repentance was not accepted—because it was not sincere" (*Commentary on Heb*, 12, 3).

The moral teaching contained in these verses has to do with fidelity. Christians are first-born, but they are capable of falling into an infidelity from which there is no return, losing the gift of faith.

18-21. The text recalls in detail all the physical signs which accompanied the manifestation of God on the heights of Sinai (cf. Ex 19:12-16; 20:18), and to these it adds other things taken from Jewish oral tradition.

All this helps to inspire feelings of religious reverence and fear, which explains why the people begged God not to speak further, for they were afraid they would die. To assert his transcendence God forbade anyone to put foot on the mountain (Ex 19:12, 21); this was a way of showing this as yet uncivilized people the difference between the true God and idols.

There is no mention in the Pentateuch of Moses being frightened of the vision he saw when God manifested himself on Sinai; when his fear is mentioned (Deut 9:19) it is in the context of the second time he went up the mountain to be given replacements for the tables he had broken in a fit of rage (Deut 9:15-18; Ex 32:19-20). His fear was that God would punish with death

tremble with fear." ²²But you have come to Mount Zion and to the city of the living God, the heavenly Jerusalem, and

Gen 4:26
Rev 21:2

---

lapidabitur"; ²¹et ita terribile erat, quod videbatur, Moyses dixit: *"Exterritus*

those who had adored the golden calf. When telling (cf. Acts 7:32) the story of God's first revelation to Moses in the burning bush, St Stephen says that "Moses trembled and did not dare to look": thus, the presence of divinity provokes in him the deepest feelings of reverence and fear (cf. the attitude of Abraham: Gen 15:12; of Zechariah: Lk 1:12; of Isaiah: Is 6:4-5; of Jeremiah: Jer 1:6; of Gideon: Judg 6:22-23; etc.).

22-24. The sacred text dramatically constrasts two scenes—that of the establishment of the Covenant on Sinai, and the vision of the heavenly city, the dwelling-place of the angels and saints. The comparison implies a rhetorical question: if the setting of the Old Covenant was so solemn and awesome, and if the Covenant itself was so supernatural and divine, what must not be said of the New Covenant?

We have therefore overwhelming reasons for staying faithful: what awaits us is not an austere and vengeful God but, rather, the joy and splendour of the heavenly city. For the Hebrew people Mount Sinai was the most important symbol of their special connexion with God, reminding them that the Almighty was also the Supreme Judge who claimed their exclusive devotion and who abominated idolatry. Similarly, another mountain, Mount Zion, on which the Temple was built, represented God's protective presence in the midst of his people. Both mountains, Sinai and Zion, prefigured the mountain from which the Messiah-King would reign and towards which all peoples would flock to worship the true God (cf. Ps 2:6; Is 2:2).

The vision which Judaism, on the basis of Scripture, had elaborated of heaven as the "new Jerusalem" is now extended: not only is it the holy mountain, the source of the light and glory of Yahweh (cf. Is 8:18; 28:16; 60:1-11; Ps 50:2; 74:2; Joel 3:17), the city of peace (cf. Is 33:20); it is the city where the angels and saints dwell and rejoice, the demesne of the living God and of Jesus—the heavenly and everlasting Jerusalem, which is also illustrated in the Book of Revelation (cf. Rev 21:15-17; 22:1-5).

The text once more recalls the Exodus (cf. Heb 3:16- 18; 4:1-2; 9:18-20; 10:19-22). Christians are making their way to heaven, their lasting homeland, their true place of rest, just as the ancient Israelites made their way out of Egypt and crossed the desert to reach the land promised to their forefathers.

However, despite this parallel there are differences: the Old Covenant, although it did include expressions and promises of joy and jubilation, was set in an atmosphere of religious fear and trembling; whereas the New Covenant is full of joy and exultation, although in the midst of suffering.

"It is a question [. . .] of the glorious and supernatural joy, prophesied for the new Jerusalem redeemed from the exile and loved with a mystical love by God himself [. . .]. Through the course of many centuries and in the midst of

to innumerable angels in festal gathering, [23]and to the assembly[z] of the first-born who are enrolled in heaven, and to a judge who is God of all, and to the spirits of just men

---

sum et tremebundus." [22]Sed accessistis ad Sion montem et civitatem Dei viventis, Ierusalem caelestem, et multa milia angelorum, frequentiam [23]et ecclesiam primogenitorum, qui conscripti sunt in caelis, et iudicem Deum omnium, et spiritus iustorum, qui consummati sunt, [24]et testamenti novi

---

most terrible trials, these promises wonderfully sustained the mystical hope of ancient Israel. And it is ancient Israel that transmitted them to the Church of Jesus Christ, in such a way that we are indebted to ancient Israel for some of the purest expressions of our hymn of joy. And yet, according to faith and the Christian experience of the Holy Spirit, this peace which is given by God and which spreads out like an overflowing torrent when the time of 'consolation' comes, is linked to the coming and presence of Christ" (Paul VI, *Gaudete in Domino*, 2-3).

22. The mention of Zion recalls the other mountain on which the Covenant was made (Sinai), as also the many prophetical texts which proclaimed that the Messiah's reign would begin on Zion, his holy mountain (cf. Ps 2:6; Is 2:2-4; 25:6; Zech 14:4). Thus, Mount Zion, the city of the living God, and the heavenly Jerusalem all mean the Church in triumph in heaven.

St Thomas emphasizes that part of eternal happiness in heaven consists in the vision of the heavenly assembly: "for in the glory of heaven there are two things which most cause the blessed to rejoice—enjoyment of the Godhead and the fellowship of the saints" (*Commentary on Heb, ad loc.*).

"Proceeding from the love of the eternal Father (cf. Tit 3:4), the Church was founded by Christ in time and gathered into one by the Holy Spirit (cf. Eph 1:3, 5, 6, 13-14, 23). It has a saving and eschatological purpose which can be fully attained only in the next life. But it is now present here on earth and is composed of men; they, the members of the earthly city, are called to form the family of the children of God in this present history of mankind and to increase it continually until the Lord comes" (Vatican II, *Gaudium et spes*, 40).

23. "The assembly of the first-born who are enrolled in heaven": the blessed, including the righteous of the Old Testament, the Apostles and all Christians who have attained the beatific vision. They are called first-born because, as in the case of the Patriarchs, they were the first to have faith; because, as in the case of the Apostles, it was they who received Christ's call initially, to pass it on to others; and, finally, because, as in the case of faithful Christians, they were chosen by God from among the pagans (cf. Rom 8:29; Phil 3:20; Col 1:18; Rev 1:5; 14:4). Their names are written in heaven (cf. Lk 10:20; Rev 2:17; 3:5; 13:8; 17:8).

[z]Or *angels, and to the festal gathering and assembly*

184

made perfect, [24]and to Jesus, the mediator of a new covenant, and to the sprinkled blood that speaks more graciously than the blood of Abel.

Heb 11:40
1 Pet 1:2

[25]See that you do not refuse him who is speaking. For if they did not escape when they refused him who warned them on earth, much less shall we escape if we reject him

Heb 2:3

---

mediatorem Iesum, et sanguinem aspersionis, melius loquentem quam Abel. [25]Videte, ne recusetis loquentem; si enim illi non effugerunt recusantes eum, qui super terram loquebatur, multo magis nos, qui de caelis loquentem avertimus; [26]cuius vox movit terram tunc, modo autem pronuntiavit dicens:

24. As Incarnate Word and High Priest, Jesus is the mediator of the New Covenant (cf. Heb 8:6; 9:15; 1 Tim 2:5; cf. Heb 2:17; 13:1; 7:25). The letter focusses for a moment on the most significant point in the alliance—the shedding of our Lord's blood, which ratifies the Covenant and cleanses mankind (cf. Ex 24:8; Heb 9:12-14, 20; 10:19, 28-29; 13:20; 1 Pet 1:2). This blood "speaks more graciously than the blood of Abel", "for the shedding of Christ's blood was represented figuratively by the shedding of the blood of all the just there have been since the beginning of the world [. . .]. Therefore, the spilling of Abel's blood was a sign of this new spilling of blood. But the blood of Christ is more eloquent than that of Abel, because Abel's called for vengeance whereas the blood of Christ claims forgiveness" (St Thomas Aquinas, *Commentary on Heb, ad loc.*). The confidence the blood of Christ gives us makes us feel happy to be sinners who, repentant, take refuge in his wounds.

"Sinners, says the Epistle, you are fortunate indeed, for after you sin you have recourse to the crucified Jesus, who shed all his blood so that he might stand as mediator to make peace between God and sinners, and win you forgiveness from him. If your evildoing shouts against you, the Redeemer's blood cries aloud in your favour, and divine justice cannot but listen to what this blood says" (St Alphonsus, *The love of Jesus Christ reduced to practice*, 3).

25. The Old Covenant was ratified in a solemn manner in order to inspire respect and veneration. The much greater importance and dignity of the New Covenant, sealed with the blood of Christ, carries with it an increased obligation of fidelity. If those were condemned who opposed Moses, who "received living oracles to give us" (Acts 7:38), there is much more reason for us to be punished if we cut ourselves off from "him who warns from heaven".

"There is never reason to look back (cf. Lk 9:62). The Lord is at our side. We have to be faithful and loyal; we have to face up to our obligations and we will find in Jesus the love and the stimulus we need to understand other people's faults and overcome our own. In this way even depression—yours, mine, anyone's—can also be a pillar for the kingdom of Christ" (Blessed J. Escrivá, *Christ is passing by*, 160).

who warns from heaven. 26His voice then shook the earth; but now he has promised, "Yet once more I will shake not only the earth but also the heaven." 27This phrase, "Yet once more," indicates the removal of what is shaken, as of what has been made, in order that what cannot be shaken may remain. 28Therefore let us be grateful for receiving a

---

"*Adhuc semel ego movebo* non solum *terram* sed et *caelum*." 27Hoc autem "*adhuc semel*" declarat mobilium translationem tamquam factorum, ut maneant ea, quae sunt immobilia. 28Itaque, regnum immobile suscipientes, habeamus

26-27. Quoting from the prophet Haggai (Hag 2:6), the sacred writer shows that just as the earth trembled at Sinai when God sealed the Covenant with Moses, so too did earth, and heaven also, tremble when the New Covenant was made (cf. Mt 27:51-52). He is stressing that the New Covenant will last forever, whereas the Old was provisional. The Law of Moses disappeared insofar as it was temporary and earthly; everything of permanent value in it remains.

Although it is more likely that the text is referring to the establishment by Christ of the New Law in place of that of Moses, this passage can be interpreted in an eschatological sense, as some Fathers of the Church have done: "Scripture teaches us that heaven and earth will be destroyed 'once more', as if this event had already happened. I think that it refers to the irresistible establishment of a new state of creation. We must believe Paul when he says that the final upheaval of the world will be nothing other than the second coming of Christ and that the existing universe will be transformed and will give way to another, definitive and unchangeable universe" (St Gregory Nazianzen, *Oratio* 21).

Whichever interpretation applies, the practical consequences of this teaching are the same. Earthly things are impermanent; therefore, we should desire things which last—heavenly things. "Why do you grieve when you suffer in this world which cannot last, in this world which soon will pass away? [. . .]. No one does any building in a city which is going to be destroyed. Tell me, please: if someone told you that in a year's time a particular city was going to be completely demolished, and also that some other one was going to endure: would you build in the one which was going to be pulled down? That is why I am telling you now: let us not build in this world; in a little time it will all collapse and disappear" (Chrysostom, *Hom. on Heb, ad loc.*)

28-29. The high point of the epistle is v. 28, which proclaims the establishment of a "kingdom that cannot be shaken", that will last forever. This Kingdom is the heavenly Jerusalem, of which the Church is an anticipation. Christians who are true to their calling are preparing the way for the coming of the Kingdom and in some way they make it present on earth. "A kingdom that is ruled by truth, by the dignity of man, by responsibility, by the conviction of being (made in) the likeness of God. A kingdom where there takes effect the divine plan for man, a plan based on love, true freedom, mutual service and

kingdom that cannot be shaken, and thus let us offer to God acceptable worship, with reverence and awe; ²⁹for our God is a consuming fire.

Is 33:1
Deut 4:24; 9:3
Rom 1:9

13

Duties towards others—charity, hospitality, fidelity in marriage

Rom 12:13
1 Thess 4:9
Gen 18:2f;
19:1-3
Judg 6:11-24;
13:3-20
Tob 5:4f

¹Let brotherly love continue. ²Do not neglect to show hospitality to strangers, for thereby some have entertained angels unawares. ³Remember those who are in prison, as

---

gratiam, per quam serviamus placentes Deo cum reverentia et metu; ²⁹etenim *Deus* noster *ignis consumens* est.
¹Caritas fraternitatis maneat. ²Hospitalitatem nolite oblivisci, per hanc enim quidam nescientes hospitio receperunt angelos. ³Mementote vinctorum

---

reconciliation of men with God and with one another" (John Paul II, *Audience for young people*, 3 November 1982).

Christians are full citizens of this kingdom, with a perfect right to share in the benefits which flow from it. However, these rights at the same time create certain obligations—to keep the grace of God and offer him acceptable worship. Some translations, including the RSV, take the original Greek to mean "let us be grateful to God": however, it seems more likely, given the context, that it means that it is grace which enables us to offer God acceptable worship. In other words, let us jealously hold onto this supernatural gift—sanctifying grace and the other supernatural graces—which makes us subjects of the Kingdom established by Christ's covenant.

The description of God as a "consuming fire" is evocative of various Old Testament passages (cf., e.g., Deut 4:24; 9:3; Ex 24:17; Is 33:14). God's justice will deal severely with those who do not accept the grace Christ offers them: it will follow its course inexorably.

1-3. The teaching on moral questions which takes up this chapter follows on logically from the trend of the whole letter, particularly the previous chapter: faithfulness to Christ means being faithful to him as a person and to his teaching. As he himself said, "If you love me, you will keep my commandments" (Jn 14:15). Among the essential teachings of our faith is the supreme importance of charity: "A new commandment I give to you, that you love one another; even as I have loved you, that you also love one another. By this all men will know that you are my disciples, if you have love for one another" (Jn 13:34-35). As Tertullian attests, pagans bore witness to how well the early Christians practised this virtue, when they would say, "See how they love one another: they are ready to die for one another" (*Apologeticum*, 39).

Brotherly love expresses itself in all kinds of ways. One of them is hos-

Jas 6:11-24
Mt 25:36
Heb 10:34
Eph 5:5

Deut 31:6, 8
Gen 28:15

though in prison with them; and those who are ill-treated, since you also are in the body. ⁴Let marriage be held in honour among all, and let the marriage bed be undefiled; for God will judge the immoral and adulterous. ⁵Keep your

---

tamquam simul vincti, laborantium tamquam et ipsi in corpore morantes. ⁴Honorabile conubium in omnibus et torus immaculatus, fornicatores enim et

---

pitality, which is one of the traditional corporal works of mercy. The virtue of hospitality is given high praise in this passage which contains implicit references to episodes in the life of Abraham and Sarah (Gen 18), Lot (cf. Gen 19), Manoah (cf. Judg 13:3-22) or Tobit (cf. Job 12:1-20), who gave hospitality to wayfarers who turned out to be angels. Similarly, Christians who practise this virtue are in fact welcoming Christ himself (cf. Mt 25:40). They should also see Christ in everyone who is experiencing any kind of suffering. "He himself is the one who in each individual experiences love; he himself is the one who receives help, when this is given to every suffering person without exception. He himself is present in this suffering person, since his salvific suffering has been opened once and for all to every human suffering" (John Paul II, *Salvifici doloris*, 30).

4. For anyone to practise charity towards God and towards others, the virtue of chastity is essential. It expands one's capacity for love. The text earnestly exhorts Christians to show their appreciation of marriage by practising marital chastity. Marriage is a personal calling by God to seek holiness in that state in life. "In God's plan, all husbands and wives are called in marriage to holiness, and this lofty vocation is fulfilled to the extent that the human person is able to respond to God's command with serene confidence in God's grace and in his or her own will" (John Paul II, *Familiaris consortio*, 34).

However, this also calls for marital chastity, which is a manifestation and proof of true love. "Human love—pure, sincere and joyful—cannot subsist in marriage without the virtue of chastity, which leads a couple to respect the mystery of sex and ordain it to faithfulness and personal dedication [. . .].

"When there is chastity in the love of married persons, their marital life is authentic; husband and wife are true to themselves, they understand each other and develop the union between them. When the divine gift of sex is perverted, their intimacy is destroyed, and they can no longer look openly at one another" (Blessed J. Escrivá, *Christ is passing by*, 25).

5-6. In teaching against love of money and exaggerated desire for material things, the text may be echoing what our Lord said: "Do not lay up for yourselves treasures on earth, where moth and rust consume and where thieves break in and steal, but lay up treasures in heaven [. . .]" (Mt 6:19-20). The epistle is encouraging us to trust God at all times and to be detached from earthly things. "Detach yourself from the goods of the world. Love and practise poverty of life free from love of money, and be content with what you have; for he has said, "I will never fail you nor forsake you." ⁶Hence we can confidently say,

"The Lord is my helper,
I will not be afraid;
what can man do to me?"

Religious duties—obeying lawful pastors; religious worship

⁷Remember your leaders, those who spoke to you the word of God; consider the outcome of their life, and imitate

---

adulteros iudicabit Deus. ⁵Sint mores sine avaritia; contenti praesentibus. Ipse enim dixit: *"Non te deseram, neque derelinquam"*, ⁶ita ut confidenter dicamus: *"Dominus mihi adiutor est, non timebo; quid faciet mihi homo"*. ⁷Mementote praepositorum vestrorum, qui vobis locuti sunt verbum Dei; quorum intuentes

---

spirit; be content with what enables you to live a simple and sober life [. . .]" (Blessed J. Escrivá, *The Way*, 631).

It uses some words spoken by Moses on God's behalf to remind the reader that it is God himself who has told man that he will never abandon him (cf. Deut 31:6). These words should fill us with consolation, allowing us to say with the psalmist (cf. Ps 118:6) that we can do anything provided God helps us, and there is nothing for us to fear provided we abandon ourselves to divine providence (cf. Mt 6:25-32).

"If Christ is yours, then wealth is yours; he satisfies all your wants. He will look after you, manage all your affairs for you most dutifully; you will need no human support to rely on [. . .]. Put all your trust in God; centre in him all your fear and all your love; he will make himself responsible for you, and all will go well as he sees best" (*The Imitation of Christ*, 1, 2-3).

7-19. In this passage this more practical section of the epistle examines specifically ecclesial duties, placing special emphasis on the Christian's duty to maintain unity with and to obey and respect those who have the mission to govern the community. This exhortation is made twice (vv. 7 and 17) to show the importance of obedience to lawful pastors (cf. 1 Thess 5:12-13; 1 Cor 16:16). We should see in the pastors of the Church a model of how we should practise the faith (v. 7; cf. Phil 3:17), and in particular we should see them as Christ's representatives (cf. Gal 4:12-14). Obedience to the hierarchy of the Church naturally involves accepting its teaching and eschewing heretical opinions (v. 9; cf. 1 Tim 6:3; Gal 1:6-9). Unity of faith, moreover, has to be expressed in unity of worship (v. 10; cf. Phil 3:3; Eph 4:4-5): no one may take part in Christian worship while continuing to take part in Jewish worship (cf. 1 Cor 10:16-21), nor is it lawful to regard rabbinical rules about food as still applying (v. 9; Col 2:16-18; 1 Tim 4:3-5). One needs to undergo a real conversion (vv. 11-13; Rom 3:23-26) and to put aside outdated rites and practices if one is to share in Christ's Cross (1 Cor 2:21-25; Gal 6:14-15). We must not put our trust in earthly things, but instead bear in mind that our end and goal is heaven (cf. Phil 3:20). Finally, unity of faith, discipline and sacraments must express itself in a consistent, coherent lifestyle whereby we are always in the presence of God, use everything as an opportunity for prayer and sacrifice, and practise a continuous charity towards others (vv. 15-16; cf. Gal 6:9-10; Rom 12:9-13; Eph 5:1-2; etc.). This short passage gives a very attractive outline of what Christian life involves. As Vatican II put it, "A life like this calls for a continuous exercise of faith, hope and charity. Only the light of faith and meditation on the Word of God can enable us to find everywhere and always the God 'in whom we live and move and have our being' (Acts 17:28); only thus can we seek his will in everything, see Christ in all men, acquaintance or stranger, and make sound judgments on the true meaning and value of temporal realities both in themselves and in relation to man's end" (*Apostolicam actuositatem*, 2).

7-14. The sacred text emphasizes the need to be at one with those in charge, the pastors and teachers of the Christian communities. Reference, in the past tense, to their faith suggests it is referring to those who have already obtained the crown of martyrdom—people like Stephen and St James the Greater (cf. Acts 7:59-60; 12:2), and other members of the community who were victims of Jewish persecution (cf. Acts 8:1; Heb 6:10; 10:32-34). They were admirable people; however, unity with one's leaders was not and is not conditional on the personal quality of these leaders: "What a pity that whoever is in charge doesn't give you good example! But, is it for his personal qualities that you obey him? Or do you conveniently interpret Saint Paul's *'obedite praepositis vestris*: obey your leaders' with a qualification of your own . . ., 'always provided they have virtues to my taste'?" (Blessed J. Escrivá, *The Way*, 621).

Faithfulness to and solidarity with one's lawful pastors is faithfulness towards Christ himself, for the "bishops, as vicars and legates of Christ, govern the particular churches assigned to them by their counsels, exhortations and example, but over and above that also by the authority and sacred power which indeed they exercise exclusively for the spiritual development of their flock in truth and holiness, keeping in mind that he who is greater should become as the lesser, and he who is the leader as the servant (cf. Lk 22:26-27)" (Vatican II, *Lumen gentium*, 27). Thus, it is rightly said that he who hears them hears Christ (cf. Lk 10:16). For their part, pastors should have the same love and solicitude for those in their charge as our Redeemer had; in this wonderful unity of charity the mystery of Christ will shine forth; it is Christ's right "to be the sole ruler of the Church; and for this reason also he is likened to the Head. The head (to use the words of St Ambrose) is 'the royal citadel' of the body (*Hexameron*, VI, 9, 55), and because it was endowed with more perfect gifts it naturally rules all the members, being purposely placed above them to have them under its care. In like manner the divine Redeemer wields the supreme power and government over the whole commonwealth of Christians" (Pius XII, *Mystici corporis*, 16).

their faith. [8]Jesus Christ is the same yesterday and today

---

exitum conversationis imitamini fidem. [8]Iesus Christus heri et hodie idem, et

---

The mystery of the Incarnation is indissolubly linked to the mystery of the Church, in such a way that the unity of the Church is a sign of the unity of the Lord's Body, which is one body with many different members (cf. 1 Cor 12:1-12; *Lumen gentium*, 7). Therefore, fidelity to the Church derives not from human reasons but from a desire to be faithful to Christ himself.

Fidelity to Christ, his preaching, to his commandments and the sacraments he instituted leads to loving fulfilment of everything the Church lays down with regard to worship—particularly to interior practice of the faith, repentance for sin and fervent reception of the sacraments (cf. Council of Trent, *De iustificatione*, chaps. 6 and 8; Rom 3:22-24; 11:16; Eph 2:8; 1 Cor 4:7; 15:10; 2 Cor 3:5). There are no clean or unclean foods (cf. Col 2:16; Rom 14:2-4), whether they are offered to idols or not (cf. 1 Cor 8; 10: 14-33), whether they are eaten or abstained from on certain days (cf. Rom 14:5; Col 2:16; Gal 4:10); there is no food which renders a person unclean or leads him to salvation (cf. Mk 7:15, 18; Rom 14:17, 20): for one whose heart is pure all things are pure (cf. Tit 1:15). The important thing is the grace of God, which is given us in the sacraments and which enables us to practise all the commandments out of love for God. The letter moves from these remarks about legal purity and impurity to point out that there is now an entirely new situation and what really matters is sharing in the paschal mystery of Christ, that is, in his passion, death and resurrection.

8. This verse expresses the foundation of the life of every Christian. It is a wonderful expression of faith constituting an act of adoration and reverence similar to the praise of the one God in Deuteronomy 6:4 ("The Lord our God is one Lord") or of the eternal God in Psalm 102.12 ("Thou, O Lord, art enthroned for ever; thy name endures to all generations"), only here it is Jesus Christ who is being extolled. Though their first teachers and guides may have died to bear witness to their faith, Christians will always have a teacher and guide who will never die, who lives for ever crowned with glory. Men come and go but Jesus remains for ever. He exists from all eternity, he is the Alpha and the Omega, the Beginning and the End (cf. Rev 1:8; 22:13); he lived "yesterday" among men in a specific period of history; he lives "today" in heaven, at the right hand of the Father, and he is "today" at our side providing us with grace and forever interceding for us (cf. Mt 28:20; Heb 4:14); he will remain "for ever" as High Priest and Redeemer (cf. Heb 6:20; 7:17) until he establishes his Kingdom and hands it to his Father (cf. 1 Cor 15:24-28).

It is moving to think that Christ did not take on human nature for a limited period only. The Incarnation was decreed from all eternity, and the Son of God, born of the Virgin Mary, in time and space, in the reign of Caesar Augustus, remains a man for ever, with a glorious body bearing the resplendent marks of his passion. In Christ's human nature, now indissolubly joined to the divine

191

Eph 4:14
Col 2:7
Rom 14:17
1 Cor 8:8

Heb 8:4f

and for ever. [9]Do not be led away by diverse and strange teachings; for it is well that the heart be strengthened by grace, not by foods, which have not benefited their adherents. [10]We have an altar from which those who serve

in saecula! [9]Doctrinis variis et peregrinis nolite abduci; optimum enim est gratia stabiliri cor, non escis, quae non profuerunt ambulantibus in eis. [10]Habemus altare de quo edere non habent potestatem, qui tabernaculo deserviunt.

person of the Son, all Creation is in some way glorified (cf. Col 1:15-20; Eph 1:9-10). Therefore, we can be absolutely sure that Christ's teaching cannot change: it is as immutable as he is and it will eventually transform the world. We know that all dimensions of human life—work, family life, life in society, affections, suffering—acquire in Christ a new and lasting purpose. "The Church believes that Christ, who died and was raised for the sake of all, can show man the way and strengthen him through the Spirit in order to be worthy of his destiny: nor is there any other name under heaven given among men by which they can be saved. The Church likewise believes that the key, the centre and the purpose of the whole of man's history is to be found in its Lord and Master. She also maintains that beneath all that changes there is much that is unchanging, much that has its ultimate foundation in Christ, who is the same yesterday, and today, and forever" (Vatican II, *Gaudium et spes*, 10). This is the source of the Christian's confidence. "Jesus is the way. Behind him on this earth of ours he has left the clear outlines of his footprints. They are indelible signs which neither the erosion of time nor the treachery of the evil one have been able to erase. *Iesus Christus heri, et hodie; ipse et in saecula.* How I love to recall these words! Jesus Christ, the very Jesus who was alive yesterday for his Apostles and the people who sought him out—this same Jesus lives today for us, and will live forever" (Blessed J. Escrivá, *Friends of God*, 127).

9. This verse contains two commandments. The first is to hold on to sound teaching and not be led astray by those who argue that the precepts of the Old Law still apply (cf. Acts 20:29-30; Gal 1:6, 7; 3:2-4; 5:12). Christians should not yield to the attraction of new teachings which are "diverse" (that is, contradictory and changeable, whereas there is only one truth and it does not change) and "strange", that is, alien to the teaching of Christ.

The second commandment, stated implicitly, was probably very clear to the first readers of the epistle, who were familiar with the strange practices of religious sects of the time. It states a basic principle: what strengthens one's resolve and leads to upright conduct is not special regulations about food but Christ's grace. Grace and food are counterposed, but the latter is not said to be something bad. Special dietary laws or food-related religious practices are of no use to anyone; but grace is always useful. This is very reminiscent of John 6:63: "It is the spirit that gives life, the flesh is of no avail."

10. Very probably the term "altar" refers to the "eucharistic table" and

the tent[a] have no right to eat. [11]For the bodies of those animals whose blood is brought into the sanctuary by the high priest as a sacrifice for sin are burned outside the camp. [12]So Jesus also suffered outside the gate in order to sanctify the people through his own blood. [13]Therefore let us go forth to him outside the camp, bearing abuse for him. [14]For

Lev 16:27

Mt 21:39
Jn 19:20
Acts 7:58
Heb 11:26

Heb 11:10
Phil 3:20

---

[11]Quorum enim animalium infertur sanguis pro peccato in Sancta per pontificem, horum corpora cremantur extra castra. [12]Propter quod et Iesus, ut sanctificaret per suum sanguinem populum, extra portam passus est. [13]Exeamus igitur ad eum extra castra, improperium eius portantes; [14]non enim habemus

---

possibly also to Christ in the Eucharist. It is not possible to take part in Christian worship if one has another religious allegiance, and vice versa (cf. 1 Cor 10:21).

The text is saying that the Old Testament form of worship has been replaced by Christian worship: Christian worship is the real thing; Old Testament worship was only its shadow or prefigurement.

11-13. This passage should be read against the background of the Old Testament rites of the Day of Atonement (cf. Heb 9:7-9; 4:14; 9:24; 10:20; Lev 16:27). Jesus Christ, crucified outside the walls of Jerusalem (for the mound of Calvary was outside the gate of Ephraim, to the northeast of the city) has acted out what was prefigured by the sacrificed victims which were burned outside the camp. By sacrificing the heifer and the male goat to atone for the sins of the people, the high priest was enabled to enter the sanctuary; so too the shedding of Christ's blood has opened the way to the sanctuary of heaven. The skin, bones and flesh of the victims were burned outside the camp; so too Christ went out of the city; but his exit is symbolic in another sense also: it means leaving Jewish worship behind and declaring it obsolete. The people to whom the epistle was initially written obviously Christians of Jewish background— are being invited to leave behind the comfortable position they enjoyed as Jews (Judaism being recognized by the Roman Empire as a "lawful religion") and not to be afraid of the risks—the "abuse"—involved in following Christ (the enmity of Jews and persecution by Gentiles).

"Abuse" may be a reference to the fact that contact with the remains of animals sacrificed on the Day of Atonement meant legal impurity (cf. Lev 16:24, 26, 28); but it clearly refers to the Cross (or "stumbling block" to Jews: cf. 1 Cor 1:23) and to the contempt suffered by our Lord. This exhortation also has a wider application—to Christians of all times, who need to leave behind anything which prevents them from being good disciples of Christ. "We too have to imitate him who chose to undergo the cross for the sake of our salvation; we have to leave this world, or, better, leave the empty affairs of this world" (Chrysostom, *Hom. on Heb*, 33).

14. Using the cyclic method found elsewhere in the epistle (cf. 9:18-22, 25),

---

[a]Or *tabernacle*

here we have no lasting city, but we seek the city which is to come. ¹⁵Through him then let us continually offer up a

---

hic manentem civitatem, sed futuram inquirimus. ¹⁵Per ipsum ergo offeramus hostiam laudis semper Deo, id est fructum labiorum confitentium nomini eius.

---

the sacred writer links the notion of atoning sacrifice to the Exodus. In fact, three points in salvation history are linked together. Firstly, the Exodus, with the celebration of the Passover and the establishment of the Covenant on Sinai. This first episode is set in the framework of the sacrifice of expiation on Sinai, when Moses sprinkled the blood over the people and the book of the Law. A second episode, or, better, a second reference point, is the ceremonial of the Day of Atonement which was celebrated in the encampment during the pilgrimage in the wilderness and later on in the temple of Jerusalem. Both the Exodus and the Day of Atonement had a spiritual meaning: the people were petitioning God for forgiveness of their sins and were asking to be set free of them; and God's mercy was being celebrated, as was the Israelites' entry into the promised land. The third episode is, clearly, the passion, death and resurrection of Christ, the fulfilment and perfecting of everything symbolized by those earlier "types".

The life of Christians is an exodus (cf. Heb 4:1-11) because it involves leaving sin behind and living in union with God, sharing in our Lord's cross. It is an exodus because we shall have to leave this earth in order to enter heaven. Death, which is a punishment for sin (cf. Rom 6:23), is something we must undergo if we are to become fully identified with Christ (cf. Rom 6:10-11): "For whoever would save his life will lose it; and whoever loses his life for my sake, he will save it" (Lk 9:24; cf. Mt 10:39; 16:25; Mk 8:35; Jn 12:25).

The verse also points to the need for Christian detachment (cf. 2 Cor 5:1-2; Phil 3:20; Col 1:5; 1 Pet 1:4): " God did not create us to build a lasting city here on earth, 'this world is the way to that other, a dwelling place free from care' (Jorge Manrique). Nevertheless, we children of God ought not to remain aloof from earthly endeavours, for God has placed us here to sanctify them and make them fruitful with our blessed faith" (Blessed J. Escrivá, *Friends of God*, 210).

The Second Vatican Council also points to this tension which Christian life involves: "the expectation of a new earth must not weaken but rather stimulate our concern for cultivating this one. For here grows the body of a new human family, a body which even now is able to give some kind of foreshadowing of the new age. Hence, while earthly progress must be carefully distinguished from the growth of Christ's Kingdom, to the extent that the former can contribute to the better ordering of human society, it is of vital concern to the Kingdom of God" (*Gaudium et spes*, 39).

15-16. The text presupposes the Old Testament distinction between the "sin offering" and other offerings. The sin offering was made publicly on the great Day of Atonement. The other offerings, particularly those not involving the

sacrifice of praise to God, that is, the fruit of lips that acknowledge his name. [16]Do not neglect to do good and to share what you have, for such sacrifices are pleasing to God.

[17]Obey your leaders and submit to them; for they are keeping watch over your souls, as men who will have to give account. Let them do this joyfully, and not sadly, for that would be of no advantage to you.

[18]Pray for us, for we are sure that we have a clear conscience, desiring to act honourably in all things. [19]I urge

Is 57:19
Hos 14:3
Mal 1:11
Phil 4:18
2 Cor 8:4

1 Thess 5:12
Ezek 3:18

Rom 15:30
Eph 6:19
Col 4:3
Philem 22

---

[16]Beneficientiae autem et communionis nolite oblivisci, talibus enim hostiis oblectatur Deus. [17]Obocdite praepositis vestris et subiacete eis, ipsi enim pervigilant pro animabus vestris quasi rationem reddituri, ut cum gaudio hoc faciant et non gementes, hoc enim non expedit vobis. [18]Orate pro nobis; confidimus enim, quia bonam conscientiam habemus, in omnibus bene

---

shedding of blood—first fruits, fruit and loaves, which the faithful presented to God in thanksgiving and praise—were called "peace offerings", among which the most prominent was the "sacrifice of thanksgiving" (cf. Lev 7:12; Ps 50:14; 116:17).

In the New Testament the faithful, exercising their spiritual priesthood (cf. Rom 12:1; Heb 12:28), offer sacrifices acceptable to God—prayer (made by lips which confess God), good works, alms, etc.

Already, through the prophets, God had made it plain that he abhorred sacrifices which were merely external (cf. 1 Sam 15:22; Is 1:11-17; Jer 6:20; Amos 5:21-22): what he wanted was a pure and humble heart (cf. Is 58:6-8). Jesus said the same (cf. Mt 5:23-24; Mk 11:25; Lk 18:9-14). So too, in the New Covenant, Christ wants all followers to exercise that priesthood which consists in doing good and offering to God all the little sacrifices each day involves: "Since he wishes to continue his witness and his serving through the laity also, the supreme and eternal priest, Christ Jesus, vivifies them with his spirit and ceaselessly impels them to accomplish every good and perfect work" (Vatican II, *Lumen gentium*, 34).

17-19. Emphasis is put here on the duty all Christians have to pray especially for those who are placed in authority over them.

"We owe two things to those who govern us in the spiritual sphere. First, obedience, to do what they tell us; and then reverence, to honour them like parents and accept the discipline they propose" (Chrysostom, *Hom. on Heb*, 13, 3).

"You are under an obligation to pray and sacrifice yourself for the person and intentions of whoever is 'in charge' of your apostolic undertaking. If you are careless in fulfilling this duty, you make me think that you lack enthusiasm for your way" (Blessed J. Escrivá, *The Way*, 953).

you the more earnestly to do this in order that I may be restored to you the sooner.

EPILOGUE

Is 63:11
Zech 9:11
Is 55:3
Jer 32:40
Ezek 37:26
Jn 10:11
1 Pet 2:25
Rom 16:27

2 Tim 4:3
1 Pet 5:12

20Now may the God of peace who brought again from the dead our Lord Jesus, the great shepherd of the sheep, by the blood of the eternal covenant, 21equip you with everything good that you may do his will, working in you[b] that which is pleasing in his sight, through Jesus Christ; to whom be glory for ever and ever. Amen.

22I appeal to you, brethren, bear with my word of

volentes conversari. 19Amplius autem deprecor vos hoc facere, ut quo celerius restituar vobis. 20Deus autem pacis, qui eduxit de mortuis pastorem magnum ovium in sanguine testamenti aeterni, Dominum nostrum Iesum, 21aptet vos in omni bono, ut faciatis voluntatem eius, faciens in nobis, quod placeat coram se per Iesum Christum, cui gloria in saecula saeculorum. Amen. 22Rogo autem

20-21. The epistle ends in the same kind of way as the Pauline epistles do—with a doxology and some words of farewell. In these verses "the God of peace" is invoked; he is the only one who can give true peace, decreeing that men should be reconciled to him through the action of Christ; and Jesus is described as "the great shepherd": once more there is this paralleling the Exodus/Old Covenant with entry into heaven. Just as Moses brought the people of Israel into the promised land the way a shepherd leads his sheep (cf. Is 63:11), so Jesus Christ, the shepherd par excellence (cf. Jn 10:10-16; 1 Pet 2:25; 5:4), has led his sheep into the glory of heaven.

Verse 21 links Christian teaching on grace with man's response to that grace. Commenting on this passage St Thomas Aquinas explains that the words "equip you with everything good that you may do his will" is the same as saying "may God make you desire everything good", because it is God's will that we act of our own free will. If we did not act freely, our will would not be good; if we do God's will we will always be doing what is good for us (cf. *Commentary on Heb, ad loc.*). God has disposed man's will to choose to do what is right. It is up to man to respond to God's design. In this sense God "equips us with everything good that you may do his will".

22-24. The "word of exhortation" conveys the idea of a speech or text that seeks to give consolation and encouragement. It may even be an allusion to the type of addresses given in synagogues (cf. Acts 13:15)—as if the author were conveying in written form something he was unable to do orally.

bOther ancient authorities read *us*

exhortation, for I have written to you briefly. [23]You should Acts 16:1 understand that our brother Timothy has been released, with whom I shall see you if he comes soon. [24]Greet all your leaders and all the saints. Those who come from Italy send you greetings. [25]Grace be with all of you. Amen.

---

vos, fratres, sufferte sermonem exhorationis, etenim perpaucis scripsi vobis. [23]Cognoscite fratrem nostrum Timotheum dimissum esse, cum quo si celerius venerit, videbo vos. [24]Salutate omnes praepositos vestros et omnes sanctos. Salutant vos, qui de Italia sunt. [25]Gratia cum omnibus vobis.

"Our brother Timothy": a reference to that well-known figure in the early Church, a disciple and travelling-companion of St Paul, to whom the Apostle wrote two letters that bear his name.

The greeting to the "leaders" shows the respect and reverence people had for those in charge of the community (cf. Heb 13:7, 17). On the phrase "all the saints", see the notes on Rom 1:7; 1 Cor 1:2; Eph 1.1.

"Those who come from Italy": as many Fathers and early commentators thought, this letter was almost certainly written in Rome.

25. The ending is similar to that of letters of St Paul, especially Ephesians, Colossians, 1 Timothy, 2 Timothy and Titus. "Grace" is the whole ensemble of supernatural gifts which God gives man through Jesus Christ. It is what all apostolic endeavour is seeking—that all men should obtain grace and that none should lose it. Theodoret, commenting on this passage, points out that "he adds the customary ending, praying that they all be partakers of grace. Let us praise the lawgiver of both old and new [laws] and, in order to obtain his help, let us pray that by fulfilling his divine commands we shall attain the promised good things to come, in Jesus Christ our Lord, to whom belongs glory together with the Father and the Holy Spirit now and for ever and for ever more. Amen" (*Interpretatio Ep. ad Haebreos, ad loc.*).

Headings added to the text of the Epistle for this edition